UBUNTU AND THE EVERYDAY IN AFRICA

D1598271

Edited by
James Ogude and Unifier Dyer

AFRICA WORLD PRESS
TRENTON | LONDON | CAPE TOWN | NAIROBI | ADDIS ABABA | ASMARA | IBADAN | NEW DELHI

AFRICA WORLD PRESS
541 West Ingham Avenue | Suite B
Trenton, New Jersey 08638

Copyright © 2019

Book design: Lemlem Tadesse
Cover design: Ashraful Haque

Cataloging-in-Publication Data may be obtained from the Library of Congress.

ISBNs: 978-1-56902-616-8 (HB)
　　　 978-1-56902-617-5 (PB)

CONTENTS

ACKNOWLEDGEMENTS vii

Introduction: THEORISING UBUNTU AND THE
EVERYDAY 1
James Ogude and Unifier Dyer

Chapter 1: EVERYDAY AND OTHER DAYS: WHAT'S
THE DIFFERENCE? 25
D. A. Masolo

Chapter 2: ENTRENCHING THE MORAL VALUES OF
UBUNTU IN EVERYDAY LIFE 65
Oriare Nyarwath

Chapter 3: UBUNTU AND THE POLITICS OF
MIGRATION 89
Anke Graness

Chapter 4: UBUNTU, INEQUALITY AND EVERYDAY
LIFE: SOME REFLECTIONS ON A MAJOR
EXISTENTIAL CHALLENGE 113
Aloo Osotsi Mojola

Chapter 5: "THE HISTORICAL DIMENSION OF
UBUNTU IN EVERYDAY LIFE" 135
Niels Weidtmann

Chapter 6: PARTICIPATORY COMMUNICATION IN CONSTRUCTING CONJUGAL LOVE IN AFRICA: CASE OF THE BAGANDA AND THE MA'DI 157
Dominica Dipio

Chapter 7: TRANSITIONAL JUSTICE FROM BELOW? LEARNING FROM 'EVERYDAY' LIVED EXPERIENCES IN SOUTHERN AFRICA 195
Cori Wielenga

Chapter 8: EXPRESSIONS OF RESISTANCE: UBUNTU, BLACK CONSCIOUSNESS AND WOMEN IN SOUTH AFRICA'S STUDENT MOVEMENTS 215
Unifier Dyer

NOTES ON CONTRIBUTORS 239
INDEX 243

ACKNOWLEDGEMENTS

This publication would not have been possible without the support and generous funding that we received from the Templeton World Charity Foundation to undertake a research project aimed at deepening our understanding of the Southern African concept of Ubuntu. The funding was made in honor of the Archbishop Emeritus Desmond Tutu in 2013.

The majority of the chapters published in this book originated from a colloquium held at the University of Pretoria in March 23 – 24, 2016 on "Ubuntu and the Everyday in Africa." My gratitude goes to the contributors to this volume many of whom remain "Ubuntu Fellows" at the Centre for the Advancement of Scholarship at the University of Pretoria where the Ubuntu project is housed. Their participation at the colloquium added immense insights to the debates on the concept. I want to single out Professors Aloo Mojola and D. A. Masolo for their constant encouragement and unwavering belief in the value of this project. To the other cluster leaders on the project, Professors Julian Muller, Christof Heyns and Maxi Schoeman for having shown faith in my leadership and for your insights as we battled to put together the proposal for funding. To my friend and intellectual colleague, Bheki Peterson, who always re-assured me about the value of African knowledge systems such as Ubuntu – *enkosi Mrena*.

Uni Dyer, the co-editor of this volume, carried out invaluable work on deep literature review on this vexed subject which led to the formulation of our original ideas on Ubuntu and the everyday. Her organizational skills during the range of colloquia we convened, her undying commitment to indigenous knowledge systems and her rare insights into the broader implication of the project, made her an invaluable intellectual companion on this journey. Our sincere gratitude to our Project Co-ordinator, Kirsty Agnew, who helped in proofreading, checking the references and consolidating the chapters. Further gratitude to the Center's Administrative Assistant, Cecelia Samson, who was responsible for the travel and accommodation arrangement for our delegates whenever they attended each and every colloquium. Special thanks to Mme Nthabiseng Ogude, for her background support and patience as the project unfolded. To the principal investigator's adorable grandchildren, Leo and Milla, born during the life of this project - you always provided the desired relief from time to time whenever we met to play – just like children do. Finally, we wish to dedicate the volume to Uni's father, Mr Clive James Dyer, himself a committed Africanist - who passed on too soon on 31 August 2015 at the height of this project. We know what you meant to Uni. To you all that inspired us: "We are because of you!"

Introduction: THEORISING UBUNTU AND THE EVERYDAY

James Ogude and Unifier Dyer

Introduction

W here do we find Ubuntu? Who still practices Ubuntu? These are some of the most frequently asked questions about the concept of Ubuntu whenever it comes up in academic discourse. The implication of course is that Ubuntu belongs to a forgotten African past and that the need to prove its contemporaneity is necessary. Like with most African value systems associated with indigenous resource base, their absence is often a good reason to dismiss their relevance in contemporary society. What is never asked is whether the absence of these values has anything to do with the imposition of a hierarchy of values that we now associate with the overdetermining forces of colonial modernity that either repressed or totally effaced the indigenous African knowledge base. To ask of Ubuntu's manifest presence in contemporary society is to suggest that it is irrelevant and belongs to a nativist archive that is of no use in the present. The latest buzz phrase Afropolitanism ranging from Achille Mbembe's (2007) location of it on the continent (himself writing from Johannesburg) dating it back centuries, to Taiye Tuakli-Wosornu's (2009) 'not citizens but Africans of the world' who emerge in post-colonial era ("Bye-bye Babar"), attempts to capture an identity that might close the fissure between cosmopolitanism and nativist depiction. However, what it overlooks is the intricate and intertwined relationship formed between the city/rural, global/local, national/diasporic and the multiway exchange which is messy and vibrant disrupting a linear flow from the former to the latter and which more importantly can tell us of the influence that Africa(ns) have on the rest of the world. Researching Ubuntu does not require a disassociation from the world, it in fact articulates our very presence and contribution to the modern world. This volume on Ubuntu and the Everyday is part of two other volumes that have attempted to grapple with a range of questions such as the ones we raise above in an attempt to provide fresh understanding to this vexed concept that continues to haunt South Africa's post-colonial and post-apartheid moment.

In this volume we argue that one of the best ways of 'finding' Ubuntu is to locate it in the politics and poetics of the everyday. To talk of its politics is to immerse it in the everyday power relations and to talk of its poetics is to search for a lexicon; a grammar of speaking that would allow us to situate Ubuntu in the everyday – our daily entanglements and in those rituals that define our daily encounters. But what is the everyday and how do we theorise it in relation to Ubuntu?

The everyday is that which passes unnoticed but governs the larger aspects of life. It is routine regulated by the personal and daily social interactions. This constitutes the structure around which we construct our lives. Laura Bovon articulates this poignantly when she notes that: "the everyday represents an indispensable starting point for the reconstruction of meaning" (1989, 44). What emerges from this is the potential for knowledge creation embedded in the everyday. From this we can venture to say that knowledge from the everyday allows us to orient our actions. In this volume, our interest is in thinking through how we reassert new forms of agency in the way we govern our daily lives. The question we seek to pose is: how can Ubuntu, when understood through the prism of the everyday allow us to disrupt certain norms prescribed by modernity that have denigrated all other forms of knowledge that do not fall within its category of meaning making? How are certain types of knowledge normalised at the expense of indigenous forms and methods of knowledge creation? In other words, how does Ubuntu continue to remain manifest in our daily lives and in what ways does it saturate the everyday? Alternatively, how do the practices of the everyday threaten the full realisation of Ubuntu?

To answer the above questions fully we need to provide a brief conceptual understanding of the everyday first. In the history of European idea of aesthetics, the everyday has always been seen as the opposite of high culture and associated with low and ordinary culture. It is therefore antithetical to the dominant culture that it strives to mimic. The everyday is thought of against high culture, ceremonies, the spectacular, tradition and the official. The aesthetics of the everyday is one such theory of the everyday which situates the origin of the everyday outside of ideal judgments of beauty and aesthetic appeal. Due to its ordinariness, to notice and apprehend the everyday one has to work through estrangement − defamiliarize it and render it visible. It is this hierarchy that sets it apart from so-called high aesthetics and its ways of meaning making. This almost normalises what it is set against − the fine arts and philosophy of art in twentieth century Western tradition. At the core of the everyday in this theory is the way people experience objects and their attitude to activities which are defined as negative aesthetic qualities of life; the banal, normal, redundant. It is the process of defamiliarization that endows the everyday with a semblance of beauty and presence, especially when it is transformed into a space where we re-experience the ordinary as extraordinary.

Our position in this volume is that the everyday need not operate at the bottom of the cultural hierarchy, rife with banality. It is not limited to sensory prescriptions that guide, regulate, and direct aesthetics but instead it is a space where norms, notions, ideas and practices bud and immediately come into contact with their multiple applications and the textures of meanings that unfold from this. Instead, it should be able to encompass spaces of engagement, interaction and contact that people have. This necessarily includes—diverse people, ideas, cultures, languages, systems and beliefs, institutions and knowledges. The European idea of aesthetics has made us more engaged with the object and its appeal, use, and value and yet the human seems to be altogether excluded and removed from the object, relating to it from a space of distancing. It is such readings of aesthetics that give rise to what has come to be known "art for art's sake." The artist and product are removed from the everyday and yet it is impossible to create beauty that is not steeped in day to day living. Beauty need not be a measure of distance from our surroundings and others but a measure of how holistic our artistry is. To create with a holistic approach serves more than simply the hunger for inspiration.

In his work on *Philosophy and the Everyday* (2015), Finn Janning acknowledges a crucial limitation in articulating the everyday in these binary terms. These are then used to govern the everyday, creating norms that he says should be done away with by finding a new language of articulation for every person's everyday. This requires that we develop a poetic language for the everyday. Janning articulates this as follows: "Our language is not sufficient to grasp what happens, (in the everyday) although we can try to make it more poetic" (2015, 3).

To seriously consider how Ubuntu relates to the everyday, it has to be extended to overcome the limitation Janning articulates. The binary created by hierarchizing spheres of life is what contributes to the limitation which can be overcome by finding a new language for the everyday. Indeed it is within the everyday that Ubuntu becomes apparent, from a simple act of greeting in acknowledgment of another human being/person, to hosting a stranger or even being courteous to all regardless of their station in life.

Furthermore, the everyday does not begin or end at one or another point. Ceremony in the everyday does not break time; time is not fragmented into totalising events and time is not a set of prescribed expectations for ordering. Rather, there is little distinction between the formal and informal. To access the everyday Bovon suggests a shift in time, noting that "the cyclical time of the everyday means that the teleology of linear time has to be given up" (1989, 42). What this entails is that there is no pronounced break in time between defined formalities and informalities. Engaging with any element of the everyday does not require a break in time but rather a negotiation of movements. The danger of the everyday being an offspring of what is considered formal or authoritative is that it becomes an imitation of authoritative ideas. Our attention is diverted away from looking at the everyday for what it distinctly offers.

James Scott's *Weapons of the Weak* (1985) recognises that oppression disrupts everyday functions of livelihood and this is what makes it an important site of resistance. In this instance oppression is defined as the overbearing governance of the everyday. Resistance here is framed along class struggle lines – a response to institutions of repressive power. The collective acts of foot dragging, dissimulation, false compliance, pilfering and feigning ignorance all require that workers defy the status quo anonymously. To this end resistance is towards an individualistic self-help, it is an individual act of defiance reliant on a level of invisibility on the part of the actor. It is informative to bring to attention how Scott likens public resistance and everyday forms of resistance stating that both "intend to mitigate or deny claims made by superordinate classes or to advance claims vis-à-vis those superordinate classes" (1985, 32). Here the everyday is located in opposition to the dominant regime, it is a site of response to a system of dominance which seeks to impose a form of governmentality on it and threatens its scope of performance.

Of interest too is how Scott again tells us that, "the peasantry often finds it both tactically convenient as well as necessary to leave the formal order intact while directing its attention to political ends that may never be accorded formal recognition" (1985, 33). Already here it is quite clear that a distinction is drawn between the everyday and formal institutions and that the levels of interaction between the two are largely governed by publicity, the spectacle, and visibility. Everyday resistance as articulated here is fashioned by going through the loopholes within officialdom and its repressive structures – finding ways to get by in the system through acting out small forms of resistance through self-effacement – deploying temporary strategies of containment, while undermining those institutions that regulate the everyday in self-constricting ways.

While the theory of aesthetics focusses on what it sees as high and low aesthetics and associates the lowly with the everyday, Scott locates the everyday within the realm of struggle, specifically non-institutionalized forms of struggle. Our aim in this volume is to collapse the artificial binary created in theory of aesthetics and to see the everyday as hidden in those rituals, ceremonies and struggles that saturate the public and private spaces, even when these may sometimes go unnoticed. While informal resistance that Scott draws attention to is often enacted in the everyday, this must not be seen as an end in itself. Everyday experiences, even when they take the form of struggle, must be seen to be linked to practices, rituals and ceremonies, even ways of being, that define most communities. To talk about Ubuntu and the everyday is to talk about ways in which Ubuntu finds expression in the everyday; in people's daily encounters with their environment and not least, with those power structures that seek to impose their regime of meaning on the everyday. It is also a recognition that the everyday within which Ubuntu dwells is in constant motion; a state of flux that defies any form of fixity. This is how Ubuntu itself a living practice gets mediated, transformed and redefined within the everyday currents. In this sense too time and space also become a fluid continuum within which everyday practices such as ceremonies, rituals, rites and daily struggles are performed, challenged and revised.

Everyday Ritual and Meaning

Within the everyday is a tapestry of norms and practices that constitute society's function. Of note are rituals, performed acts of everyday norms and practice that are formal in construct and informal in their relationship to the everyday. In Africa ritual is still pervasive today and continues to inform the everyday social relations, beliefs, values and perceptions passed down from one generation to another orally and through performance. Rituals punctuate all of life and act as navigation tools for norm creations. The everyday is particularly informative of African ways of being. It follows that it is a source of significant knowledge(s).

The historical baggage African knowledge is forced to grapple with is that too often it is relegated to the traditional, pre-historic and even ahistorical, and unchanging. In this instance value judgments are made on culture and frameworks of knowledge making. Such value judgment is made by privileging hard science, the universal measurement imposed on all knowledge and meaning making. The burden is having to present hard proof or manipulate knowledge to fit a prescribed mould, or else face being reduced to the irrational, magical, and mystical. This follows from the way in which European technological advancement has been "promoted as technological superiority ... extrapolated not only as a cultural advantage but also ... as a qualitative superiority" (Keita 2014, 24). This has been at the expense of other technologies that people who were colonised had advanced although quite differently from the colonisers. In an environment of politicised and ideological knowledge formation, defined by the privileging of certain knowledge systems and exclusionary culture, it is important to ask questions about the ways in which the formal canon of "knowledge economy" is structured and gets to inhabit our spaces. Intellectual heritages, become practices of governance in knowledge where rationality and the science are often framed by the logic of capital. In this instance what needs to be interrogated is certain knowledge presented as legitimate and authorized; the

7

technologies that create 'real' knowledge; "and the entanglement of such knowledge with capital" (Green 2014, 45). What is central is that the way we choose to develop knowledge on Ubuntu and the everyday informs an approach to it.

In Sindiwe Magona's *Chasing the Tails of My Father's Cattle*, Shumikazi is a young girl who attends missionary education and participates in traditional rituals and ceremonies at home but with some initial scepticism over what the practices of her people can teach her which missionary education does not only teach but surpass. The following scene unfolds when she undergoes *Intonjana* - her ceremony into womanhood:

> Shumikazi was mildly surprised at some of the 'secrets' for, to her they seemed plain common sense. She had received better guidance, she felt, at school - but then, she quickly reminded herself, that was regarding education and the attainment of a profession of one kind or another. This was different. As the days went on, Nosapho worked on the girl, giving her all her know-how, including reasons certain things are done, in certain ways, at certain times, clearer and clearer did it become to the girl she had been hasty in her judgment. *Intonjana* was much more than being a woman. It was about being a human being among other human beings, about the meaning of life and one's role as a woman in that life, and the unravelling and support of that eternal mystery called life (Magona 2015, 216).

Ubuntu has its foundation and roots in the community, but it extends well beyond the family and even community. It is expressed through the everyday engagement between people, from greetings to court proceedings and peer institutions. It governs relations between people who are part of the larger cosmos— the relationship persons have with the land, animals, plants, mountains, water sources, the ancestors etc.

Ubuntu is therefore in part, about how one conducts themselves in the presence of other persons. The philosophical principle is that we are all inter-connected by mutual recognition. We are always connected and we are governed by these connections and their changes. Because of our recognition of this we are required to learn and uphold prescribed ways of being. From this foundation of oneness are born our institutions. These we practice in all the fundamental stages of life continuously reaffirming our Ubuntu— that we are the product of the union between two people who themselves are the product of the union between another two people and so on. From this recognition the being relates with the rest of the community and indeed all persons, and the totality of their universe.

The most intimate aspects of shared life are where people perform Ubuntu. The values of Ubuntu emanate from the daily necessities of life. To draw once more an example from Magona's novel, a mother named Miseka is with a child and daily chores burden her full body. The Red women (AmaXhosa) take it upon themselves to project Ubuntu by collecting wood for her, presenting it before her and leaving with a smile of understanding and joy for the blessing she carried— one they all fully comprehended the weight of. With gratitude Miseka's mother bursts into song: "Behold! Behold! And be grateful! Behold! Behold! And give thanks! We are as we are, this beautiful; wealthy we are. Verily; here inside, we are truly wealthy, happy in ourselves, rightly beautiful we are!" (2015, 18). In joy she proclaims her connectedness to the other women and celebrates that which Ubuntu stands for. Ubuntu becomes a way of being, a way of becoming more integrated. Life is organised around relationships and how these relationships are formed, expressed and forged.

The everyday challenges how knowledge is studied and how we perceive of it. The everyday experiences of people are what they use to navigate life and what informs everything that they do; the rituals they perform, how these are performed, changed, cast out, altered, and what they are replaced with. Knowledge is produced here in the most fundamental way – those who have knowledge of the everyday ways of their people and interrogate them or guard them are thus the knowledge bearers and preservers. This knowledge of the everyday in the African context is closely intertwined with the wisdom of Ubuntu. Knowledge bearers are inevitably challenged by those who have similar knowledge and are forced to critically interact with assumed communal or individual norm.

In his seminal work on *Sage Philosophy*, Odera Oruka (1990) positions African philosophical thought within an oral tradition anchored in critical engagement with the communal norms and practices, and intellectual critique. Everyday language, ritual and performance are made meaning of by those in the community who study them. This means that the everyday already has its intellectuals, institutions of questioning, and preservation. The so called informal is formalised in these incubatory spaces of thought and dialogue with the community's everyday activities. What is germane here is the ambiguous web of interaction which serves to disrupt a clear distinction between what is formal and what is 'everyday.'

Philosopher Ikuenobe tells us that "moral thought or moral philosophy is an everyday practical enterprise that ordinary people engage in during their daily living when they examine how they lead their lives and in their effort to apply moral principles to their daily lives, it is not an activity that only professional experts in philosophy can engage in" (2006, 102). But, neither is it simply utilitarian. Rather, this should reflect the spirit of African philosophy and critical thought.

Could Ubuntu and the everyday lead us to a break from looking at Ubuntu historically—basically through the lens of European discourse making, a perspective that is bound to make us unaware of the ways in which it has survived and the significance of things that have kept Ubuntu accessible to us to this day? These modes of preservation and continuation were not only overlooked by Europe and its historicising of Africa but they have been discarded, silenced and devalued. If we include them then what do they do to time? If we seriously consider them and apply them as a theory then what does Ubuntu look like to us and what does the pattern of its existence look like?

Performing Ubuntu in the Everyday

By virtue of the way modernity is constructed, individualistic traits inform the institutions we are in contact with on an everyday basis. With this in mind we want to ask what institutions inform what Ubuntu entails. This is a question that would best be answered by practitioners of Ubuntu, those who are knowledgeable about institutions steeped in the principles of Ubuntu and those who are the custodians of the institutions as well as those who have been initiated into these institutions. And yet Ubuntu's embeddedness in the everyday requires that anyone who practices it reflect upon their personhood. We are therefore required to undertake the task of collectively and personally re-envisioning Ubuntu. The majority of South Africans continue to practice in African institutions and modern institutions with little contradiction. Marriage, initiation and naming practices evoke very specific principles of Ubuntu both in the urban and rural space thus merging the two. Acts of Ubuntu continue to play out in the everyday alongside institutions of individualism. The everyday is embedded in Ubuntu which should not be mistaken for a fixed and pre-colonial phenomenon but rather a flexible moral compass and a product of the society it comes from. Ubuntu and the everyday should not be fixed, instead both would benefit from continuous rework and re-imagination as the community of persons change to suite their times and environment. We can search for and identify Ubuntu and what informs it, all the time attempting to tease out any clues of the changes it has undergone - for we may not be able to at first, and with clarity, see it for what it is. What we cannot do is to outright dismiss it.

The everyday is the space where Ubuntu collides head on with the motion and movement of human interactions, where it experiences its greatest changes, use or neglect. Because of its dependence on human relationality it is determined by all connections and disconnections. Religion, politics, ideology, identity, culture all brush against the shoulders of Ubuntu. Janning's metaphor of the everyday as a saucepan illustrates this

11

image best. The everyday is the point of interaction between multiple realities. Within the postcolonial saucepan Ubuntu is one of the multiple ingredients and adds its own flavour to the mix and is enhanced, complicated or simply repressed and undermined, especially under authoritarian regimes, both in the political and social arena; spiritual and economic sphere. And even under these intolerable conditions, Ubuntu continues to haunt our conscience and to offer hope since Ubuntu is the obligation we have to others and the spirit with which we perform these obligations. These are obligations to the living, the non-living and yet-to-be-born – the totality of human ecology. What Ubuntu recognises is that relations are unavoidable and indeed necessary; the question is how to navigate these and develop them for the benefit of all parties, the community and the growth of each person. What defines the everyday most starkly is interconnectedness— meeting points. All the basics of life involve weaving one's own tapestry of Ubuntu— becoming a person through one's relationship with others. All relations are connections; all things are connected and inform the continuity of generations before and generations to come. It is what Weidtmann in this volume calls a historical dimension as a defining aspect of Ubuntu – a historical trajectory that provides us with a genealogy of our connectedness and a common lineage and history that binds us together, even if within difference.

Let us place into context what has been thus far articulated by turning to greeting. One of the first interactions a child has with older people is identification and greeting. He or she learns to identify their name among a range of other sounds and words, and naturally, responds. With time they are taught how to respond and the initiation of that response is coded in aspects of greeting. Greetings can also make children very anxious because they stand before elders and have to perform an act that is long drawn out and it expects varied answers from them, they all too often may try to get away from the ritual as soon as possible. The child learns that greeting is done on all occasions and saturates every aspect and space of life. Greeting is done when you enter the home, when you meet someone in the street, in the taxi/kumbi/matatu/boda-boda, in the que, at a social function, in a meeting, out at an eatery and so on. Even if greetings have undergone changes in modern contexts there still remains an obligation to acknowledge people. This is most noticeable in instances where people are not greeted and take offense that someone would enter their space and not pay any recognition to them. The establishment of a connection with others is lost when greeting is abandoned; the great ritual of reciprocity is missed out on. Children are therefore encouraged almost immediately to learn to greet and to internalise the ritual and perform it in every aspect of their lives.

Greeting is observed in most if not all societies. Greeting is a mode of recognition. The way it is performed is informed by the relationship created/formed between the two parties. Rituals of recognition are inclusive or exclusive. They are introductory and are loaded with meaning. Greeting acknowledges the other person in a way that places them in relation to the broader and larger relationships between the parties engaged in the courtesy. The acknowledgement is the beginning of a familial relationship. This acknowledgment is not only for the person but their position as someone who has some information of importance to the greeter. Greeting reaffirms connections between two people, families, groups, communities etc. It is this recognition of African concepts, philosophies and practices that is a central theme of our work thus far. It is in the process of this recognition that we can begin to unravel our myriad and complex make up. How we have changed but also how our influence goes beyond geography, institution, language, culture and practice.

Looking at Basotho greetings, Dele Akindele tells us that this sociolinguistic event is informed by rules of conduct, and is an inevitable part or everyday conversation. She goes on to say that it "regularizes patterns of reciprocal behaviour among group members. It facilitates predictability and stability in interpersonal relationships and, at the same time, minimizes negative feelings or general misunderstanding" (2007, 2). In her paper Akindele is specifically concerned with Sesotho greetings but we can agree that this sentiment resonates with diverse African communities. For instance, we witness that in most if not all African greetings the parting is always a well wish regardless of the weight of the news shared amongst people or the antagonistic relationship between parties. When closing the greeting both should establish neutrality on the spoken matters and extend generous parting words that necessarily rebuild and repair the relationship. Akindele reaffirms this by saying that "among the Basotho, greeting is considered as an aid to peaceful social relations because it is very much part of the daily experience of the group members" (2007, 2). To engage in a critical reflection of Ubuntu is to initiate a long process of reflection and healing, projects that should never be overlooked in our intellectual endeavours as we are reminded by Ayi Kwei Armah in *The Healers* (1979). We should approach Ubuntu with the same spirit as we would engaged in a greeting and begin an important dialogue.

When we investigate the overall makeup of greeting and its reach into all moments of relationality then we can see that greeting is the universal ceremony that flavours human interaction. All dialogue is a performance of greeting, it sets the parameters for engagement and strict protocol is observed in its initiation. This permeates through to the level of informality where greeting amongst friends or loved ones embeds in these relationships a level of high esteem and respect for one another. Greeting is not only prefatory, meaning used for simply introducing a conversation, it also frames both form and content of the conversation. This includes the way you approach a person or group of people, the required exchange, critical questions and responses made and the mood of the closure of the exchange. There are examples of the importance of greeting which always includes sharing of food, an example is the breaking of kola nut sometimes mixed with alligator pepper among West Africans and drinking *mqombothi* (traditional brew) in Southern Africa. Within this ritual are the ingredients that make up relations of Ubuntu amongst *abantu* (people).

We will turn to an engagement with the posture of greeting and its position as a site of meaning making. The posture of greeting is a very significant aspect of greeting among most societies. Bows, squatting, kneeling, lying down, nodding, waving are just some greeting postures. Firth tells us that "The body as a whole can be a greeting or parting instrument in three main respects: by maintaining a distance gap between the parties; by adopting an overall posture; and by moving to meet or farewell the other party" (1972, 18).

To greet is to display a deep respect for the necessity of acknowledgment between people. The respect is to the greeted but it goes beyond that too, it is respect to those both the greeter and the greeted know— the extension of relationships they both share. It is also about respect for the ancestors since they are part of the community. There is an interpretation of greeting which is ritualistic, defined as "that aspect of customary behaviour that makes statements about the hierarchical relationship between people" (Goody 1972, 39). But there is another way in which greeting can be understood without having the hierarchal act as an imposition, but rather as a form of guidance as to how one should behave or the manners they should portray in a given circumstance, in this case greeting.

When a young person kneels before an older person, a man before a woman or a woman does so before a man, further going to the extent of lying down on the ground they are not simply doing so as an inferior, in fact such an interpretation belies the rich meaning and significance of greeting. What is problematic about this perception is the gendering of greeting and its equation to women as submissive and men as dominating. The posture interpretation is made through the prism of Western gender distinctions and binaries now adopted widely as standard critique. Subordination is turned into symbols that are dictated by Western thought and the internalisation of this is then imposed on African ways of being. The tyranny of universalism makes women from all corners of the earth who have taken their divergent trajectories of social behaviour come under the same scrutiny by Western feminism. These women are blanketed with the burden of being submissive— this being a stigma endorsed and perpetuated by Western feminism. Masculinity, femininity, ritual and performance are all subject to gendering (Oyewùmí 1997).

The rich meanings we get from exploring greeting are but one glance into how foundational Ubuntu is but also how universal (not universalist) its principles are. Rituals of greeting may vary from culture to culture but greeting itself is a universal form of recognition. How it is coloured and textured is the wealth we have to learn to surface.

One other trend that has persistently survived in the postcolonial African landscape is the culture of hospitality. Hosting is at the interface between relationality and reciprocity and signals a powerful idea of human connections beyond kith and kin thus cutting across boundaries of difference. It goes beyond the superficiality of categories of difference, which are often malleable and thus manipulated to create tensions among groups of people. The clearest example of this is found in the acts of Afrophobia and xenophobia across the continent, where historical borders and boundaries are cemented into distinct lines of warring sides that can be traced back to political subterfuge. In contrast to such hostility and violence, hospitality is a deeply rooted act of sharing information, burdens, joys, ills, wealth and emotions.

By welcoming a visitor, we openly invite them to share the modest home and meal we have and by extension the community's wealth. Whether familiar or stranger, passer-by or resident, a visitor is immediately attended to with the greatest of care taken to ensure their comfort. The attitude adopted when accepting visitors is one that makes no distinction between a familiar or unfamiliar guest. Suspicion is cast aside and the wellbeing of the guest is made of paramount concern, the activities of the day are immediately altered to suite the guest. Whatever chores were in progress are paused for the benefit of interaction and this becomes an occasion to eat the best food available. Receiving a guest is a celebration of interaction, of the presence of life and its extension and of the spirit of sharing which makes life all the more enjoyable. A central part of hospitality is sharing food. One never considers oneself inconvenienced by an unannounced visitor; anyone can pass by or "pop in" for no prescribed amount of time nor any particular reason except to inquire on the wellbeing of the residents and the homestead at large. Visitors are reassured that they are not considered to be encroaching on the privacy of their host or in any way inhibiting them from enjoying their own home. Visitors come with gifts, of news from afar or nearby, material items, and it can generally be agreed, that a visitor never comes empty handed. The everyday is no private, individual, consumptive affair, instead it is engaging, all encompassing, productive and the requirement is that one generously extends themselves to offer comfort, reassurance, nurturing and aid.

Hosting encompasses a broad spectrum of participants who form a reciprocal relationship with one another so that hospitality is never one sided. It includes the household that is doing the central hosting, family from the community, community members who can offer a hand, guests who honour the family both from near and far places and the ancestors who are an extension of the family and indeed guests since they too will receive libation and offerings and be included in the ceremony at the home as it is considered nothing can be done to their exclusion. Family, friends and neighbours are usually considered as part of the hosts but prominent members of the community are treated as guests to the family. The show of hospitality comes more from the heart and the art of the work put into hosting than the materiality of the hosting. It is assumed each will host according to his or her means but this is not always practically implemented, and this is presumably due to the spectacle involved in hosting. Despite how far people extend themselves to host others there are words of caution such as those from the Swahili proverb: *Mgeni siku mbili, siku ya tatu mpe jembe akalime*—"a visitor is a guest for two days; on the third day, put him or her to work" (Gathogo 2007, 116). What is important to take note of here is that "hospitality demands that we teach not only life skills but also specifically economic skills in order to prevent dependency and parasitism" (Gathogo 2007, 116). There is a need for collective work in hosting so that no single member is burdened but that everyone participates in sharing the increasingly rare gift of Ubuntu.

Hosting is an offering made to others on behalf of a family, for there is no individual who can host without the assistance and blessing of other people and those who preside over them in their daily lives. As with most of life, hosting involves specific rituals which are to be observed throughout the period of hosting. There are a variety of activities that accompany a ceremony or celebration: food, gifts, song, dance, and acts of gratitude. All the stages of hosting require a great level of work and ought to be conducted gracefully. The art of work we call hospitality is linked to the manner in which a person shares their life with others and is connected to the way people will celebrate a lived life according its contribution to life and how well a person enriched the lives of others.

What we can deduce from this brief discussion is that the everyday is the material foundation upon which Ubuntu is shaped and takes form. The everyday is Ubuntu's locus of enunciation, where we make meaning of those aspects of life that go unnoticed and unsearched and yet brim with the rich makeup of human life. Ubuntu is also the aesthetic expression of human generosity and spirit. Greeting and hospitality are but two examples from the human spectrum of being and expression, and Ubuntu is but one tool we have in our archive to explore these everyday acts and countless others.

These said, it is also important to acknowledge that the advent of modernity has led to unprecedented changes in basic human relations in Africa and notions of greeting as an object of recognition and hospitality as a gesture of sharing and obligation to the Other, have been transformed, especially within the urban context. Although as Fabian (1997) reminds us, networks of kinship relationships are continuously re-invented within urban spaces in spite of the difficult living conditions underpinned often by individualism. Nevertheless it is still difficult, as de Certeau (1984) avers, to speak about the everyday outside power relations. Both in pre-colonial Africa and post-colonial Africa, the space of connection; of recognition and affirmation of humanity, has always been threatened by repressive regimes of tyranny, often driven by power, greed and forms of self-gratification that are inimical to the values of Ubuntu. When ideologies such as apartheid are allowed to thrive and get normalised through social institutions such as the school and the church, our humanity is dented and our connectedness is brought into question. Indeed, all forms of power domination, whether gender, class, race or ethnic based, often work to undermine our human worth, and not just of the subordinate classes but also the humanity of those who subordinate others is damaged. It is for this reason that the Archbishop Desmond Tutu (2013) has argued that apartheid as a system did not simply deprive the oppressed of their humanity, it also robbed the oppressor of their humanity. In this sense the everyday, at least in the context of apartheid, had been turned into a space of control, of boundaries and daily humiliation of the Other. The tyranny of the everyday here ensues from the tyranny of governmentality and surveillance in which mutual human entanglement is stifled (Foucault 1977). As Graness shows in this volume Ubuntu continues to face challenges from state institutions, but we must read this as part of the limitations imposed by varied and long standing power relations.

Most of the chapters in this volume speak to the spectre of authoritarian control and economic deprivation on what ought to be the site of mutual respect. And yet even under the most tyrannical conditions, the sheer fact of the Master/slave having to share the same space, often complicates what may appear to be a clear-cut relationship of domination in which the dominated are rendered helpless. The ordinary people working through the everyday actions of appropriation and evasion subtly resist power. De Certeau (1984) sees strategy as the structures and institutions of power set in place to discipline and gain from the subordinate groups; while tactics are the practices employed by ordinary people to evade, manipulate and survive power's desire for absolute control as Dominic Dipio argues in her discussion of the role of the *Ssenga* (the woman who negotiates the thin line between patriarchal control and its subtle opposition all at once as she imparts traditional wisdom to the young female initiates) among the Baganda of Uganda.

While several chapters (Aloo Mojola, Oriare Nyarwath, Anke Graness) are interested in overarching powers that Ubuntu principles – flailing against these—must negotiate through active participants of democratic states. The dependency is on the material quantification of a life of dignity which is fundamental, certainly after political independence won by some African countries more than half a century ago. We would like to however add that Ubuntu is often performed despite political instability, economic deprivation, violence and lack of recognition of basic human dignity (Ogude and Dyer Forthcoming). While a complex and intricate relationship is formed from dominant power and acts and experiences of violence the capacity for Ubuntu is not regulated by this relationship even though its affects are both wide scale and intimate. Indeed, it is this which made it possible for Archbishop Desmond Tutu to facilitate the Truth and Reconciliation Commission through Ubuntu, imploring South African's (even when it seemed it was mainly Black South Africans who were called and responded) to reach beyond what is humanly expected of them and perform this act after the most heinous crimes had been committed in the name of apartheid. This capacity to show Ubuntu by the most marginalized in society can easily be abused and should never overshadow the immediate and necessary basic needs and dignity people ought to be afforded wherever they are in the world.

Finally, most of the chapters in this volume draw attention to how Ubuntu has always worked in a power dynamic. The greatest challenge it has faced is effacement and yet it continues to exist in the everyday relational encounters between people who share its basic tenets. These it must be mentioned are not provincial but universal principles which is what makes Ubuntu relatable and indeed familiar to even strangers to its vocabulary. It is however founded on seemingly simple ideas which build, inform and guide complex societies and operates in an ever changing and expanding world. It is the yardstick which though steeped in each community, is not limited to it, as all human beings are judged by this fundamental and this highest per*form*ance of being. It is true that it is not enough to simply be human, but similarly to have Ubuntu and perform it is an exceptional trait which is required of all human beings— to go beyond simply meeting the biological minimum of the human species.

Bibliography

Akindele, Dele F. 2007. "Lumela/Lumela: A Socio-Pragmatic Analysis of Sesotho Greetings." *Nordic Journal of African Studies* 16 (1):1-17.

Armah, Ayi Kwei. 1967. *The Healers*. London: Pearson Education.

Bovon, Laura. 1989. "Theories of Everyday Life: a Search for Meaning or a Negation of Meaning?" *Current Sociology* 37 (1):41-59.

de Certeau, Michel. 1984. *The Practice of Everyday Life*. Berkeley: University of California Press.

Fabian, Johannes. 1997. "Popular Culture in Africa: Findings and Conjectures". In *Readings in African Popular Culture*, edited by Karin Barber, 18-28. London: James Currey.

Jennings, Finn. 2015. "Philosophy for Everyday Life." *Journal of Philosophy of Life* 5:1-18.

Firth, Raymond. 1972. "Verbal and Bodily Rituals of Greeting and Parting." In *The Interpretation of Ritual Essays in Honor of A I Richards*, edited by J.J. La Fontaine, 1-19. Oxfordshire and New York: Routlege.

Foucault, Michel. 1977. *Discipline and Punishment*. Translated by Alan Sheridan. New York: Random House.

Green, Lesley. 2014. "Re-theorizing The Indigenous Knowledge Debate." In *African-Centred Knowledges: Crossing Fields and Worlds*, edited by Brenda Cooper and Robert Morrell, 36-50. London: James Currey.

Goody, Esther. 1972. "'Greeting', 'begging', and the Presentation of Respect." In *The Interpretation of Ritual: Essays in Honor of A I Richards*, edited by J.S. Fontaine, 39-73. Oxfordshire, New York: Routlege.

Gathogo, Julius M. 2007. "Revisiting African Hospitality in Post-Colonial Africa." *Missionalia* 55:108-130.

Ikuenobe, Polycarp. 2006. *Philosophical Perspectives on Communalism and Morality in African Traditions*. Oxford: Lexington Books.

Keita, Lansana. 2014. "Validated Knowledge: Confronting Myths about Africa." In *African-Centred Knowledges: Crossing Fields and Worlds*, edited by Brenda Cooper and Robert Morrell. London: James Currey.

Magona, Sindiwe. 2015. *Chasing the Tails of My Father's Cattle*. Johannesburg: Seriti sa Sechaba.

Mbembe, Achille. 2007. "Afropolitanism." Trans. Laurent Chauvet. In *African Remix: Contemporary Art of a Continent*, edited by Simon Njami and Lucy Duran, 26-29. Johannesburg: Jacana Media.

Ogude, James and Unifier Dyer. 2018. "Utu/Ubuntu and Community Restoration: Narratives of Survivors in Kenya's 2007 Post-election Violence." In *Ubuntu and the Reconstitution of Community*, edited by James Ogude. Bloomington: Indiana University Press. Forthcoming.

Oruka, Henry Odera. 1990. *Sage Philosophy: Indigenous Thinkers and Modern Debate on African Philosophy*. Koln: E.J. Brill.

Oyewùmí, Oyèrónké. 1997. "The Translation of Cultures: Engendering Yoruba Language, orature and world-sense." *The Invention of Women: Making an African Sense of*

Western Gender Discourses. Minneapolis/St. Pauls MN: University of Minnesota Press.

Scott, James. 1985. *Weapons of the Weak: Everyday Form of Peasant Resistance*. New York: Yale University Press.

Tuakli-Wosornu, Taiye. 2009. "Bye-bye Babar (Or What is Afropolitan?" *Afrololis* 26. http://afropolis.wordpress.com/2009/.

Tutu, Desmond. 2013. *God is not a Christian: Speaking truth in times of crisis*. London: Rider/Random House.

Chapter 1: EVERYDAY AND OTHER DAYS: WHAT'S THE DIFFERENCE?

Introduction

When you wake up in the morning, what goes on in your mind about what you are just about to get into—the day—and what are the factors by which your day is likely to be directed and determined? We usually do not start our days with these kind of questions, so this is a reflective, second-order question. Instead, we wake up with one objective: to go about our day as our awareness of who we are may allow. So, are you in a position to consciously have a sense of an objective for the day? Are you waking up in a familiar place that gives you an unconscious sense of security, and of the day as desirable? Maybe you want to go to work, to school, to visit a relative, to run an errand, or to perform any other action as your specific calling may have set up for you. But a person waking up in a prison cell or in a hospital room might not have their thoughts on *this* day like you, but rather on a far-off and only imaginary day away from *this* here and now. What goes through their mind may be mere desires thrown into their imagination by the thoughts of the possibilities of freedom. So ask yourself: how desirable is my present? On the other hand, although it does not even occur to us as part of our ordinary consciousness of the moment, you are either a male, a female, of a specific racial or ethnic identity. You may be broke, or unemployed, or unencumbered by financial limitations. And then your waking is certainly happening in a specific rural place or city neighborhood with its own specific social, cultural, and economic make up under the umbrella of a specific political atmosphere. All these factors will affect how your day is likely to turn out as we enact our subjectivity by navigating through them. No day is the same for any given two people even as many people, sometimes large portions of populations, may share the circumstances which these factors make real as shared conditions. What is "everyday"? If we are all human - are we? And are citizens in the same measure - is it? Then why is "everyday" so different for everyone? And for different groups of people? Indeed, the very idea of subjectivity - its presence, growth, and fullness - emerges out of considerations of how we operate (talking, moving about and making decisions) through these circumstances in a calculative application of our will and intelligence. At the end of the day, if we consciously have one (a mentally impaired person, or the terminally ill, of the barely conscious person in their death-bed is regulated by biological cycles rather than the hourly cycles of the day defined by alternating activities), how many narratives would we be able to construct to describe its contents to reflect not just the actions we performed, but also the desires and other thoughts that ran through our minds, and the failures we experienced? And now that I have set you up to reflect about the circumstances of your life in different ways, do you think of your life as one of privilege, or of grave economic limitations? To what causes do you attribute your circumstances? And what would you ever want to have done differently in order to change your circumstances for the better? And would such changes be to benefit you personally, or to benefit a vast number of other people in circumstances similar to your own? Why, or why not? Definitely, questions about the "everyday" can be unending, but those we have asked, and a few others below, help to throw some light on how complex our lives are. They show that individuality is a rich and complex notion, shaped by many factors. In other words, individuality is a product of the forces of systems within which we operate. And now our key question: how do we make sense of these complexities by thinking of them through the idea of Ubuntu? Isn't it the case that when we go out there, for those of us who are able to, we will be acting as our own situations will dictate to us? Yet, our rationality in those actions is shaped by the exigencies of life to be lived in response to needs that flow out of things we did not create? When we wire funds to relatives far away, don't we just participate in a web of financial processes, and in response to needs that have been imposed upon us? Yet it is not the case that our actions, and the needs to which we respond, are exactly as envisaged by those who "created" the economic conditions, and the financial facilities we have become consumers of. We make concrete and personal that which is general and undefined, and mold into our private truths and language the patterns of the abstract metaphysical system. In other words, meanings are produced by the specific uses of language and the games to which we put it. Similarly, and in the general sense of language, we put to the service of our specific needs and uses, within shared value systems, the language of economic resources, and we do this every day as social subjects. Regardless of the conditions under which we live, we will always find "ways of coping," of bending, translating, or taming that which is imposed to our own uses. Michel de Certeau refers to this as operational tactic. Here is what he says:

> We must therefore specify the operational schemas. Just as in literature one differentiates "styles" or ways of writing, one can distinguish "ways of operating" - ways of walking, reading, producing, speaking, etc. These styles of action intervene in a field which regulates them at a first level (for example, at the level of the factory system), but they introduce into it a way of turning it to their advantage that obeys other rules and constitutes something like a second level interwoven into the first [for example, a factory worker may transform an order of social importance back in his village because of his access to a

new economic resource and goods unique to his village - this is how "Jopango," the salaried laborers who worked far away from home, caused a new social order of importance by virtue of their newly-acquired image]. These "ways of operating" are similar to "instructions for use," and they create a certain play in the machine through a stratification of different and interfering kinds of functioning... He ...creates for himself a space in which he can find *ways of using* the constraining order of the place or of the language (De Certeau 1984, 30).

We are constantly translating in order to be able to operate at all, functioning within the constraints of systemic orders.

Constraints and Tactics of Taming the Everyday

Frantz Fanon (1967) analyzes the psychological tribulations of the everyday person as the embodied manifestation of the deadly racism and racialized history; Steven Feierman (1990) describes them as intellectuals in their own right; Sydney Littlefield Kasfir (2007) describes them as in control of symbolizing their own histories by means of differentiating between generations through carefully designed material cultural productions in the form of artefacts such as, for example, the Maasai and Samburu do with the spear and other materials of metal work; Clapperton C. Mavhunga (2014) describes them as transformative or innovative agents who are constantly thinking about and designing ways to tame, exploit, and adjust to the varying environmental conditions and topologies through technological innovation; Mike McGovern (2011) describes them as the people whose beliefs about the management and strengthening of personhood has driven an almost endless conflict that produces the national political picture in Cote d'Ivoire; Corinne Kratz (1994) describes them as the people responsible for creating for individuals and whole communities at large the norms by which they regard themselves as "proper" or not, thus defining whole narratives for individuals, families, and clans based on how the contours of cultural appropriateness are defined in such a manner that give individuals and age-groups as well as their families lasting identities. Alexis Kagame (1956) describes them as those who speak the ontologically structured language that reflects the complete understanding of Being as structured into its different categories based on an understanding of the role of reason or intelligence in the world. Henry Odera Oruka (1991) described them as practitioners of different levels of sagacity. Heidegger (1962) claims that *Dasein* is the special being whose ways, epitomized in the concomitance of *ratio* with language, is what gives nature its reality in the plurality of the meanings of finite beings or identities that make it as opposed to nothing. In other words, language, the ordinary language spoken by Adongo and Opiyo, by Wanjiku or John and Jean Does in its primitive form, is the language that manifests the revelation of Being. In other words, all these scholars, in their different interpretations of the everyday experiences of humans, concur in a broad sense that the everyday expression of basic humanity is anything but simple. Yet we are accustomed to speaking of Wanjiku, or Opiyo and Adongo, or John and Jean Doe of Americans as the "everyday person," the unsophisticated and simple-minded version of the rest of us.

So why have we invented phrases such as "the everyday person," or "in everyday life", etc., and become accustomed to thinking of the person in these spaces as inhabiting some marginal lands away from what really matters? The answer is to be found in our fixation with written narratives and the culture of print. "Since texts are what count as primary," say Mark Taylor and Esa Saarinen, "the diagnostics of our era are carried out vis-à-vis textualities." While they lament the neglect accorded by postmodern writers to the earth-moving implications of the techno-structures of world-production and commerce as well as administrative networks, we have only to think of the gulf between those who have school and those who do not. That divide is what defines the texts by or on Africans that I have mentioned above. Obviously, their authors are driven by a

29

protest against the meaningless divide between the so-called "everyday person", whether it is Wanjiku or Opiyo, or Adongo, and someone else whose mind is directed by what is written as opposed to the oral method of these folks. The debate cannot have been stronger than in Odera Oruka's idea of philosophical sagacity. Like I have said before, at the World Congress of Philosophy in Brighton, UK, in 1978, he shouted, in apparent frustration, "Who says that the West must monopolize philosophy?" In hindsight, it could only have been a frustration with the idea that because so-called "true philosophy" takes place only with texts, that is, in the context of written texts, anything else could not be regarded as "true philosophy." To be sure, Taylor and Saarinen are concerned with the on-going or still-happening practices of contemporary technology and its effect in shaping human lives today, but what they say easily translates into noticing how other things folks do daily are equally important tools that transform social reality. According to Taylor and Saarinen, the popular appeal of the *métarécit* obscures the fact that the metanarrative of our age is not a written product. The metanarratives of ecocatastrophe, the world economy, the technologizing of the lifeworld are not first literary creations that are later materialized. To the contrary, incipient metanarratives involve material practices that have not yet been theorized. In other words, it is not just the new phase of the media, as manifested in the habitation of a vast segment of human population today, that is telling us that the written is quickly becoming obsolete, it is the turning to the value of doing, of praxis in general which embraces the praxis of the Wanjikus and Apiyo and Adongos that is making the written narrative a threatened species of the modalities of human expression of thought. Thus, one can surmise, philosophy will not survive beyond this century unless it overcomes its fears of the oral and other media as contaminants of the discipline's core.

Nobody theorizes the "everyday" better than Pierre Bourdieu, at least since the publication of his *Esquisse d'une théorie de la pratique, précédé de trois études d'ethnologie kabyle* in 1972 (English translation as *Outline of a Theory of Practice*, 1977). In this work, Bourdieu left an indelible mark in teaching how the informal works in holding societies together, in other words, how the unwritten works meticulously and just as effectively as, if not better than, the juridical code. His idea was that the precepts of custom, very close in this respect to sayings and proverbs (such as those which govern the temporal distribution of activities), have nothing in common with the transcendent rules of a juridical code.

> [In it] everyone is able not so much to cite and recite them from memory, as to reproduce them (fairly accurately). It is because each agent has the means of acting as a judge of others and of himself that custom has a hold on him: indeed, in social formations where... there exists no judicial apparatus endowed with a monopoly of physical or even symbolic violence and where clan assemblies function as simple arbitration tribunals, that is, as more or less expanded family councils, the rules of customary law have some practical efficacy only to the extent that, skillfully manipulated by the holders of authority within the clan (the 'guarantors'), they 'awaken', so to speak, the schemes of perception and appreciation deposited, in their incorporated state, in every member of the group, i.e. the dispositions of the *habitus* (Bourdieu 1977, 17).

In other words, the so-called "everyday", customary, is equally structured and with its own mechanisms of effective self-sustenance and with its own metanarratives. In other words, the practice of the "everyday" produces its own discourses about the practice itself. Control of the grammar of practice, meaning of the rules of practice, has its own elasticity to account for occasional aberrations and rules of adjustment when there occurs a broken link between dispositions and the structures within which they operate.

Bourdieu stresses the effectiveness of custom in the regulation of conduct, both private and public, where Wiredu argues that according to the Ghanaian philosophical tradition, a penchant of many Ghanaians with inclination toward abstract thought, custom is put in use for the feeble-minded who cannot reason out moral right on their own. The difference, Wiredu argues, is that philosophical inclination in sorting out the basis for moral conduct is given to many people in his community, and custom to only a few. Thus, to him, long before Tempels, the Akan were, as a matter of traditional inclination, already accustomed to engaging in philosophical discourse, and this is not just in the manner of Tempels' Bantu whose philosophical delineations were passively buried in their practices. Rather, Wiredu (1992) claims, it was the *modus vivendi* for the majority of Wiredu's Akan to engage in vigorous philosophical debates, much like Kai Kresse's ordinary Mombasa folks engage in vigorous debates over the correct philosophical interpretations of the teachings of Islam. This way, they subject their own readings and understanding of the different denominational interpretations of Islamic teachings to analysis and scrutiny. But that is not the issue for Bourdieu. Rather, for Bourdieu, the objective is to study how social structure and practice affect each other over time; while the structure determines how members of a group conduct themselves, those behavioral practices sustain the social structure only so long as they are adhered to. In other words, his concern is the production of society by means of the multi-faceted systems of control. He says that unlike scientific estimations which are corrected after each experiment in accordance with rigorous rules of calculation, practical estimates give disproportional weight to early experiences. As families deal with procurements of necessary needs, the practice of actually satisfying the needs brings about the structuring of the social domain in which the needs are identified or defined, as the space of practice, the *habitus*. For example, the decision to make procurements to satisfy a specific need, say getting flour for making *Ugali* , or *Fufu* (bread) for the family dinner may result in such practices as gender division of labor (whose task is it to go to the family farm to fetch the farm product from which the flour will be pounded), domestic morality (how is each member of the family expected to conduct themselves as everyone gets to do something related to the preparation of the family dinner), cares (whose role is it to take care of those members who are still dependent, like babies), strife (competitions and complaints arise between different members of the household), tastes (the general expectation of how every component of the dinner should be prepared for it to be appreciated as delicious according to individual expertise, as well as family and cultural standards), etc. These structures in turn become the basis of perception and appreciation of all subsequent experiences. In other words, custom, like most practices of the social, always looks back to find precedents that suggest how similar issues have previously been successfully managed.

There is a difference between Wiredu and Bourdieu in regard to how they view custom. Wiredu's opposition to custom as a source of morality is about the use of custom as a source of morality because it negates the use of individual reason as the ideal source of norms. In Wiredu's naturalist view, appeal to custom as authority does not reveal any connection between a past or transcendental view and how the propriety of a present action should be determined. In other words, an action does not become right only because some person in the past, like an ancestor, or a general customary belief serves as a command that it is so, nor does such an action become wrong because such ancestor said it was. This critique of citing custom as the basis of our moral choices is a re-enactment of the classic Socratic argument about the meaning of piety as narrated by Plato in *Euthyphro*, the dialogue between Socrates and the young Euthyphro. According to this original argument, an action ought to be good (or right) on an account that is independent of its being liked, whether by the deities as transcendental authority, or by anyone else. In other words, since being liked is not a quality but a possible result of a quality, it cannot be the basis of a choice. Hence, something or an action must be liked due to a quality that belongs to it on account of which it becomes likeable, such as being good, right, or helpful, and not simply because the deities like it. For something to be good, it must bear some characteristic about it, like its quality, that is found to be independently appealing. The deities' liking of it cannot be such quality because it has nothing to do with the thing itself. So, for even the deities to like it ought to depend on this independent quality of the action or object itself, and not on the attitude of the deities or any such transcendental figures like ancestors. So, for Wiredu, as for Plato's Socrates, something or an action is liked by the deities or ancestors because it is good, but it cannot be good because the gods like it. Also, an action cannot be good because "it is what has been done from time immemorial," nor can it be bad merely because "nobody has ever done it." This is appeal to custom as authority. Instead, there must be a reason why something or an action was done, or was prohibited. Such reason addresses the quality of the matter, and so it is such reason which must be examined in the effort to determine its acceptability. Such quality can only be discovered by reason, and not by appeal to the attitudes of the deities or ancestors toward it. Thus, custom, religion, or ancestors, cannot be the source of norms of how we ought to conduct ourselves.

For Bourdieu, on the other hand, the object of analysis is practice. For him, as for his compatriot Michel Foucault, everyday practices depend on a vast ensemble of procedures as discourses which are schemas of operations, and of technical manipulations. At this level, Bourdieu's concern is not exactly philosophical in nature but rather - or almost - sociological. In other words, his concern is to clarify the structure of everyday practices in relation to discourse which Foucault calls "ideology" and Bourdieu calls *habitus*, the system or network of acquired modes of conduct, all complete with the norms, principles or beliefs which support them as "the way people in the specific cultural system ought to behave." Both concerns do, however, reveal in their argument and analysis, respectively, the idea that, at least from a moral point of view, the everyday is a complex, structured "ideal reality" which is always about the conflict between the real and the ideal as indicated by the question: on the basis or what principle ought I to act now? The *habitus*, he says, "is constituted in practice and is always oriented towards practical functions...one has to situate oneself within 'real activity as such', that is, in the practical relation to the world, the preoccupied, active presence in the world through which the world imposes its presence, with its urgencies, its things to be done and said, things made to be said, which directly govern words and deeds without ever unfolding as a spectacle" (Bourdieu 1990, 52). For Bourdieu, we practically inhabit, and are immersed in the world that conditions us in our thoughts, speech, and conduct. He challenges us to reflect on whether there are any instances, and under what circumstances, when we make free choices of a rootless, unattached, pure subject. This reality, for him, does not exclude the practice of individual rational guidance toward the best normative principles because we always act in view of an idealized picture of society. In other words, it easily absorbs variations, exceptions, and accidents without drastically transforming itself.

According to Foucault's and Bourdieu's analyses of ideologies and *habitus* respectively, we are both products as well as producers of "the world." What we do, and how we do it, is made possible by this vast system of conditionings, and in turn our practices become exactly its many bolts and screws that hold it together. Each agent, says Bourdieu,

> Wittingly or unwittingly, willy nilly, is a producer and reproducer of objective meaning. Because his actions are the product of a *modus operandi* of which he is not the producer and has no conscious mastery of, they contain an 'objective intention' ... which always outruns his conscious intentions... It is because subjects do not, strictly speaking, know what they are doing that what they do has more meaning than they know. The *habitus* is the universalizing mediation which causes an individual agent's practices. Without either explicit reason or signifying intent, to be none the less 'sensible' and 'reasonable' (Bourdieu 1977, 79).

Bourdieu's rambling description of *habitus* and the mutual productivity it has with its subjects whose practices sustain it can be found in *The Logic of Practice* (1990, 53-54).

So, who are we as agents in the realm of everyday? We are someone's child, as son or daughter, of our father or mother; we are another person's sister or brother, grandchild, again as male or female, of grandmother or grandfather; we are a brother, a sister, or a cousin to differently gendered people; we are someone's in-law; we are someone's current or former classmate, pupil, and all these things. We are also professors, scholars, or employees of different ranks and performers of different roles and duties at non-academic institutions; we are friends to many people, a barber's client, a client of a whole lot of other vendors, both occasional ones as well as those we patronize frequently like the grocer, the car mechanic or service station manager or technician, the gas station attendant; someone else is a student, and so on. We are a neighbor, a wife, and a husband. According to observation of practice, we are part of the different networks that these facts about us place us in, and the conduct of everyone that these relations bring together are determined by what we come to acquire as the expectations or etiquettes that determine the behavior of everyone in the relations we participate in. Our daily practices are structured by the structures of these many relations and their objectives. Each one has its rules for everyone who engages in the practices that define the relations at any given time. The variations and homogeneities of the practices in these different domains are what we call "the world." Engaging in the practices that these relations demand is what produces our humanity. To paraphrase Paulo Mboya's now popular title (*Luo Kitgi gi Timbe-gi*, 1938), they are what amount to *Dhano, kite gi timbe-ne*, which can be translated roughly as *"How to be human."* This is why the everyday opens itself up to analysis by multiple, multi-disciplinary approaches—namely because it's accomplishment is organized by many objectives whose meanings are defined and guided by the structures and the prescriptive norms which sustain them by spelling out the roles through which the structure is manifested. Jean-Paul Sartre, the famous French existentialist philosopher, had problems with the psychology (authenticity) of acting. With several examples (the grocer, the student, the soldier, the gambler, the flirt, the waiter, and others) he tells us in *Being and Nothingness* that no performance of any role in everyday life is ever wholly what it seems, that in numerous instances we have to pretend to "be ourselves," that there is only a difference of degree between the real, "sincere," unselfconscious performances in which we act ourselves, and the "dishonest," calculating, fully conscious staging of a scene for a given public, in short that it is impossible ever fully to be oneself. Yet he still affirms that this playing of roles is essential to society. Don't we call up our best but uncharacteristic manners when a mother in-law is in the house, while keeping under restraining watch those who, when left to "be themselves," are likely to run us into finable embarrassment? So when we think of *Utu*, *Kit Dhano*, or Ubuntu, we think of these roles, usually in their ideals, as what characterize him or her in relation to others in any number or all of these dimensions that his or her practices unveil. But the practical world is different from, and usually falls short of its idealized and desirable one, which is why everyday practice is inherently subject to normative regulation. Good, bad, right, wrong, equality, justice, fairness, respect, friendship, are some of the key values of the normative world. They are directed at regulating the quality of our actions, not only in respect to how they measure up to their desired ideals, but also, or especially, in respect to how they affect others. In other words, they are norms which are meant to regulate how we play our roles.

There are acceptable exceptions to some rules of engagement in everyday practices, and the room accorded such exceptions usually marks the boundaries of creativity. I am thinking, for example, of the realm of grammar as the body of rules of speech and the universal acceptability of poetry as a way in which the violation of grammar qualifies as an artful creativity in the unusual use of everyday language. Like in old times, including in classical Greece and Middle Eastern cultures, poetry, such as is revealed in song, is an important aspect of artistic use of language that defies the regulations of ordinary language. Like scientific and other forms of specialized language, poetry is often reserved to a few creative specialists or experts, yet its recital is part of the structure of the everyday because the latter includes the creation and enjoyment of art. *Shairi* in Kiswahili, poetry remains an important aspect of most cultures. Among the Swahili and other Islamized communities of the East African coastal region, poetry intertwines with the everyday recital of prayers but is also used to sing praises as well as to express traditional myths and general wisdom. In other cultures, poetry appears predominantly in the form of song and is intertwined with musical traditions. In Luo culture, for example, poetry is the foundation of the *Dodo* genre of song.

The expressive role and value of poetry cuts across entertainment and serious thought. In other words, poetry both expresses ideas and reveals the mind and emotions of the poet. Straddling the two domains defies the rivalry between them once witnessed in ancient Athens. There, as indicated in Book X of Plato's *Republic*, art was once seen as the rival of serious thought as represented by the sophists. Their attack on poetry and poets - as belonging to the world of irrational inspiration to talk of things they neither understood nor could teach while pretending to be wise - does not cloud or prevent the flourishing of poetry and song in the history of cultures. Cast to the realm of mythology by some traditions, poetry becomes one of the oldest expressions of human emotions, wisdom, and imagination of human relations with the surrounding universe.

Everyday and the Body

Nothing surrounds humans in terms of its unavoidable presence like the body itself, and nothing beats the body in grabbing our attention each and every day. It is our visible identity. The material concerns we have for the body beat every other concern. We are not described as *homo somaticus* for nothing. It is the primary possession any human has, for it is there before our ideas set in. It grabs our attention when it runs low in nutrition and hydration. It governs the instincts of the baby or child to draw the attention of the mother or substitute care-giver because its well-being requires regular feeding and hydrating. Its physical malaise result in similar calls for attention. The child's cry, or the adult's complaints, are equally aimed at signaling the need for the body's restoration to its average well-being. Poor or rich, royal or commoner, the needs of the body do not discriminate. A Luo folktale about when the fabled chief Odera Akang'o took revenge against a poor woman who denied him food when he felt hungry teaches that the natural dispositions of the body knows no class. Nor does the body's disposition to discharge its wastes happen according to our social class.

But the body's primacy is not only in relation to its bio-physical needs. It is also an epistemological as well as a social entity, a private as well as a public object with which people interact in socio-cultural contexts. Ancient Egyptians once owned the idea of immortality, believing that once life here on earth came to an end, people transitioned to another realm beyond here, and their bodies had to be prepared for this second run of life. Either this belief inspired them, or the long-lasting funerary rituals led to decomposition and unpleasant conditions prior to the burial of the dead, they invented the famed mummification process to preserve the body. This practice has since given influence to the modern science of embalmment. The dead do not have to look repulsive to those who interact with them prior to interment. Rather, they were adorned according to their social class and family status. The Christian doctrine and belief in the resurrection at the end of time may well have traced its roots to these ancient traditions of North Africa. Since Plato and Aristotle differed on the epistemological value of the body, their difference has continued to divide the Western world that is philosophically descended from them. While Plato placed the immortal soul above the body as the seat of true, universal, and durable knowledge, Aristotle's realism led him to put the senses at the source of our relationship with the external world, and therefore at the foundation of empirical knowledge. The differences have continued to separate not only idealists from realists, or rationalists from empiricists in metaphysical and epistemological matters respectively, they separate equally vigorously their more recent representatives in the philosophy of mind and the seat of consciousness. The lineage of thought that springs from Plato down through the Medieval period often viewed the body negatively, as exemplified in the thought of Origen and represented in veiled bodies in medieval and early modern art, regarding it as the source of sin, always threatening to contaminate the soul. Descartes, the modern representative of this tradition, repudiated the body, casting the senses as unreliable in their delivery of the perceptions of the external world, thus reenacting Plato's theoretical dialectic which turns the mind away from the everyday world of "shadows." The African statesman and philosopher Léopold Sédar Senghor opposed this Cartesian privileging of reason, arguing instead that the African self is essentially embodied, hence his/her perception of reality does not depend on or spring from pure reason alone. Senghor's controversial and widely discussed dictum - namely that "*emotion is black as reason is Greek*" (Senghor 1964, 24)[1] - emphasizes embodiment as central to how people acquire knowledge. It is his view that knowledge claims are always contingent upon the circumstances of the claimant. Everyone defines knowledge, and makes claims thereof on the basis of the virtues that his or her society provides, and which he or she just takes for granted. Embodiment, as the expressive tool of emotion, that is, e-motion, from to e-move, makes it possible for the subject, the knower, to approximate the object (of knowledge), to bring it closer instead of keeping it at a distance where it remains fixed

---

1   See also, Senghor, Léopold S., *On African Socialism*, English transl. Mercer Cook (New York and London: Frederick A. Praeger, Publisher, 1964), p. 74. In the latter, the expression is a little more elaborate: "European reasoning is analytical, discursive by utilization; Negro-African reasoning is intuitive by participation."

and lifeless. In other words, embodiment is the medium of participation. According to Senghor, the Negro-African "feels the object before he sees it... thereby entering the object, so to speak, in order to get to its essence, beyond the mere mental image of it that pure reason forms" (Senghor 1977, 92-93). Senghor's insistence, by constant use of the qualifying adjective "Negro-Africaine, or Black African", in contrast to "les Blancs, or the Whites" that this epistemological scheme is essential to the Negro-African, can be interpreted as indicative of his belief that the "modes" of applying human faculties such as how reason (actually) works, are racially distributed, and so forming racial essences. In "Orphée noire," Jean-Paul Sartre is ambiguous in his description of Negritude. In one sense he describes it as the Black man's (Negro's) way of being in the world, but then also calls it a historical contingency, an antithesis, brought about by the alienating cultural domination of the Whites, the thesis, in a dialectical historical progression (Sartre 1948, xi-xii). It is to be noted, however, that the Senghorian stance on embodiment as the basis of participative apprehension is different from the position of physicalists or quasi-physicalists. The latter, like the Ghanaian philosopher Kwasi Wiredu, stand in opposition to the dualist view of the constitution of humans. In contrast to the view that mind and body are separate substances, physicalists contend that mind is a capacity generated by the biological functioning of the specifically human body. Wiredu qualifies as a quasi-physicalist because he argues that although mind is not a separate substance, it cannot be reduced to matter either, but rather to a capacity generated by the biological functioning of the body specific to humans. It is the nature of the human brain to generate mind in cognitive experience.

To summarize, the body is central to how we make sense of everyday as the spatio-temporal location of human experience. Also, how we value it in the everyday experiences and discourse, as opposed to professional or specialized knowledge, is significant in the idea of the structures that Bourdieu analyzes. It is key, not just to the experience of our own selfhoods and identities, it is also morally structured. Many cultures consider parts of it with sacredness, as having a holy status that warrants concealment from the public view. Contemporary hyper-sensitivity toward the sexualized body is indication of the recognition of this status, and of sex as an act of holiness and privilege. But cultures differ on what or how many parts of the body are symbols of sex and so must be concealed from public view. While the public display of sexual organs was and continues to be banned universally, Africans in traditional settings related the female breast with sustenance of life and nutrition for the young, hence breast-feeding was considered normal, and its practice in public was not considered inappropriate. The influence of Western attitudes as well as availability of alternative baby feeding products has plunged Africans into debating the appropriateness of breast-feeding in public even as the West itself struggles with the idea. Relatedly, the definition of nudity separates many cultures, especially Western and non-Western definitions and practices. One wonders whether Western visitors who take pictures of bare-chested village women did not use their prints as pornographic pictures when the victims of their distorted intentions did not think of exposure of breasts as nudity.

Opponents of the Cartesian notion of the self, including empiricists, think of the body as our epistemic connector to the external world. It is also that part of the self that allows itself to be viewed as an object of which we can speak as if it were a thing out there, one that we can decorate, or even use, misuse, or abuse. In all these senses, the body is central to human discourse.

While we do not give much attention to the whys and hows of the body's biophysical demands - because they just happen to us - like being able to see when we open our healthy eyes, hearing with our healthy and unblocked ears, or feeling when we touch, and so on. On the deliberate side, we care about how our own bodies and those of people under our care are perceived by others around us. In other words, we care about how our bodies fare socially or in public. The Queen of England is not expected to appear at the Trafalgar Square in her underpants or sleeping wear, let alone in her birth suit. And she would not knowingly appear in any of those modes. Her handlers would not let her. And we would not expect you to come to meetings in your birth suits either. It is possible that you might be reading this in nothing other than your birth suit, but we want to assume that you are able to do so only in the privacy of your home, alone, or perhaps only in the company of that special person with whom you are in tacit agreement to have privileged mutual access to such confidentiality. That means that the rest of society is closed out of your private bodily posturing. We might not require of you in public appearance what we are likely to expect from the Queen of England, but some adornment of the body is expected. Perceptions of the public space, or what we know or suspect them to be drive how we prepare our bodies for presentation to such spaces and attending audiences. Mutual perceptions of the public space - who I am aware to be in the social world, and who I am aware to be presenting myself to, as well as my awareness of other people's perceptions and expectations of me - determine the details of the socialization of the body.

Everyday is defined by how we respond to a variety of expectations which society expects us to know. We are praised when we meet them, and rebuked when we fail, and both judgements are measured according to our status within the community where the exchange takes place. Not only does what I present to my guests matter, but also how I prepare and present it. These modalities of presentation may differ from one guest to another based on the social status that I bestow upon them. In other words, while all my guests might still be relatively well fed biologically on some green leaves, unless some of the guests were allergic to them, I may deem a meal of meat or fish more appropriate because of who my guest is to me, meaning that it is the social standing I give them that determines the selection of the material objects that I put before them. Because society already defines, in a graded manner, which objects symbolize the different levels of status, my selection "objectifies" the status of my guest according to this social scale of the community. My selection of items to present to my guests claims for them a specific spot in society's social scale as symbolized by the items on which society has bestowed a symbolic social status, for my selection of them is dependent on this "objective" value that the objects possess.

Similarly, I groom and dress well before I visit my friend, or before I present myself for an interview, because of the social meaning accorded different appearances. Aestheticization of the body in the broader and diverse socio-cultural terms is the oldest expression of art. Think of body paintings, piercings, and scarifications, and other modifications of the original natural body, or of its adornments, coverings and bearings. The body is the oldest object of art that we know. Before people painted rocks in caves, and before they invented canvas and used it for expressing imaginations in paint, they painted the body and cosmetized it to enhance its public appearance in everyday social presence.

Equally, when we think about the gendered and gerontocratic factors in the division of labor of which Bourdieu talks, we are engaged in socializing the body in terms of sex and the body's duration. It is no wonder, then, that philosophers like the pioneer French feminist, Simone de Beauvoir, talked of the social genesis and construction of womanhood as coterminous with the kind of labor that was born out of industrial revolution, although cultural womanization of the female body was far older and more ubiquitous than that which accompanied labor roles in the family and society at large starting with industrialization.

We are not talking of practices that are reserved for special moments. We are *homo laboris* to the extent that we are *homo somaticus*. We are *homo aestheticus* in so far as we are *homo somaticus*. We work and we adorn ourselves everyday. That is who we are daily. Our survival depends on our ability to direct our bodies to safe locations, healthy nourishments, and control. In private and in public, the body is both a moral, aesthetic, and cognitive object even as it is the physical basis of our mind and thoughtfulness whence springs the agency that coalesces our personhood. By describing humans as *homo laboris*, Marx aimed at putting man and his economic interests at the center of the universe, claiming thereby that through the use of his body, man is the principal transformer of the material world. History, he theorized, is the dialectical social progression that results from the contradictions dictated by the alienating economic inequities engendered inside this transformation.

The different views of labor, whether capitalist, Marxist, or peasant, valorizes the body as the primary and natural possession for which we ought to be compensated in a certain way. And Marx's idea that it is an inherent logic of capitalism to exploit the bodies of others for profit suggests that the body is always susceptible to abuse. It is the window through which we enter negotiations with others, and our moral regard for others is judged by how we define, valorize, and hierarchize body types. Simone de Beauvoir argues in *The Second Sex* (1952) that although the perception of female bodies as inferior to that of males is both old and ubiquitous, the perception of females as objects of male satisfaction or comfort the same way the couch in the living room is can be traced to the age of industrialization and salaried labor outside the home for males. In other words, industrialization invented womanhood as the social status of females who were already considered to be inferior by many cultures around the world. It is the perception of the African body as a free economic asset that gives birth to the modern slave even if the idea of race and the practice of racism were much older. Because our subjectivity is borne by the inalienable primacy of the body, we experience every day as victims or perpetrators of these conflicts which center a round perceptions of certain body types. It is hard to imagine experience in a world in which one was constantly reminded of the spatial margins and corners in which their bodies were to be confined, and the violence - moral, judicial, political, social, and physical - to which they were subjected as part of how the human dermatological geography was imagined, drawn, and enforced.

There is a saying that beneath their skins, human beings are all the same.[2] The scientific refutation of the idea of race as a biological reality has exposed the banality of the idea of race and the practice of racism as belief and practice based on a politicized illusion. Yet, despite this relatively recent scientific debunking of the idea that is as old as people started to travel to faraway lands populated by people who looked different from them, the atrocities meted on individuals and whole populations on the basis of the false belief have continued to ignore the scientific findings even as scientific findings have exposed the serious irrationality of the beliefs in racial differences and their alleged respective differences in capacities. The point is clear. Racial prejudice did not start as a scientific idea, but attempts have been made to manipulate or misinterpret science to support this mythical belief.[3] Eugenics sprang up as a science in the United States in the early twentieth century before it was used in Nazi Germany with aims to protect and improve the capacities of the white population as a superior race in discrimination of Jews and non-whites. As evidenced by Nazi Germany as the worst recorded example in human history, the power of the myth has driven political ideologies and policies and resulted in systematic and systemic exterminations of fellow human beings like unwanted household trash or pests. In the United States, South Africa, and throughout much of the colonial world, policies of

---

2   A remark by Stephen Jay Gould (1941-2002), the American paleontologist evolutionary biologist, and historian of science, in the documentary, "Race: The Power of an Illusion."

3   Ideas of race and classification of people into races is a modern Western creation whose uses coincided with the spread of European ideology of economic, and then military and political intrusion into far reaches of the world, occasioning its use, especially since the eighteenth century as a mechanism to stratify society and to accord privileges, benefits, and rights to some and not to others, with the justification that the groups called 'races' are innately different and that their differences cannot be transcended" (Smedley 1999, xii). By contrast, ancient peoples stigmatized "others" based on language, custom and especially religion, but they did not sort people into "races."

legal segregation, discrimination in the administration of justice, and in the distribution of resources kept non-white populations at the bottom of their nations' societies. Racial prejudices or mythical beliefs developed during these periods have long outlived the dismantling and delegalization of the formal racist policies and practices and have recently been emboldened by political gains and ascendancy to power by members of conservative, ostensibly racist groups.[4]

Everyday, whether or not we are aware of it, we are real or potential victims of discrimination by virtue of how we look as embodied subjects. When not explicitly stated in public discourse, the evocation of the idea of Ubuntu as a moral and political critique (of race and racism) reminds us of the flimsiness of segregation, apartheid, or discrimination in general on the basis of the stigmas falsely attached to skin color. Its emphasis on freedom, respect, and equality as the right ideals of any society is an affirmation of the shallowness of the differences in skin color and a negation of the social construction of race. While the superficial perceptual variations among peoples is obvious

---

4   Individuals and groups will usually express their biases only when they believe that their ideas and actions have support among influential segments in society either by law or unofficial but widespread social endorsement. Neo-Nazi and other white supremacist organizations in the United States, while not official or recognized for their ideological positions, manage to enjoy social support and legal protection under the free speech laws which allow them to openly and publicly express their racial hatred for target groups. Some members of these groups do not rationalize their hatred as they might not know either why exactly they hate non-white people, or in what regard(s) exactly they believe to be superior to non-white people, or whether they themselves would show to be superior to any one non-white person, let alone to all of them, or, conversely, show how at least some non-white persons are inferior in any one or more of those regards, but they hate non-whites nonetheless. On the other hand, we infer the grounds for rationalized racism from practices which differentially apportion responsibility to non-white people from how they do to whites. Because non-white people are either *a priori* discriminated out of positions, or they are *a priori* held to be culpable of wrongs, we infer that they are held in such systems to be intellectually and morally inferior.

47

enough for everyone to see, proponents of a universal Ubuntu argue, like Smedley says, that such "variations among peoples have no social meanings except what we humans give them" (Smedley 1999, xii). In other words, if there are no biological races, it then follows that the judgements crucial to racist beliefs such as intellectual and moral differences must be false.

Our bodies are constantly under scrutiny and judgement by others, and living successfully in the public domain means in part being able to navigate these rough terrains by knowing and being able to anticipate and preempt responses to the scrutiny of the public sphere. Awareness of this public presence affects and shapes our embodied agency in some general way, but long-standing traditions of masculine domination and control of the conceptual keys of valuing the body have made feminist voices better positioned to assess sexually biased beliefs and practices. Throughout the world, the social structures that Bourdieu talks about left females in subordinate positions in relation to their male counterparts, and often left to perform tasks that were considered less important and "beneath" a man's status. His sociology arose in the shadow of the work of Simone de Beauvoir who pioneered the philosophical critique of the naturalization of what in reality were social constructions and assignment of roles in line with such constructions. To the question, "what is a woman?" she famously observed in her opus magnum, *The Second Sex* (1952), some would respond, "woman is a womb (*Tota mulier in utero*)," thereby assigning a meaning, womanhood, to a biological femininity, giving it an essence or definition that fixes its social role. "But conceptualism has lost ground," she writes. The biological and social sciences no longer admit the existence of unchangeably fixed entities that determine given characteristics, such as those ascribed to woman, the Jew, or the Negro. Science regards any characteristic as a reaction dependent upon a *situation*" (Beauvoir 1974, xvi). Her work, then, starts what would become in the ensuing years and decades a feminist exploration of the psychological, sexual, and social roles of women and their historical and contemporary situation in

Western culture at the middle of the 20ᵗʰ Century. Society imposes its "readings," or, in our cases, and generally, its discourses on who we are and how we ought to act in virtue of those definitions. Sartre thought that these *situations*, the perennial platform of our existential everyday, are insurmountable. According to him, the particularities of these situations are everywhere encountered by human-reality, which is free choice, as resistance and obstacles which it has not created. "It is *my place, my body, my past, my position* in so far as it is already determined by the indications of Others, finally my fundamental relation to the Other. [They form] various structures of the situation" (Sartre 1956, 629; emphasis in original). Cultural structures are a network of limitations which we encounter everyday. "...the limit imposed does not come from the *action* of others...when we give in we do so *freely*... [And this may apply even to my] encounter with a prohibition in my path ('No Jews allowed here,' or 'Jewish Restaurant. No Aryans allowed,' etc.), and this prohibition can have meaning only on and through the foundation of my free choice. In fact, according to the free possibilities which I choose I can disobey the prohibition, pay no attention to it, or, on the contrary, confer upon it a coercive value which it can hold only because of the weight which I attach to it. Of course the prohibition fully retains its character as an 'emanation from an alien will'; of course it has for its specific structure the fact of *taking me for an object* and thereby manifesting a transcendence which transcends me. Still the fact remains that it is not incarnated in *my* universe, and it loses its peculiar force of compulsion only within the limits of my own choice and according to whether under any circumstances I prefer life to death or whether, on the contrary, I judge that in certain particular cases death is preferable to certain kinds of life, etc." (Sartre 1956, 672; emphasis in original). Sartre's words sound like they are a description of the not-so-distant past in South Africa. Both de Beauvoir's *Second Sex* and Sartre's *Being and Nothingness* were written at a crucial time in world history. They were revelations that historical military, political, and socio-cultural experiences of conflict finally threw into the open the fundamental evil hidden in the psyche of people. Sartre thought that navigating the resistances and obstacles that this drive creates was the existential human reality; it was permanent and unresolvable even if its resolution, freedom, was the fundamental goal and motivation in authentic life. de Beauvoir, on the other hand, thought that situations of oppression were historical, brought about under specific circumstances, hence they could be overcome and freedom could be restored. But what, exactly, does this freedom imply?

The idea of a resolution, or the end-goal, resonates with Nietzscheanism

In *The Genealogy of Morals* Nietzsche says this:

> Granting that political supremacy always gives rise to notions of spiritual supremacy, it at first creates no difficulties (though difficulties might arise later) if the ruling caste [appoints itself to be] also the priestly caste and elects to characterize itself by a term which reminds us of its priestly function. In this context we encounter for the first time concepts of pure and impure opposing each other as signs of class, and here, too, good and bad as terms no longer referring to class, develop before long (Nietzsche 1956, 165).

For Nietzsche, there are two moralities, one for the Master class, and the other for the subordinate class, the slave class. Over time, the values of the ruling class become the ideal norms of society in which the term "good," he argues, denoted a class of powerful, aristocratic individuals who innocently celebrated their power and concomitantly took for granted their assumed superiority over the powerless common folk. The morality of these aristocrats celebrated as virtues such character traits as pride and arrogance, strength and egoism, wealth and leisure, simply because these were the values they themselves already possessed at the deliberate exclusion of others. The aristocratic person regards himself as the determiner of values; he does not require to be approved of; he passes the judgement: "What is injurious to me is injurious in itself." He knows that it is he himself only who confers value on things and practices; he determines who ought to live where and do what, all in service of what is favorable to himself; he is the creator of values; he honors whatever he recognizes in himself. Such morality is self-glorification.

Thinking historically, Nietzsche argues that the next stage of morality is the revolt of the subordinate class against the aristocratic master morality. The oppressed, the abused, the suffering, the unemancipated have a resentment for the morals of the oppressor as well as a suspicion and skepticism for everything defined as "good" in the value system set by the dominant class. In eagerness to alleviate the sufferers of their condition, the new morality brings into prominence such values as sympathy, kindness, mutual recognition and respect, humility, friendliness, diligence, fairness, and justice to replace the values of the master-morality as the core values of humanity. According to Nietzsche,

> The slave revolt in morals begins by rancor turning creative and giving birth to values - the rancor of beings who, deprived of the direct outlet of action, compensate by an imaginary vengeance. [While] All truly noble morality grows out of triumphant self-affirmation...Slave ethics, on the other hand, begins by saying no to an "outside," an "other," a non-self, and that no is its creative act. This reversal of direction of the evaluating look, this invariable looking outward instead of inward, is a fundamental feature of rancor. Slave ethics requires for its inception a sphere different from and hostile to its own. Psychologically speaking [as psycho-socially conditioned by the history of oppression], it requires an outside stimulus in order to act at all; all its action is reaction (Nietzsche 1956, 170-1).

How, then, does the concept of Ubuntu - as invoked or used both in present-day social, political, and moral discourse in South Africa, and in its core definition, if any, and therefore broader application - envisage "everyday" as a different situation, or condition, or place, in the sense of a value system? Such a view can be gleaned only indirectly from considerations of derivative meanings of the concept, and, negatively, in relation to what it rejects as unacceptable. Like we indicated at the beginning, we walk into our days from different stations of life. Some of these may be things we might be responsible for while others may have been imposed on us. If our education was stunted or limited in scope due to unfair constraints, then each day of our lifetime may be lived in constant imagination of what it could have been. But if the job I have today is the result of my own past free choices under fair circumstances, then I bear responsibility for how my days are lived with all the limitations that my past choices have made real. As the economic world changes around me, my limitations may become more glaring, but they are, to some degree, my making. In this respect, believing in the social ideals of Ubuntu may involve accepting social diversity, and some social dissimilarities, so long as they are produced under circumstances of fairness, and so long as this idea of fairness is applied to making access to decent basic goods and resources within the reach of everyone in society. In practice, we all will remember that during the apartheid era, black native Africans could not access markets and other retailing outlets or facilities of their choice, so it was hard to assess if they were having access to goods of the same quality as those in Whites-only facilities. The invocation of Ubuntu against this restriction as unjust and immoral argues, to the contrary, for an open-market system where anyone can get procurements at any place of their choice free of arbitrary restrictions produced by unjust and immoral policies.

In the same vein, we can all see the differences that describe us by age, language, or gender, or by the specific cultural beliefs and practices by which we claim our diverse ethnic identities. They are some of the differences that make the human family a beautiful tapestry that is made up of the different paths of ancestry and the cultures our ancestors have lived by and passed on to us over a long time. None of these ways is better than, or superior to another, and they are not indicators of any fundamental differences between us. Hence, by interrogating, and condemning the practice of establishing policies that draw demarcations between peoples on the basis of a vertical moral and political ordering of society based on such differences as incompatible with the moral tenets of Ubuntu is to claim that deep down all humans are equal despite their superficial or outside dissimilarities and diverse cultural practices. From a moral point of view, the principle of Ubuntu urges us to believe in this fundamental equality and, consequently, to treat each other with equal respect that allows affiliations across the lines of these superficial differences. In other words, the invocation of Ubuntu calls for the deconstruction, and destruction of the evil social imaginations and constructions of apartheid and their replacement with a boundaryless social order that reflects a different, better or higher moral order that recognizes the basic equality between all people.

As illustrated by Nelson Mandela's now famous pronouncement – "Never, never and never again shall it be that this beautiful land will again experience the oppression of one by another" (Mandela 1994). Replacing the master morality is not a matter of mere preference of one moral system over another between competing moralities. Rather, it is a commitment to a higher value system, one that aims at improving the human condition for all. Before Mandela, the Ethiopian Emperor Haile Selassie had himself made an equally powerful pronouncement against the values of evil. He said:

> Throughout history, it has been the inaction of those who could have acted; the indifference of those who should have known better; the silence of the voice of justice when it mattered most; that has made it possible for evil to triumph (Selassie, as quoted in Kinni 2015, 12).

Invoking the idea of Ubuntu as a counter-discourse critical of the practices of apartheid directs itself at the fallacious inference of intellectual and moral differences between people from the superficial varieties of human skin complexion, or from the cultures they practice. In the same vein, Ubuntu criticizes sexism and tribalism as practices which, like apartheid, circumvent social and judicial justice on unjustifiable grounds. In this regard, it is a call, or reminder, that human rights apply equally to all, and that everyone must be accorded equality before the law, and everyone must be accorded fair treatment in the distribution of resources as no one must be prejudged, favorably or negatively, based on the color of their skin, or their ethnic or gender identity.

As time has shown, ethnic and gender equality have proven to be special challenges to an anxious South African society as it emerges out of complex forms of inequality, hence the invocation of Ubuntu as an ideal against that background promises to battle two of Africa's biggest sources of social injustice. In a continent where women's rights, and general respect for women lag behind any social and economic gains since independence from colonialism, deriving such ideals from moral considerations of the concept of Ubuntu may present the biggest cultural, social and political challenge yet to Ubuntu as an ideal that is expected to permeate all segments of society as the guiding principle of thought and practice.

Considering Africa in general, much has changed over the past several decades. In some cases, Africa has shattered some of the misconceptions regarding gender suppression of women in her traditional systems. Africa has had women revolutionaries in the fight against both foreign and local injustices. Ali Mazrui's famous documentary, "The Africans," documented African women's membership and participation in wars for social, political, and cultural change. Winnie Madikizela-Mandela is a world-recognized example. Africa has had women elected presidents. Again, a lesson from Simone de Beauvoir may be helpful here. The present image of womanhood as the second sex is the result, and development, of what emerged in Europe at the time of industrial revolution and the significant resultant transformation of the idea of labor. It is no accident that this predicament for the African woman sprang from the implantation of colonial economy. Left at home as the new economy took men away to work in colonial establishments - whether these were in the transport industry, in the factory, in the farms and plantations, in the mines, in the domestic service industry, or in the often-forgotten support services like tailoring, shoe cobbling, barber shop services to fellow African urban migrants or other marginal occupations - African women stayed behind at the ancestral home to keep and sustain the integrity and interests of the family. They learned to be autonomous and to be depended on for the social and, to a large degree, also economic well-being of the family whose peasant farm interests and daily needs she took care of. She became the unwilling head of household, because this new role was not voluntary. Because of this and other biases, she lagged behind in education in a system that favored patriarchy in the "manufacture" of the new local workforce that, as a result, created the new sense of "elitism," one defined by active participation in the new economy. She would later become a teacher or a nurse, both professions which, by virtue of their gender domination by women, would themselves struggle to gain respect or prominence in local senses of job status.

Although the African woman has made strides in many sectors of life, the majority of African women make a significant portion of the world's women who continue to be marginalized from access to the resources that enable self-development and autonomy, and from critical decision-making positions in society. She is still so much less educated than her male counterpart, because we continue to think of the values of society, and of its development (better life defined by better knowledge or education, better jobs, better health, and more wealth) through the interests of males. So, as we go about our lives and mingle in our everyday preoccupations, in the village or in the city, we move around either as the beneficiaries of and accomplices to the values and policies of inequality, or as the victims of historically unjust institutions of modern economy or cultural structures. In other words, the everyday realism of the body as subject is subject to varieties of measures that make it the avenue to either social privilege or victim of the imposition of social meanings and roles.

The body is also often abandoned as subject when it is objectified, not only as a detached object of cognitive experience, but as an object of abuse in our everyday encounters with it, in the course of our living inside it. The body can be either part of the I-subject or the me/it - object. As object, it can be sexualized and exploited in practices that defy the capitalist-socialist divide. The body is not just sexualized, it is sexualized in differing degrees, and to different ends based on the socio-economic conditions of everyday life. The reification or "thinging" of the body, or its commodification as some would put it, whether female or male, its reduction to carnage for the pleasures of the Other, is one of the oldest forms of human commercial exchanges in both formal and informal settings. Anything can be reduced to a commodity for purchase. Thus it cannot be assumed that prostitution is inimical to egalitarianism, but the courage or audacity to put on sale that which is our most sacred and intimate of all values spells a condition of unequal access to "normal" resources.

The reification of the body of the prostitute is problematic on different levels in respect to how we regard the everyday. While the latter is structured by rules, some of which create or sustain inequality by setting up the norms of expectation and predictability, encounters with the prostitute are the suspension of the regulations of the everyday. The single rule that drives prostitute-client relation is exchange, the *quid pro quo*, in which the prostitute is reduced to the level of the dirty money he/she vies for. She/he becomes less than human under those terms as a transition is made from the I-subject to it/me-object. The prostitute becomes instead a nameless piece of flesh for consumption. Many social theorists have suggested that the violence meted frequently against prostitutes is hinged on precisely this fact: that they cease to be seen as persons. They are dehumanized, robbed of their *Utu*. In fact, therefore, there can be no true relationship between a prostitute and his or her client. What happens between them is guided by the image of the unfamiliar, the impersonal - namely the things that defy, or are removed from the rules of the everyday. Because they are outside it, the non-everyday practices are treated as exotic B they escape the jurisdiction of known rules. No-one checks on them because there are no known norms to check them against, and they also stand outside the realm of everyday discourse, whether normative or descriptive. Instead, the exotic is always either holy or very perverse. It is left to the imagination of the participating consumer.

Everyday and the Pursuit of Happiness

Finally, the "everyday" is often marked by things as simple as telling one's family, "I'll see you tonight," or children telling their parent, "See you later, Daddy," "Have a nice day, Mommy," and so on. Yet, in the apartheid South Africa, the long list of "the missed, and the missing," or the "presumed dead" tells us that no-one could count on their day, any day. Many individuals left home and then vanished without trace or witnesses. This is what happened to the now-famous "Cradock Four," all School teachers whose "everyday lives" would have been expected to be as stable as anybody's. What about the "everyday" of the many captives imprisoned on the Roben Island and other illegitimate places of captivity - people whose "everyday" was defined only by the fact that they would still be breathing when the sun came up again? What about those whose "everydays" were defined by the endless torture in secret police captivities? So the question is: how would their families think of their days? What would "everyday" mean to them? What about the entire population whose days, any day, were so indeterminable? And what about the sick and immobilized? What about the poor for whom "everyday" has no sense in human terms? And what about those permanently on the run, whether for reasons of their own making, or for reasons of political and social instability that robs them of a guarantee of seeing the next sunrise, or sunset? The idea that one can be on the run permanently for reasons of their own making is a description of a person with mental health problems. Normal people do not just go on the run. We cannot take lightly the saying that "home is where one's heart is." Everyone would like to be in the place he or she calls home, and to be with family. Whether it is limited or extended, family is the anchor of humanity, and being in the midst of family is how life should naturally ground the basic idea of humans. Away from, or despite the negative challenges of the antagonisms of history, waking up into the company of family is fulfilling and reassuring, and this is so despite the structural rules discussed by Bourdieu. It is the family that is expected to give us the normative ropes with which to navigate the rest of the world.

Being with family, and with others generally, gives or restores to us our basic sense of humanity. Hence despite the antagonisms fostered by the forces of history, we still recognize in each other our respective and mutual humanity. This problematic relationship involves a dialectical opposition in which the Self is constrained to act in a manner that recognizes the other as a potential threat, or as having the ability to dis-order and destroy the state of the Self. In this respect, the self-image of the Self is real only to the extent that the Other feeds it by acting in a manner that recognizes the Self as a Subject at par with the Other. Our actions in these situations are purely relational in a direct manner - they are how we relate with friends, with family or relatives, and even with colleagues at work. As humans, we possess the rationality of congregation, the capacity that enables us to stand above the values that separate us into social categories by virtue of the material tools by which our daily practices and values are defined. We need each other in order to live our different lifestyles. The owner or driver of that expensive car needs that mechanic at the service shop, and the attendant at the gas station, and the manual laborer who works daily to maintain the roads; the person who eats at the expensive table needs that vegetable vendor at the open market, or the cashier at the supermarket, the butcher at the slaughter house, the fisherman in the treachery waters, the fishmonger at the shore and market, and the cook in the kitchen; when we get lost, we ask for directions from that young idle-looking person by the roadside because they have the useful knowledge we don't have. And when we look into the face of the family member at the end of the day, or when we wake up, we do not read these roles in their eyes; instead we see the person we love and care about. Alongside the serious talks about our pursuits in the course of the day, we also have those moments when we just enjoy the simple things like food, the company of others, and with them, also conversations and laughter. And still with them, or alone, we may enjoy entertainment such as by listening to music or telling and listening to stories. When we lose one of these people, whether they are family or friends, we experience abandonment and sadness. These encounters and experiences are purely human, and they force us, if we did not already, to realize that as humans we are connected and are interdependent.

It is in view of the above seemingly simple but deeply human values that we have developed the concept of the basic rights of humans, also called the rights of man. The idea is that there are certain practices, or needs, that every human being must have just on account of being human, namely the conditions that enhance rather than hinder the enjoyment of what is deeply or basically human. And we hold every government, and every unit of social order, accountable to everyone that they ought to live under conditions that make it possible for them to pursue and enjoy these basic human experiences. We believe, for example, that everyone has a right to a humanly decent and economically rewarding engagement; to a humanly decent shelter; to decent clothing; and to education. Thus, negatively, any view of humanity ought to start with thinking of those conditions under which all humans enjoy protections - from hunger, from homelessness, from involuntary nakedness, and from ignorance. When individuals or groups face or are victims of any one or more of these threats to basic humanity, it is our duty to question ourselves as societies whether we are doing everything right. It is unjust for anyone to be a victim of any one or more of these basic human rights.

It is the case, however, that Africans are fleeing home in disproportionate numbers in search of opportunities for themselves and their families because they face hunger, homelessness, nakedness, and ignorance at home. This flight is not voluntary. Their human rights are denied or threatened at home. Flight from home is also and predominantly caused by strife at home due to and resorting to undemocratic means of expressing political disagreements and finding resolutions. From the early stages of political independence from colonial domination, much of Africa has failed to practice or believe in democratic means of settling political differences. Under normal conditions, our thoughts about the "everyday," each day, include the stability of our expectations of each day as reasonably predictable. Barring accidents as happenings that stand outside reasonable responsibility and control, we all plan our lives, whether by days, weeks, months, or longer by correlating what we do now to outcomes they should produce in determinable time in the future. Fundamentally, freedom allows us to think of ourselves as agents of our own futures or destinies within the circumstances availed fairly to everyone under the principle and conditions of equality. In the absence of freedom and equality, or in the absence of the practice of fairness, victims of such conditions are robbed of the ability and meaningfulness of the basic agency by which every normal human being, *Mtu*, or *Muntu*, is expected to exercise the simple things of their humanity like to plan their days, weeks, months, or longer spans of their lives, or simply to have the uninterrupted hope for a tomorrow. Application of the laws of inequality under apartheid, or rampant and unjustified arrests and violence against non-Whites in South Africa stripped "everyday" of its worth. Unpredictable disappearance reduced life for the Black majority South Africans to a matter of chance, and each day a bivalent (either good or bad) encounter with luck - any given day could be the last - rather than an occasion to execute one's short-term-cum-long-term plans. Addressing itself to these conditions, Ubuntu as a moral idea stands out against the repression of the human spirit as directed at the unfolding of the human potential through the formation and execution of the ideas of self-cultivation and realization. During the apartheid days many South Africans left their homes on diverse mornings to start what for free people should have been normal days but disappeared without trace as victims of official state terrorism. They were perceived to be a threat to white supremacy and privilege. Because every black person was perceived as a potential threat to the daily survival of the terroristic regime, their "everyday" was stripped of the reasonable normalcy that guides all normal persons' sense of stability that allows reasonable planning and life projections. To be denied this normal certainty is to be robbed of the core of humanity itself. In a similar manner, disease and sickness, poverty and socio-political instability, all rob humanity of the meaningfulness of "everyday" as space, both mental and temporal, in which life is given sense by exercising human deliberation in thought and practice. The critique of the violence of domination by way of invoking Ubuntu is an attempt to put the basic but essential sense of humanity, Ubuntu, back into how people normalize their lives again.

Bibliography

Beauvoir, Simone de. 1974. *The Second Sex*. Translated by H. M. Parshley. New York: Vintage Books.

Bourdieu, Pierre. 1977. *Outline of A Theory of Practice*. Translated by Richard Nice. Cambridge, UK: Cambridge University Press.

Bourdieu, Pierre. 1990. *The Logic of Practice*. Translated by Richard Nice. Cambridge, UK, Polity Press jointly with Stanford University Press.

de Certeau, Michel. 1984. *The Practice of Everyday Life*. Tranlated by Steven Rendall. Berkeley: University of California

Press.

Fanon, Frantz. 1967. *Black Skin, White Masks.* Translated by Charles Lam Markmann. New York, Grove Press.

Feierman, Steven. 1990. *Peasant Intellectuals: Anthropology and History in Tanzania.* Madison, WI: University of Wisconsin Press.

Heidegger, Martin. 1962. *Being and Time.* New York: Harper and Brothers.

Kagame, Alexis. 1956. *La Philosophie bantu-rwandaise de l'être.* Bruxelles: Académie Royale des Sciences Coloniales.

Kasfir, Sidney Littlefield. 2007. *African Art and the Colonial Encounter: Inventing Global Commodity.* Bloomington, IN: Indiana University Press.

Kinni, Fongot Kini-Yen. 2015. *Pan-Africanism: Political Philosophy and Socio-Economic Anthropology for African Liberation and Governance.* Volume 2. African Books Collective.

Kratz, Corinne A. 1994. *Affecting Performance: Meaning, Movement, and Experience in Okiek Women's Initiation.* Washington, D.C.: Smithsonian Institution Press.

Kresse, Kai. 2007. *Philosophising in Mombasa: Knowledge, Islam and Intellectual Practice on the Swahili Coast.* Edinburgh, Scotland: Edinburgh University Press, for the International African Institute, London.

Mandela, Nelson. 1994. "Nelson Mandela at his Inauguration as President of South Africa." Speech Pretoria, South Africa 10 May 1994. http://www.mandela.gov.za/ mandela_speeches/ 1994/940510_inauguration.htm.

Mavhunga, Clapperton C. 2014. *Transient Workspaces: Technologies of Everyday Innovation in Zimbabwe.* Boston, MA: The M. I. T. Press.

Mboya, Paul. 1969 [1938]. *Luo Kitgi gi Timbegi.* Nairobi: Equatorial Publishers.

McGovern, Mike. 2011. *Making War in Cote d'Ivoire.* Chicago: University of Chicago Press.

Nietzsche, Friedrich. 1956. *The Genealogy of Morals.* Translated by Francis Golffing. Garden City, NY: Doubleday

&Company.

Oruka, Henry Odera. 1991. *Sage Philosophy: Indigenous Thinkers and Modern Debate in African Philosophy*. Leiden, The Netherlands: Brill Publishers.

Plato. 1992 [ca. 380 B.C]. *Republic*. Translated by G. M. A. Grube, revised by C. D. C. Reeve. Indianapolis: Hackett Publishing Company.

Sartre, Jean-Paul. 1948. "Orphée noire". In *Anthologie de la nouvelle poésie nègre et malgache de la langue française*, edited by Leopold S. Senghor, pp ix-xliv. Paris: Presses Universitaires de France.

Sartre, Jean-Paul. 1956. *Being and Nothingness*. Translated by Hazel E. Barnes. New York: Washington Square Press, Pocket Books.

Senghor, Leopold S., ed. 1948. *Anthologie de la nouvelle poésie nègre et malgache de la langue française*. Paris: Presses Universitaires de France.

Senghor, Léopold S. 1964. *Liberté 1: Négritude et Humanisme*. Paris: Le Seuil.

Senghor, Léopold S. 1977. *Liberté 3: Négritude et civilisation de l'universel*. Paris: Le Seuil.

Senghor, Léopold S. 1964. *On African Socialism*. Translated by Mercer Cook. New York and London: Frederick A. Praeger, Publisher.

Smedley, Audrey. 1999. *Race in North America: Origin and Evolution of a Worldview*. Boulder, CO: Westview Press.

Tempels, Placide. 1969 [1959]. *Bantu Philosophy*. Translated by Rev. Colin King. Paris, Présence Africaine.

Wiredu, Kwasi. 1992. "The Ghanaian Tradition of Philosophy." In *Person and Community: Ghanaian Philosophical Studies, I*, edited by Wiredu, Kwasi, and K. Gyekye. Washington, D.C.: The Council for Research in Values and Philosophy.

Chapter 2: ENTRENCHING THE MORAL VALUES OF UBUNTU IN EVERYDAY LIFE

Oriare Nyarwath

Introduction

Ubuntu is a moral concept which is often understood to mean humanness. But for such a concept to be recognized and applied in everyday life requires that its values or basic tenets be exposed and synthesized. Just to claim that the concept means humanness does not demonstrate its moral quality nor show how it is to be practiced in everyday life. Again, to say, as is often done, that Ubuntu means a person becomes a person through other persons, does not clarify sufficiently its meaning. The very meaning of Ubuntu, its cognate moral values and the process by which one becomes a person through other persons need to be explained. In this work, I attempt to do exactly that. I try to explain the meaning of humanness and show its relationship to the moral values constitutive of the concept of Ubuntu that defines the very moral quality characteristic of personhood. Finally, I examine some key areas of society from which the values of Ubuntu may emanate, be nurtured and then permeate into the rest of society becoming an important resource for both the moral formation of the character of the young and a lived culture of society.

Concept of Ubuntu

The term Ubuntu is often used to refer to various meanings in different contexts (Gade 2011, 304-329). Two such meanings stand out. One is Ubuntu as being human (Gade 2011, 308; Ramose 1999, 52). This reference remains unclear and ambiguous. In one sense it could mean simply being a human being – *humanness*; referring to the essential or common qualities that define a human being. But this is least likely to be what is often meant when we use the term Ubuntu since the qualities that define a human being are common to every human being. It would imply that everybody has 'ubuntu' yet quite often we express the doubt that some people have Ubuntu when we say, for instance that 'so and so is not a human person'. However, being human could also mean possession and expression of *humaneness*. There is a difference between humanness and humaneness. Humaneness refers to the possession and nurturing of moral qualities that express the best of human character; instilling in a person moral disposition towards fellow human beings, namely– feeling, acting out of sympathy to sentient beings, devotion to general human welfare and goodwill towards all human beings. Though there is a difference between humanness and humaneness, they are intricately related. A proper understanding of the meaning of a human being (humanness) necessarily informs how we should treat and relate with other fellow human beings (humaneness). The normative qualities that enable us to properly relate with other human beings in accordance to the nature of a human being are the most integral part of the meaning of Ubuntu.

The other meaning of Ubuntu that stands out is that a human being becomes a person through other persons (Shutte 2001, 25; Tutu 1999, 35; Ramose 1999, 120; van Niekerk 2013, 4; Mbiti 1969, 108-109). Without explaining the meaning of a person and how one becomes a person through other persons, this meaning of Ubuntu does not help much, especially if we are to examine the meaning and significance of Ubuntu in the everyday life. Among the most important aspects of the meaning of a human being or human person is the possession of the capacity to reason and development of the moral character. In philosophy, sometimes a distinction is made between a human being and a human person. But where such a distinction is made, a human being is simply understood to mean belonging to the human species while a human person refers to having the capacity to acquire moral character (Masolo 2010, 241; Wiredu 1996, 19). However, the minimum that is required for one to be subject to humane treatment is that one belongs to the human species.

However, one can grow in moral character (in Ubuntu) beyond mere belonging to the human species. This growth requires the participation of and the nurturing by other human beings (persons). From now, I use human being and human person interchangeably. The whole of one's existence from birth throughout one's life requires and involves the participation of other human beings. Therefore, from the perspective of Ubuntu, a person is moral, social, and relational (Praeg 2014, 253). The concept of Ubuntu is therefore anchored on the consciousness of the inescapable interconnectedness of human beings and the sociality of the human self (Masolo 2010, 228). This calls for the recognition of the unity of humanity, human dignity and human well-being. An individual's dignity and well-being is necessarily tied to the dignity and well-being of other human beings. Ubuntu refers both to the fact that to be human is to recognize the humanity of others and that one's humanity is inextricably intertwined with the humanity of others. This means that an individual cannot truly flourish at the expense of others. One's dignity and well-being is equally bound up to the dignity and well-being of others. Ubuntu therefore calls for behavior and relating to fellow human beings and the environment in ways that ought to promote the well-being of all (Tutu and Tutu 2010, 47). Ubuntu also entails the nurturing of certain normative values that not only enhance the good of all but also bring out the moral character of a human being and which essentially define our humaneness. These values include generosity, hospitality, friendliness, caring, compassion (Tutu 1999, 34), love, forgiveness and a sense of fairness (justice), (Bell 2002, 82-89; Tutu 1999, 34-35; Tutu and Tutu 2010, 39-54; Shutte 2001, 17-25, 32).

Ubuntu is projected towards and calls for a life of solidarity, social harmony and community. Solidarity is a feeling of unity characterized by firm commitment to the common good of all and of every individual. Solidarity is based on the recognition not only of shared humanity and dignity but also interdependence of people. This calls for actions that are mutually beneficial and directed toward mutual flourishing and wellbeing, or common good. It implies that we have responsibility to look after the needs of others by caring for the quality of their life. It calls for mutual support and unity of purpose or sympathy. To be uninterested in the wellbeing and flourishing of others or to express ill-will such as hostility or cruelty is antithetical to the principle of solidarity (Masolo 2010, 240; Metz 2011, 538).

Much of the suffering in the world today due to selfishness, greed, conflicts, poverty and killings of fellow human beings, exhibits lack or decline of solidarity and humaneness in the world. On the contrary, it seems that these problems would effectively be addressed through solidarity and cooperation. In fact, to some extent, these distressful conditions have been tempered by expression of solidarity through acts of charity (Masolo 2010, 251-252). In relation to Ubuntu, charity is an expression of care, compassion and responsibility to the needy. It helps in building a sense of unity, solidarity, social harmony and community. However, from another perspective, charity may be seen as a practice that condones and perpetuates inequality in society by temporarily assuaging the negative effects of social inequality. Of course, social harmony requires that there should be less inequality in society. But charity and care for the needy need not be practiced only in an egalitarian society (Gyekye 1997, 158-162).

Social harmony refers to people living together, getting along well and cooperating for the benefit and wellbeing of everyone. It is a life of peaceful co-existence among people, on the one hand; and between people and nature, on the other hand. For the people living together, social harmony implies respecting and being tolerant to different opinions even if one does not agree with them. It emanates from recognition and emphasis of social complementariness which brings about tolerance, equality, sense of justice, cooperation and greater cohesion. It creates a feeling of connectedness and oneness. We increase our humanness or become more humane by belonging, participating and sharing in the community. When we enhance other people's well-being, we enhance our well-being too. When we dehumanize others, we dehumanize ourselves also. From the perspective of Ubuntu, social harmony is the greatest good (Tutu 1999, 35). Gyekye concurs with Tutu that, in a communitarian social structure and according to communitarian ethic, social harmony and sense of community are social goods (Gyekye 1997, 72-76). Masolo correctly and aptly argues that social harmony is essential for human well-being when he observes that material well-being alone cannot guarantee general human well-being without a sense of security, unity and good neighborliness (Masolo 2010, 250-251).

Therefore, any threat to or subversion of social harmony is considered the greatest evil because it is seen as diminishing the dignity and quality of life of all people in the community (Tutu 1999, 35). Therefore, the solution to such subversion requires all efforts and takes priority over everything else. This explains why a society oriented towards Ubuntu considers reconciliation a virtue and thus places great importance on it. Since our dignity, well-being, self-fulfillment and survival depend on other human beings then we are all bound up together. Any cruelty to one human being diminishes the dignity of all other human beings and kindness to one person enhances the quality of life of everyone (Tutu and Tutu 2010, 15). The underlying point in reconciliation, on which Tutu and Masolo concur, is that it aims at restoring the humanity and dignity of both the victim and perpetrator (Tutu 1999, 35; Masolo 2010, 238).

It is by positively participating in the lives of other human beings – the community— that we become human (Masolo 2010, 240-241). A human being therefore derives meaning and purpose of his existence from the society and in turn gives meaning and purpose to society. It is instructive, at this point, to clarify that the human society or community is not limited to the family, relatives or political entity, but to the whole of humanity. Thus, an individual and society are inextricably bound together in terms of meaning and purpose. It is from this perspective that we may understand the famous statement "a person is a person through other persons" or "I am because we are; and since we are, therefore I am" (Mbiti 1969, 108-109). The corporate nature of human existence lends credence to the claim that human life is a gift received through others not only from the perspective of individual survival and growth, but also in the acquisition and development of those qualities that define a human being and that make community life possible (Shutte 2001, 24-25; Kirwen 1987, 71-12).The qualities of care, compassion and generosity entail sharing not only in individual joys and successes but also in hardships and disappointments. The sharing in life involves offering support and comfort to one another and thus makes community life possible (Tutu and Tutu 2010, 44-45). This is what the Tutus mean by the life of wholeness; conducting ourselves in such a way that gives meaning and sustains life hence creates social harmony (Tutu and Tutu 2010, 44-52). The life of wholeness is a life of community and not a solitary life. It is not living a life of selfish concerns but a life of flourishing together and for the pursuit of collective good. This is a life of community in which people care for one another, share in their joys and sorrows, successes and failures; as well as take good care of the environment for common good (Tutu and Tutu 2010, 47-48).

The conception of the person as inextricably embedded considers self as a necessary part of community, contrary to the conception of the person as unencumbered where the self is not considered a necessary part of the community. The two different conceptions of the self result in two diametrical conceptions of community; the communitarian and libertarian respectively. According to the libertarian conception, community is merely a collectivity of persons contrary to the communitarian conception according to which the community is not merely a collectivity but organic and therefore conceived of just as "another self" (Shutte 2001, 25-27); as a web of personal relationships in which a member relates to another member as well as to community as he would relate to another self. Masolo clearly articulates the nature of the relationship between the self and community in this passage:

> The sense of belonging, or the realization and acceptance that the self is located in the midst of others, becomes the basis of his or her moral outlook within the context of a common set of values. Within this mode of thought, no person is considered to be a self-sufficient entity in and for him or herself. Rather, it posits the existence of others as an essential part of the very structure of the self, from which emanates the communitarian exigency. The community is thus crucially differentiated from the "mass". It is not just a collectivity. Rather, it is built through deeds in which are inscribed a person's contribution to the building of the community (Masolo 2010, 249).

Community becomes a pool of moral resource into which a member contributes for common good and from which a member, especially the young, learn through socialization. The ethic of communitarianism is learnt through the teachings of the society (Masolo 2010, 249). Throughout one's life one is taught and constantly reminded of the values that would promote common good, social harmony and ideal conditions for human life (Masolo 2010, 240, 251-252). Masolo identifies charity, politeness and benevolence as among the most cherished values in African communitarianism. But these values also capture most of the values that are often associated with Ubuntu. Charity is very close to compassion. Politeness entails friendliness, showing respect and being considerate. Benevolence entails care and several other associated values such as kindness, compassion, being considerate and altruism. In some sort of summary benevolence has to do with avoiding harming others, preventing harm to others, helping those in need (removing suffering from others), promoting good or well-being.

Mutual help or contributing to other people's well-being is not only to contribute to common good (Masolo 2010, 238-239) but is also part of one's moral growth and an expression of that growth on the part of the giver (Shutte 2001, 30). Showing unwillingness to contribute to the common good of the community or being indifferent to the suffering of fellow human beings is often considered evil, wicked (Masolo 2010, 248) and a manifestation of inadequate personal growth, the kind of people Masolo refers to when he says, 'that they become known as the proverbial "unpollinated grain stalk" of the village' (Masolo 2010, 239).

However, the society can also have a negative moral impact on a member depending on the very moral content of its everyday culture or way of life. If the community has sound, dominant or pervasive moral values then it will have a positive moral influence on her members but if its everyday life is characterized by all sorts of vices then it will have negative influence on her members. This is so, because an individual's moral beliefs and outlook are to a great extent influenced by the moral character of the society of which one is a member. A society which is morally disintegrated produces most members who are equally morally disintegrated. There is need for consistency between the values that people claim to hold and their conduct. This is part of the meaning of what Masolo calls the principle of practical altruism, which is an important social virtue (Masolo 2010, 246-247), geared towards the creation of humane condition in society. Many people tend to forget that effective influence on people's behavior requires both imparting knowledge through teaching and living out the knowledge. Shutte claims that the growth of an integrated self requires an integrated society (Shutte 2001, 24). Such an integration, be it of the self or community, takes place at two levels. One of the levels is when there is harmony of the core values that an individual or society believes in. Such harmony prevents actions based on conflicting moral values that create moral ambivalence and that often result in conflicts between personal or sectarian interests and ethical demands within an individual or among members of society. The other level is when one acts in accordance with the values in which one believes or claims to believe. In an integrated society all members should have common core values as guiding principles for their conduct. Though this is more of an ideal situation, in reality, especially where there are competing systems of values such as moral values, cultural values and religious values, there is bound to be conflict between the values. In the absence of integration of values, we find disintegration where members of society follow different values some of which are even conflicting. But effort should be made to minimize disintegration of values in society. Moreover, a disintegrated self either holds conflicting values or, does not even act according to the values he holds or claims to hold. Such a person manifests ambivalence over the values that should best guide personal conduct or relations with other people.

These values of Ubuntu are not given in every person or else our lives would always be characterized by social harmony, but that is not always the case. Neither are they all manifested in everybody's life nor exist in equal measure. They are to be learnt, nurtured and safeguarded through institutions in society. There are moments in the life of an individual and society when Ubuntu is at its lowest ebb and overshadowed by greed, selfishness, conflicts, violence and even destruction of human life.

As Masolo aptly observes, it is taught and nurtured (Masolo 2010, 236, 249). And only few people seem to have acquired the consciousness. There is still need for awakening the consciousness in the majority of people; "it is not true that Ubuntu is all the time in evidence and its impact felt. It remains a strong virtue that needs reawakening and celebration" (Okello 2012, 50). Casting our eyes not only across Africa but the whole world, we realize several instances of dehumanization resulting variously from wars, poverty, disease, and environmental degradation which do not manifest extensive awareness and practice of Ubuntu (Biney 2014, 40-46). Therefore, we would agree with an observation by Biney that: "For the ordinary people of Africa, both the colonial and post-independent experiences have been replete with brutalities that fly in the face of the philosophy and practice of African humanism/Ubuntu" (Biney 2014, 40).

However, the paradox in human life is that both humanization and dehumanization often co-exist (Biney 2014, 40; Tutu 1999, 36). Both in society and a person's life there are moments when Ubuntu and lack of it are manifested in various ways in which we relate to one another. Though this remains an issue, there is need to raise awareness on the meaning and practice of Ubuntu so that we may reduce the contrary behavior in society.

The holistic interconnectedness has normative implications. A human being is therefore to develop certain normative imperatives or qualities such as love, care, generosity, compassion, hospitality, forgiveness and sense of fairness (justice) (Bell 2002, 82-89; Tutu 1999, 34-35; Tutu and Tutu 2010, 39-54; Shutte 2001, 17-25, 32) in order to sustain the web of relationships. The normative values that relate to Ubuntu and that define humaneness can be categorized into two (Shutte 2001, 31-32); the ones that relate to oneself and the very moral status and definition of a human being, and those that pertain to one's relationship with other human beings. This categorization is important in the sense that Ubuntu is based on the two aspect; proper understanding of the very nature of humanity and how that understanding informs the kind of relationships that should exist between human beings. The latter, proper understanding of the meaning of humanity definitely dictates how we should treat and relate to a human being.

The single most important value in relation to oneself is *integrity* (Shutte 2001, 32). The Latin root of the concept integrity is *integer,* which variously means intact, solid, wholeness or completeness. As a moral virtue integrity is therefore understood simply as intact character in relation to one's feelings, judgements, decisions and actions. It refers to coherence between one's actions and one's moral values, beliefs and principles. It is a manifestation of strong moral character and acting in good faith. It is a virtue (individual moral excellence) that entails other values such as courage, endurance, confidence, honesty and self-respect (Shutte 2001, 32). Because it expresses consistency in moral character, integrity is often understood as moral uprightness. This consistency is understood in two ways. In one way, it refers to harmony in the moral values that one holds or believes in. Often one is faced with holding conflicting values. In order to harmonize the values one needs to critically examine and analyze the values so that one attains accurate knowledge and understanding of the values. The second meaning of consistency is to act in accordance with the moral values that one holds and knows to be right. Lack of moral integrity refers to moral fragmentation of character. This fragmentation means either acting from conflicting moral values or acting contrary to the moral values that one holds (Archer 2017, 437). It is this fragmentation which is sometimes associated with corruption. Corruption is rooted in Latin words; *rumpere, cor-rumpere, corruptus;* that partly mean, break up in pieces, violate, or contaminate. So, corruption can be understood to mean violation of integrity.

The issue of integrity is important especially in relation to imparting values of Ubuntu through role models. We should remember that in the acquisition and nurturing of character, people tend to learn more through imitation rather than mere instruction. And if the person giving moral instruction lacks moral integrity then the instruction is least likely to influence and transform the character of the recipient. Moreover, if a society lacks people of integrity in important positions as role models who can exert influence on the moral character of most members of society then that society cannot be morally integrated and consequently cannot develop a sound moral culture. This is because people of fragmented moral character send mixed moral signals which lead to conflict in values in society. Society requires coherent value systems to guide and harmonize the conduct of her members in order to create social cohesion and harmony. If the values of Ubuntu have to be embedded in society then having people of moral integrity is vital across levels of society from the family through educational institutions, religious institutions and various professions to political leadership.

The other values of Ubuntu that pertain to how one relates to other human beings can be subsumed under *caring*. Caring is used here to refer to a feeling and expression of concern and responsibility for other people's dignity and wellbeing. Shutte claims that some of the fundamental virtues in our relationship with other people are the virtues of respect and sympathy (Shutte 2001, 32). Respect entails the recognition of the shared humanity and consequently giving due regard to other people's feelings and rights. In respecting others, we indeed express how we would wish to be treated. Sympathy refers to sharing feelings with people who are in need or afflicted by misfortune. But feeling of sympathy seems to emanate from feeling of empathy – the ability to share other people's feeling by imagining how it would feel to be in their situations. Empathy and sympathy are central in the development of the feeling for caring. That is why Masolo argues that communitarian ethic builds on empathy and other altruistic feelings that enable one to feel the necessity of others as a means of creating humane and ideal conditions for human life and flourishing (Masolo 2010, 247-249). Caring therefore entails other values such as generosity, honesty, compassion, tolerance and forgiving.

Generosity refers to being kind, friendly and considerate. So in sharing what we have with other people or extending a helping hand to the needy (compassion), or welcoming and caring for strangers (hospitality), we are not only affirming their humanity and contributing to their wellbeing and common good but we are also expressing our moral quality. In sharing, we offer ourselves as a gift to others, which is an expression of love and high moral value. Honesty is vital for social life. Central to the meaning of honesty is truthfulness and fairness. Truthfulness and fairness build trust and thus improve human relations and communication. Community would be unbearable if not impossible without trust. Honesty not only reflect respect for others but also self-respect. Dishonest people call upon themselves dis-respectful treatment. Tolerance is another test for our respect of other human beings. The willingness to live with people with differing opinion or behavior that we may even dislike or disapprove of is being considerate and acknowledging the fact of human diversity. Tolerance is necessary for social harmony. Conflict is a fact and is bound to happen in society, but the test for our humanity and humaneness is our capacity to forgive and reconcile in order to restore social harmony and improve the quality of social life.

The values associated with Ubuntu are to help human beings grow into moral persons and to create a worthy human community.

Entrenching Ubuntu in Everyday Life

In order for the values of Ubuntu to be part of our everyday life, they have to be part of the core contents of socialization in society so that they are internalized and become the quality of our personal character. They have to be taught and emphasized right from childhood through our formal education system and everyday life. We tend to forget that teaching and talking about these values alone without actually living them in everyday life will not help much, or may not help at all in the internalization of these values. Teaching and exhibiting these values in our everyday relationships and dealings with fellow human beings must go hand in hand.

In an effort to entrench the values of Ubuntu in our everyday life and society, certain issues need to be addressed. One of the issues is where to begin in imparting the knowledge of Ubuntu; do we begin at the family with the children or reinforce the values of the existing society by injecting the values of Ubuntu in order to transform the prevalent culture. We are aware and we have mentioned it that the society and its prevalent culture can exert enormous pressure on an individual to the extent that an individual would find it difficult to internalize and nurture the values of Ubuntu if the values are contrary to the prevailing values in society. We know, for instance, that a society that has entrenched a particular dominant culture of violence, aggressiveness, theft, corruption, tribalism, racism or gender discrimination would, to a great extent, socialize its members into these vices. But we are also aware that some individual members of society in positions of influence can transform the values of society. That is the case with people like Julius Nyerere, Nelson Mandela, Mahatma Gandhi and Martin Luther King.

It would look prudent to employ a multi-pronged approach directed at very important levels of influence in society such as the family, the educational institutions, the religious institution and political leadership.

The family is not only the basic unit of society but also the first place where character formation of a child begins. There are at least three challenges related to imparting necessary values to a child that can be faced at the level of the family. Some parents may not have the vision of the character they would like their children to grow into and what to do in their attempt to ensure that the children acquire the character. Such a vision would require that the parents have a clear knowledge and understanding of a set of core values that constitute the envisioned character. But this can be problematic if the parents hold conflicting value systems and may not know how to choose between the values systems or how to harmonize them. Many people in African, for instance, hold religious values (contemporary religious values) and cultural values (from their traditional heritage). These values tend to be relativistic and may even be conflicting; and unless such values are properly interpreted they cannot give adequate guidance in human relationship in a multi-religious and multi-cultural society. So, such conflicting values cannot help form a consistent and adequate character in a child. The other challenge has to do with the moral integration and integrity of the parents. Effective and adequate character formation of a child requires parents with moral integrity. Children in particular and people in general learn better by imitation. Parents therefore should be of moral character and integrity worthy of imitation by their children. Such parents should always behave in accordance with the values they teach their children so that the children do not receive moral mixed signals in relations to values from their parents. In most cases, when children receive moral mixed signals, they tend to imitate the behavior of the parent rather than to follow the teachings. The third challenge but particular to families with house-helps, concerns the role of a house-help in the character formation of child. The unfortunate thing is that some house-helps do not seem to have properly formed moral character. Otherwise, parents need to be very careful when choosing a house-help or should always create a day or two when they spend time with their children alone without the house-helps in order to bond and have influence on the children. The unfortunate thing that can happen is when the house-help and a child have bonded so strongly that the child prefers the company of a house-help to the parent. In such a situation, the parent has no sufficient influence on the formation of the character of the child. In short, the point I belabor here is that the family, be it nuclear or extended, being an initial point of contact for a child should be a hub of positive values worthy of emulation if a child is to develop sound character.

School is another important institution in society with a great influence on the character formation of a child in respect to imparting humane values. In this respect, the school faces at least two challenges. The first concerns the content of value education taught in school if such a curriculum exists. Unfortunately, from my experience with school system in Kenya, there is never any particular subject in schools that directly deal with value education. The second challenge concerns the moral quality of teachers as role models worthy of emulation by the children. In modern times, children spend a lot of their early years in schools. That means a great deal of their character formation take place in and during their schooling. If teachers have to effectively and positively contribute to the formation of the character of children, then teachers must never be morally fragmented – holding conflicting values –and should have moral integrity. The unfortunate thing is that the value teaching seems not to exist in our schools or it has been relegated to the periphery of curriculum, yet the very root and meaning of education entails value teaching. The word education comes from two related Latin words *educare* which means "to mold or train", and *educere* which means "to lead out". In training and molding the character of a pupil, education aims at equipping a pupil with knowledge, skills and values that would enable a pupil to lead (lead out) a better life. Education in an ideal sense is to mold a person to fit well in society by imparting on the person the knowledge and values that would make the person not only adequately fulfil his needs and but also to sufficiently discharge his social responsibilities. A person without reasonable amount of requisite humane values cannot fit well in society. But if value teaching is not core in school curriculum, then one wonders from where is one to acquire the values.

Religion is another very important aspect of society that is or should primarily be concerned with the formation of character. Religion is both personal and social. It is personal in that it answers to individual spiritual needs and ultimate concerns. But is social in the sense that it also concerns how one should relate with fellow human beings and the kind of social organizations ideal for human life and spiritual growth. In addressing these two aspects, religion is concerned with three main questions; the question about origin, meaning or purpose, and destiny. In answering these questions, religion offers ultimate answers. Almost all religions attribute the origin of everything to a supreme being. In answering the question of meaning and purpose of everything but more so human life, religion prescribes normative rules that human being must follow in order to attain ultimate purpose of life. As to destiny, religion offers either the eternal bliss or suffering depending on how faithfully one followed the normative rules. Interestingly, the normative rules of most religions are the same as the very values that define and constitute Ubuntu. These include honesty, generosity, compassion, forgiveness and tolerance. Many people in the world in general, and Africa in particular boast of being religious yet our world today experiences a lot of vices including religious instigated wars. One may legitimately wonder why religion has not succeeded in making most of its members behave in accordance with the religious imperatives. Two reasons may explain the failure of religion to compel most of its members to live by the religious rules. Many people are born and therefore socialized into religion systems without really understanding the meaning and role of religion in one's life and society. Even those who convert later in their life to new religions may equally not understand this. To such people it is simply good to be affiliated to a religious system and regularly participate in the religious activities without realizing that religion is primarily to guide practical life. The other explanation is that the lives of many religious leaders do not inspire transformation in the character of their followers. Good leaders inspire positive action and transformation through their integrated self and integrity –through their words and deeds. It is therefore imperative that religious leaders should harmonize their conduct, both in the private and public, with the religious values. This will, to some extent, help many religious followers nurture and entrench some of the values of Ubuntu in their character and society.

Political leadership is another area of society where the values of Ubuntu seem very relevant and urgently needed if these values have to be embedded in society. Political leadership has many people as followers, includes complex mechanisms, and has the power to influence the values of society. Depending on their character in terms of both instruction and conduct, political leaders can influence the values and general behavior in society in either negative or positive ways. The kind of political vision and program of action (ideology) can create ideal or dehumanizing conditions for human life in society. Great or depraved countries (societies) are created by political leadership. Therefore, the moral stature and integrity of political leaders are very important in charting the direction of society in terms of entrenched values and general behavior of members. There are some things that may look simple but because they are associated with admirable political leadership, they are adopted as patterns of behavior by several people. For instance, in Africa, we have the signature suit of Kenneth (President of Zambia Kaunda 1964-1991) which became famously known as the Kaunda suit. There is also the signature Madiba shirt associated with Nelson Mandela (President of South African 1994-1999). Many people across the world, because of their admiration of these leaders started sporting similar design of clothes in imitation of the leaders. The dress code of political leaders does not necessarily correlate to their leadership values, but I use the examples to illustrate the parallel influence the leaders would impact on their followers and society in general if their character were to epitomize the values of Ubuntu. The most elaborate example is the case of Julius Nyerere in Tanzania (President of Tanzania 1962-1985). Through sound ideology in which national values and policies were well articulated, Tanzania through Nyerere's leadership, attained national identity, national unity, equality and respect for human dignity. Tanzania therefore became one of the countries in Africa with relatively strong national cohesion and social harmony characterized by peaceful transition of government unlike most countries in Africa. Nyerere epitomizes a leader who tried to carry out national policies in accordance with the core values articulated by the government (Malipula 2014, 60-65; Shivji 2014, 137-149). Because of the enormous influence they have on their followers, political leaders would play an important role in entrenching the values of Ubuntu in society.

Work, in a general sense, is another area in which the entrenchment of the values of Ubuntu seems significant. Work is both individual and social. Work is a means by which an individual not only fulfills personal needs but also creates and expresses one's worth. This recognition ought to also inform a just payment for work done. There is, from the perspective of Ubuntu, a connection between common humanity, dignity and social justice (Shivji 2014, 139-142). The recognition of common humanity and human dignity demands that people are justly paid for work. Though the idea of just pay is problematic, it should at least consider human worth and respect. Through work we provide for our needs and hence sustenance. Work is therefore vital for our very being, meaning and existence. Through it, we create and define our self and who we are. Our attitude towards work and faithfulness in carrying out work determine the extent to which we efficiently meet our needs as well as self-realization. From this perspective, work calls for individual integrity, honesty and self-respect. Work is also social in the sense that through it we not only acquire means to discharge our duties to people for whom we have direct responsibilities such as family members and relatives but also serve fellow human beings in general. Since Ubuntu expresses the embedment of self in the humanity of others, our service to others is necessarily informed by our conception of the very nature of human being and the normative imperative of how such a being ought to be treated. In work, therefore, we should express our recognition and respect for the dignity of fellow human beings whom we serve. Work is also social in the sense that most work is done in group or collaboration with others hence for such work to be successfully accomplished; it requires the values of Ubuntu such as community, unity, honesty, kindness, considerateness and integrity.

Language is another area vital for the entrenchment of the values of Ubuntu in society. Language is not only used to relay ideas but also expresses our attitude, feelings and perception of our interlocutors or those to whom we address. If we would like the values of Ubuntu to be part of our lives, then we should use language in a manner that expresses politeness and respect. This will show that we not only recognize but also respect the dignity of such people even if we disagree with them over certain issues. Through appropriate language, we can express ourselves firmly and clearly without humiliating or showing disrespect to the people we address. Children should be taught to use respectful and polite language without necessarily compromising on honesty and truth. Adult people should also avoid using language in ways that are insulting and disrespectful to other people or that may be bad examples to the young. In a society where adults use disrespectful or obscene language or where such usage is condoned, the young also pick on such usage. Mwai Kibaki, one time a president of Kenya, had the habit of rebuking certain people during his address to public gatherings, using such Kiswahili words as *pumbavu* (foolish), *mavi ya kuku* (chicken droppings); language that appeared impolite, disrespectful, insulting and humiliating. We should develop the habit and culture of the use of courteous language if we want the values of Ubuntu to be embedded in our everyday life. To illustrate this point. There is often a stark comparison and difference in East Africa between Kenya and Tanzania in the use of Kiswahili language in relation to politeness. Most Kenyans are less known to frequently use such polite Kiswahili phrases like 'naomba - I beg', 'tafadhali - please', when compared to Tanzanians. My own personal experience may illustrate further this point on language. One time in my secondary school, I had a teacher for mathematics and physics whom I liked and admired for those were some of the subjects I liked. One day, during mathematics lesson, I asked a question, I don't remember how I had put the question. But our teacher was not happy with me. But he told me that the question I had asked was important however I should learn how to put my question across. I really felt bad that the teacher I admired may have been offended by the way I had asked the question. Since that day I learnt to be very mindful on use of language. Being courteous, not only in our language but in our general relationship with other people is important because it not only expresses our respectful, considerate and dignified treatment of others but also our own character and our wish to be treated likewise. Therefore, courteous behavior entails some of the basic values constitutive of Ubuntu.

Conclusion

The fact that the very meaning and existence of the self is inescapably intertwined with the humanity and life of other persons, the entrenchment of the values of Ubuntu in society therefore implies the values must be part of both the character of the self and the community of which the self is an inextricable part. Efforts must be made to impart these values to both the self and the community concurrently. This approach is deemed necessary because the values that the individual self acquires, to a great extent, are derived from the prevailing values of the society in which one is born, nurtured and lives.

Since the character formation of a person begins from birth through the process of socialization, the very important and influential persons in the life of a child such as the parents, teachers and religious personages; whom the sociologists call significant others; should be people who themselves embody the very values that we would wish to be part of the character of the child. These persons should be people of moral integrity; people who guide their actions by consistent harmonized moral values.

If we grant that children learn and are greatly influenced in their character formation more by imitation than instruction, then the people who give such instructions should be worthy of emulation by the children and hence can positively influence on the development of the character of the children. Children should not be exposed to violent, impolite and disrespectful language because the way we use language mirrors our attitude, feelings and perceptions of the reality around us. It would be hard for people to express feelings of care, compassion, kindness, respect and many such values without due consideration to the courteous use of language.

Bibliography

Archer, Alfred. 2017. "Integrity and the Value of an Integrated Self." *The Journal of Value Inquiry* 15 (3): 435-454.

Bell, Richard H. 2002. *Understanding African Philosophy: A Cross-Cultural Approach to Classical and Contemporary Issues.* New York: Routledge.

Biney, Ama. 2014. "The Historical Discourse on African Humanism: Interrogating the Paradoxes." In *Ubuntu: Curating the Archive*, edited by Leonhard Praeg, and Siphokazi Magadla, 27-53. Pietermaritzburg: University of KwaZulu-Natal Press.

Gade, Christian, B. N. 2012. "What is *Ubuntu*? Different Interpretations among South Africans of African Descent." *South African Journal of Philosophy* 31 (3): 484-503.

Gade, Christian, B. N. 2011. "The Historical Development of the Written Discourses on Ubuntu." *South African Journal of Philosophy* 30 (3): 304-329.

Gyekye, Kwame. 1997. *Tradition and Modernity: Philosophical Reflections on the African Experience.* Oxford: Oxford University Press.

Malipula, Mrisho. 2014. "Depoliticised ethnicity in Tanzania: a structural and historical narrative." *Africa Focus* 27 (2): 49-70.

Masolo, D. A. 2010. *Self and Community in a Changing World.* Bloomington: Indiana University Press.

Mbiti, John. S. 1969. *Africans Religions and Philosophy.* Nairobi: Heinemann Kenya Limited.

Metz, Theddeus. 2011. "*Ubuntu* as a moral theory and human rights in South Africa." *African Human Rights Law Journal* 11 (2): 532-559.

Njue, John. 2012. "African Humanism Ubuntu: The Spiritual Lung for the Future of Humanity." In *In Ascolto dell'Africa: Contesti, Attese, Potenzialita*, edited by Alberto Trevisiol, 23-48. Rome: Urbaniana University Press.

Okello, Stephen. 2012. "Western Humanism in Dialogue with African Ubuntu for the Greater Good." In *In Ascolto dell'Africa: Contesti, Attese, Potenzialita*, edited by Alberto Trevisiol, 49-60. Rome: Urbaniana University Press.

Praeg, Leonhard, and Siphokazi Magadla, eds. 2014. *Ubuntu: Curating the Archive*. Pietermaritzburg: University of KwaZulu-Natal Press.

Ramose, Mogobe B. 1999. *African Philosophy Through Ubuntu*. Harare: Mond Books.

Shivji, Issa G. 2014. "*Utu, Usawa, Uhuru*: Building Blocks of Nyerere's Political Philosophy." In *Ubuntu: Curating the Archive*, edited by Leonhard Praeg, and Siphokazi Magadla, 137-149. Pietermaritzburg: University of KwaZulu-Natal Press.

Shutte, Augustine. 1993. *Philosophy for Africa*. Rondebosch, South Africa: UCT Press.

Shutte, Augustine. 2001. *Ubuntu: An Ethic for a New South Africa*. Dorpspruit, South Africa: Cluster Publications.

Trevisiol, Alberto, ed. 2012. *In Ascolto dell'Africa: Contesti, Attese, Potenzialita*. Rome: Urbaniana University Press.

Tutu, Desmond. 1999. *No Future Without Forgiveness*. London: Rider.

Tutu, Desmond, and Mpho Tutu. 2010. *Made for Goodness*. London: Rider.

van Niekerk, Jason. 2013. "Ubuntu and Moral Value." PhD Thesis, University of the Witwatersrand, Johannesburg.

Wiredu, Kwasi. 1996. *Cultural Universals and Particulars: An African Perspective*. Bloomington: Indiana University Press.

87

Chapter 3: UBUNTU AND THE POLITICS OF MIGRATION

Anke Graness

In the context of the topic of this volume 'Ubuntu and the Everyday', migration, a burning issue in the daily lives of millions of people worldwide, particularly in Africa, cannot be ignored in our discussions.[1] Surprisingly, the broad academic discourse on the concept of Ubuntu rarely touches on the issue of migration and gives no answer to questions such as:

a) how Ubuntu as an ethical concept, a philosophy, or worldview conceptualizes the phenomenon of migration, and

b) which ethical or political conclusions ought to be drawn in relation to the philosophical-ethical and political challenges related to migration. For example, what are the consequences of applying the concept of Ubuntu in the context of immigration policies and the duties of the nation state towards refugees?

This article cannot offer a comprehensive answer to these difficult questions; instead, it attempts a preliminary, comparative approach to them. First, the article summarizes some influential views on migration presented by 'Western'

---

1   This work was supported by the Austrian Science Fund (FWF) V 348 Richter Programme.

liberal and communitarian theorists; second, it offers a description of key features of the concept of Ubuntu and their consequences for the issue of migration, based on the ideas of two main representatives of the academic discourse on Ubuntu, Michael O. Eze and Mogobe B. Ramose. Third, I address the challenges raised by an Ubuntu-based view of migration in a world where resources are scarce. In this context, I introduce a study by Elina Hankela on migration in South Africa. Lastly, I try to provide a tentative comparative answer to the questions above.

Migration and National Boundaries

Migration is one of the most burning problems today. In the face of large migrations caused by wars, poverty, or natural disasters, both policymakers and philosophers are confronted with difficult challenges and moral questions such as the tension between the human right 'to seek and to enjoy in other countries asylum from persecution' (Article 14 of the Universal Declaration of Human Rights), and the concept of state or national sovereignty anchored in Article 21 of the declaration, which recognizes a basic right to self-government, stipulating that 'the will of the people shall be the basis of the authority of government.' Under the current regime of states, that fundamental right includes control over borders as well as determining *who* is to be a citizen as distinguished from a resident or an alien. Moreover, it includes the responsibility of governments to protect their populations. The moral questions that arise here are, for example, the question of whether it is morally legitimate for rich countries to restrict immigration to preserve their standard of living or cultural identity. Why should goods and capital be able to move freely across borders, but not people? The irony of current global developments is that while state sovereignty in economic, military, and technological domains is eroded and national borders have become more porous, they are still policed to keep out immigrants. Further questions are: Do we have a special responsibility for the well-being of our fellow citizens (the members of our community), and do we have the same responsibility for all people in the world? And, do countries have a greater moral duty to admit refugees fleeing war and persecution than immigrants fleeing dire poverty?

Regarding the issue of migration, at present the majority of industrial states (e.g. the USA, Australia, Japan, and the Member States of the EU) focus on the protection of national sovereignty and welfare systems and follows a strict immigration policy. The main concern of the European Union and its Member States is to secure their external borders at all costs, as the new high-tech border fence between Hungary and Serbia/Croatia and the establishment of Frontex–the European Border and Coast Guard Agency, built to coordinate and develop European border management, clearly illustrate. Frontex's tasks include, among others, 'Monitoring migratory flows and carrying out risk analysis regarding all aspects of integrated border management.'[2] The target is to reduce irregular migration into the EU. The strict refugee policy is usually legitimized by the argument that controlling borders is a precondition for sustaining the open societies in Europe. Thus, Hungary's Prime Minister Viktor Orbán has called mass immigration from the Middle East and Africa an existential threat to the European way of life, Europe's cultural heritage, and its Christian value system. He even calls for 'preserving ethnic homogeneity' (Orbán 2017).

As early as 1943, German philosopher Hannah Arendt, herself a Jewish refugee from persecution by the Nazi regime, criticized the closed-border policy of her time, which cost the lives of thousands of Jewish people and other victims of the Nazi regime. Even though human rights were supposed to be those rights that we have regardless of our political status, the only people who could expect to enjoy the benefits of human rights were members of a nation state. Human beings as such, lacking

---

2   See the Frontex homepage "Mission & Tasks": http://frontex. europa.eu/about-frontex/mission-and-tasks/ (viewed 20 May 2018).

nationality, found themselves without rights. Or as Arendt pointed out in her essay 'We Refugees' (1943):

> ... being a Jew does not give any legal status in this world. If we should start telling the truth that we are nothing but Jews, it would mean we expose ourselves to the fate of human beings who, unprotected by any specific law or political convention, are nothing but human beings. I can hardly imagine an attitude more dangerous, since we actually live in a world in which human beings as such have ceased to exist for quite a while; since society has discovered discrimination as the great social weapon by which one may kill men without any bloodshed; since passports or birth certificates, and sometimes even income tax receipts, are no longer formal papers but matters of social distinction (Arendt 1978, 65).

Here, and later in her famous *The Origins of Totalitarianism* (1951), Arendt clearly highlights the dilemma of the refugee, the stateless human being—with nothing other than his/her naked life–who has no legitimate legal or political status—a persistent problem, as the fragile status of refugees clearly shows today. At present, the possession of individual human rights (theoretically independent of any institutionalized source of authority) is still anchored in belonging to a certain nation state, since one can only sue for one's human rights through state institutions.[3] With the loss of the legal and political status that entitles individuals to government protection, it is almost impossible to make use of one's human rights. Thus, it is not yet the case that the individual transcends the citizen, which proves how hollow the talk of inalienable human rights still is, and how passports or birth certificates still decide if a human being will live or die. For Arendt, then, the first human right is the 'right to have rights',

---

3   An exception is the *European Court of Human Rights*, a supranational organization where suits may be brought against contracting states by any person, non-governmental organization, or group of individuals. In the *International Court of Justice*, only states can be parties to a suit.

that is, the right of every individual to belong to a political community and, thus, to humanity.

Current liberal or communitarian theories either fail to resolve the persistent conflict between the human right to asylum and the right to national sovereignty or resolve it in favour of national sovereignty. Liberal theories, for example those of David Miller, Thomas Nagel, or John Rawls, or Communitarians like Michael Sandel or Michael Walzer legitimize the foreclosure policy of the industrial states today. In these theories, despite the emphasis on (abstract, and in Rawls' case very limited) human rights, the responsibility to secure the preconditions of a decent standard of human life (for example physical security or food, i.e. matters of social justice) is mainly anchored in the nation state and limited to the citizens of the state. There are two main lines of argumentation. For representatives of Communitarianism, the anthropological basis for this limitation is the assumption that our concern and willingness to help are limited to the people who are close to us. According to this argument, homogeneous groups have a stronger moral cohesion than less homogeneous ones. In view of representatives of liberal theory, states or nations are regarded as moral and political communities that impose reciprocal obligations on their members. Such reciprocity as well as a (state) sovereign are considered as preconditions to raise and enforce claims of justice. Although there are certain moral obligations towards all human beings, including such negative duties as the prohibition of killing, social justice as a positive duty is limited exclusively to the local field and does not apply to foreigners. A duty to help in cases of emergencies or catastrophes is usually granted, but limited to situations like natural disasters, and famines without clear causes.

Even though Rawls does not explicitly deal with the issue of migration in his *Law of the People* (1999), he makes some enormously important marginal remarks on migration. He argues that the main causes of migration are the persecution of religious and ethnic minorities, political oppression, famines, and population pressure (Rawls 1999, 9). In his opinion, these causes are linked to the unjust domestic political institutions. In other words, in a world of justly governed societies, migratory movements would not be a serious problem. And thus, migration which is–according to Rawls–basically a result of domestic political injustice is not a central topic in his *Law of the People*, which, primarily envisages an international law appropriate for just and decent societies. In a footnote to his discussion of the role of national borders, Rawls argues that a people should have a qualified right to limit immigration (Rawls 1999, 39). His argument for the establishment of borders is that an asset tends to deteriorate if nobody is given responsibility to maintain it. And even though a border line might be historically arbitrary, the existence of borders is necessary for maintaining the land and natural resources of a given territory. According to Rawls, a people bears responsibility for the condition of its territory 'and they cannot make up for their irresponsibility in caring for their land and its natural resources by conquest in war or by migrating into other people's territory without their consent' (Rawls 1999, 39). The poor condition of a country, especially its economic situation, is, according to Rawls, attributable to political mismanagement and structural problems, and thus, affluent countries cannot be made responsible for the (economic or political) failures of poorer countries. In addition, 'Another reason for limiting immigration is to protect a people's political culture and its constitutional principles' (Rawls 1999, 39). The point Rawls tries to make here is based on two assumptions: first, that the political culture and the constitutional principles of a people are something of value and worthy of protection; second, that immigration threatens this value.

In a similar but more comprehensive way David Miller, a representative of liberal nationalism, argues that we have special duties to those we are attached to in some way. In his article 'Reasonable Partiality towards Compatriots' Miller argues that certain 'ground-level special duties' (Miller 2005, 65) arise from relationships that are intrinsically valuable. According to Miller, one such intrinsically valuable community is the national community. Miller argues in *On Nationality* (1995) and *Citizenship and National Identity* (2000) that the nation state performs the role of replicating the social solidarity found in local communities at the level of states, in which populations are largely anonymous. He claims that we have greater ethical duties to our fellow nationals than to nationals of other states: 'nations are ethical communities ... The duties we owe to our fellow-nationals are different from, and more extensive than, the duties we owe to humans as such' (Miller 2000, 27). Or as he pronounces in 2005: '... nations are ethical communities whose members have special responsibilities both to support one another and to preserve their community' (Miller 2005, 69). This means that nationality is bound to entail differential treatment for insiders and outsiders, evidenced by limiting or denying outsiders access to the social welfare system of a certain state. Yet, Miller acknowledges certain cases where our global duty to respect human rights takes precedence over the obligation to provide distributive justice that we owe to our compatriots. Thus, for example, our duties to protect compatriots would not extend to killing foreigners. Miller argues that duties are of different weight and suggests a weighting model for our decision-making, particularly when deciding how to use scarce resources. He pronounces: 'The first is the duty to respect the basic human rights everywhere. The second is the duty to interact with others on fair terms' (Miller 2005, 72-73). But our duties to respect human rights are of two different kinds: the first is negative duties, namely refraining from acting in harmful ways; and the second is positive duties, namely ensuring that people have access to resources necessary for subsistence. Particularly with regard to positive duties there is the substantive question of whose responsibility it is to provide the resources needed to secure basic rights. Rawls clearly delegates such distributive-justice duties to the nation state, whereas Miller suggests a weighting model, but with a clear priority for compatriots: '... if because of material shortages we have to choose between

securing the subsistence rights of compatriots and the equivalent
rights of others, we should favour our compatriots' (Miller 2005,
75). Even though Miller emphasizes that this priority is not to be
taken to its extreme (for example helping starving people in
another country cannot take precedence over our duty to supply
elementary education to fellow-nationals), he also clearly states
that 'if other agents fail in their duty, this cannot impose
additional duties of justice upon us' (Miller 2005, 76). Thus, in
most cases where the basic rights of people are threatened and
where we do not bear *outcome responsibility,* but some other agent
is responsible for creating the conditions of, for example,
starvation, we have, rather, humanitarian obligations, i.e. an
obligation that is wrong to neglect but whose performance
cannot be demanded in the way a duty of justice can (Miller 2005,
76). Thus, Miller defends a moderate, liberal form of nationalism
with a clear focus on responsibilities to our fellow-nationals, or
as he argues: 'what we owe to our fellow-nationals as a matter of
justice takes precedence over humanitarian obligations to
outsiders' (Miller 2005, 77).

Thomas Nagel's view on immigration also goes in this
direction. In 'The Problem of Global Justice' (2005) Nagel
argues:

> The immigration policies of one country may impose large
> effects on the lives of those living in other countries, but under
> the political conception, that by itself does not imply that such
> policies should be determined in a way that gives the interests
> and opportunities of those others equal consideration.
> Immigration policies are simply enforced against the nationals
> of other states; the laws are not imposed in their name, nor
> are they asked to accept and uphold those laws. Since no
> acceptance is demanded of them, no justification is required
> that explains why they should accept such discriminatory
> policies, or why their interests have been given equal
> consideration. It is sufficient justification to claim that the
> policies do not violate their prepolitical human rights (Nagel
> 2005, 129-130).

Nagel emphasizes that 'states are entitled to be left to their own devices, but only on the condition that they not harm others', and even admits that 'In extreme circumstances, denial of the right of immigration may constitute a failure to respect human rights or the universal duty of rescue' (Nagel 2005, 130). Nevertheless, like Rawls and Miller, Nagel believes that the demands a state puts on its members and the members on a state, justify exceptional obligations, particularly the positive obligations of justice, towards its citizens (Nagel 2005, 130).

To sum it up: Representatives of liberal theory defend immigration restrictions by assuming that nations or states have special obligations to protect the interests of their citizens against the interests of foreigners. This is in line with communitarian thinkers like Michael Sandel who also argue that we have special obligations to our compatriots which justify immigration restrictions, for example to protect jobs for the poor citizens of our own community or to reduce costs which immigration imposes on citizens (Sandel 1982, 2005).

But using Ubuntu, which is also a deeply communitarian concept, what answers can we formulate to the ethical and political challenges of migration? Does Ubuntu (as an ethical or political imaginary) offer an alternative way to re-think the politics of migration beyond national boundaries?

Ubuntu and the Issue of Migration

Ubuntu–as described in the academic literature–is essentially a concept of justice and solidarity. It is a principle that brings the relational character of human life into the foreground, underlines that everyone is inherently embedded in a net of social relations (a community) and, thus, cannot be thought of as independent from social relations. Or as the Nigerian philosopher Michael O. Eze expresses it:

'A person is a person through other people' strikes an affirmation of one's humanity through recognition of an 'other' in his or her uniqueness and difference. It is a demand

97

for a creative intersubjective formation in which the 'other' becomes a mirror (but only a mirror) for my subjectivity. This idealism suggests to us that humanity is not embedded in my person solely as an individual; my humanity is co-substantively bestowed upon the other and me. Humanity is a quality we owe to each other. We create each other and need to sustain this otherness creation. And if we belong to each other, we participate in our creations: we are because you are, and since you are, definitely I am. The 'I am' is not a rigid subject, but a dynamic self-constitution dependent on this otherness creation of relation and distance (Eze 2010, 190-91).

Thus, Ubuntu entails a very specific ontological approach to what it means to be human. Here, relations between humans are considered to be constitutive, i.e. the human being is a relational being. The idea of a monadic individualism is alien to the concept of Ubuntu. Due to the interdependent nature of human existence, it follows that if one person's dignity is violated, other people are also affected. And, thus, the characteristic virtues of Ubuntu are compassion towards others, sharing, kindness, respect for the rights of minorities, conduct that aims at consensus and understanding, a spirit of mutual support and cooperation, hospitality, generosity, and selflessness.

In his article 'I Am Because You Are: Cosmopolitanism in the Age of Xenophobia' (2017) Eze describes the primary consequences of Ubuntu with respect to migration. According to him, 'Ubuntu as a theory of political humanism possesses the following credentials: (i) a duty to recognize others in their unique differences, histories and subjective equations; (ii) unlike the cosmopolitan ethics evolving out of the age of reason, the sense of humanism embodied in ubuntu is not only a *recognition of our kind*' (Eze 2017, 100; emphasis in original). The famous Xhosa/Zulu aphorism *umuntu ngumuntu ngabantu* (a person is a person through other people) expresses the basic assumption of the Ubuntu concept, namely that one affirms one's humanity by recognizing the humanity of others and establishing relationships with them that reflect that recognition (see Ramose

1999, 194). Eze concludes that '... our humanity flourishes through a dialogic process of relation and distance, of difference and uniqueness' (Eze 2017, 101). This dialogic process leads to a transition from ignorance to knowledge of the other (Eze 2017, 103), and by such a dialogical process 'the stranger ceases to be an abstract entity to be feared, ostracized or disqualified as part of my humanity' (Eze 2017, 105).

Eze emphasizes that the ethical vision of Ubuntu[4] does not lead to an eradication of boundaries. He states:

> Boundaries are presupposed insofar as the traveller (stranger or kinsman) is privileged over the old as we learn in the Igbo saying, *onye njem ka onye isi awo mma*. Depending on context, the saying could mean that *the traveller is more learned than the old or the travelled (including the travelled stranger) is more cherished than the old.* The traveller or stranger is cherished insofar as s/he brings new knowledge to the community, new ways of life, a new cultural outlook. This is very instructive in a culture where respect for old people is a sacred virtue (Eze 2017, 99; emphasis in original).

Thus, an African ethical approach like Ubuntu does not negate differentiation into discrete parts such as nations, ethnicities, religions, castes, or classes, but handles them as secondary, formal, and superficial distinctions. Here boundaries are conceptualized as places of complementation, as a link and not as something divisive, or as the South African philosopher Mogobe B. Ramose emphasizes:

> According to our preferred ontological perspective, the boundary is not the point of the exclusion of 'the other'. Instead, it is contemporaneously the moment of the reaffirmation of the 'I' and the coupling point of 'the other' and the 'I'. The boundary then underlines the originary

---

4   This vision is akin to ideas expressed in many other African languages, for example the concept of *utu* in Swahili or *uwa* and *izu* in Eze's own mother tongue Igbo. See the description of *utu* in Kresse 2007, 140, and the description of *uwa* and *izu* in Ramose 2013, 33.

relationship of complementarity subsisting between the 'I' and 'the other'. In this way, 'be-ing' constitutes boundary as the recognition of the ineradicable network of complex relationships between and among beings; the 'I' and 'the other' as the human being and other beings as well (Ramose 2014, 30).

According to Eze, in an African ethics (as expressed in the concept of Ubuntu), the 'other' is not seen as a threat to the community but rather, is taken 'as an embedded gift that enriches my humanity' (Eze 2017, 101). In this view then, 'The stranger is a potential relative, a desired member of my commonwealth' (Eze 2017, 100) and has to be seen not 'as a threat but a complement to our humanity' and a 'gift that enriches my humanity' (Eze 2017, 101). Eze concludes that in an African ethical framework (and in a new approach to Cosmopolitanism) as envisioned in the concept of Ubuntu, 'we do not have the dilemma of choosing *our own kind over the stranger for even the stranger is a potential relative* (Eze 2017, 98; emphasis in original).

If we try to summarize Eze's and Ramose's description of the concept of Ubuntu, it seems to lead to the following conclusions: at an epistemological level I have to acknowledge that my subjectivity is constituted by the other human beings with whom I share my social world. Normatively, it follows that recognition of the humanity of every human being (independent of his/her original membership in any particular national, cultural, religious, or other community) is a precondition for the affirmation of my own humanity. Moreover, the violation of the dignity of another person (for example by failure to recognize their humanity) has negative effects on my own humanity or personhood and is a threat or challenge to my own humanity. Thus, the stranger is not a threat to my community, but the maltreatment of the stranger is. The rejection of the recognition of the stranger's dignity is a threat to the humanity of my community and myself. It follows that the stranger has to be considered enabling enrichment of one's own humanity, since he or she challenges me to develop my qualities of being human, qualities which are, according to the concept of Ubuntu, not primarily reason and rationality, but compassion and, to use Heideggers's term, my 'being-with-others'. Further normative conclusions may be drawn: members of our own natal or chosen community need not be given preference over the stranger, and borders or boundaries should be regarded as artificial and secondary phenomena, places of complementation, not separation.

It follows for the issue of migration that unlike the 'Western' liberal and communitarian theories briefly discussed above, which justify a policy of separation and closed borders for the sake of the protection of the nation state as a community of values, the concept of Ubuntu obliges every single person and all communities (nation states or other forms of communities) to welcome all strangers, including refugees, regardless of whether they seek protection from war, persecution, or poverty. If the recognition of the 'other' in his/her humanity is a precondition for the affirmation of my own humanity, if members of my own community do not have precedence over the stranger, and strangers have to be regarded as an enrichment of my own community, then we can turn our backs neither to people who seek protection from war, natural disasters, or poverty, nor to anyone who genuinely wants to be part of our community, for the inclusion of others in all their differences lies at the core of Ubuntu as a moral maxim.

Now, at least two further questions arise: Is this indeed the core of the concept of Ubuntu with regard to the issue of migration as it is conducted by the state? And is this practicable in a world of nation states?

Ubuntu, Migration, and the Challenges of the Everyday

Being a European scholar, I cannot answer the first question. It needs to be answered by African specialist on the concept of Ubuntu, preferably native speakers. They have to answer the fundamental question on how identities of communities—for

101

example, cultural, religious, and linguistic communities—can be preserved while maintaining a general and very far-reaching openness to strangers as described by Eze for example. This question remains unanswered at present, as do the questions of whether or not there may be good reasons to exclude strangers from a community, and what the criteria for such exclusion might be.

Here I will attempt to approach only the question of Ubuntu's practicability in a world of nation states.

Ubuntu seems to be in line with Hannah Arendt's demand for respect and protection of human beings simply as human beings–and not on the basis of their possession of a particular passport or birth certificate. However, for a nation states immigration policy the consequences of Ubuntu are far-reaching and would demand–if the concept of national borders is considered to be artificial and of secondary importance–more or less open borders, and, moreover, wide-ranging help and integration programmes. Regardless of the reason why a stranger wants to immigrate to a community (such as a nation state), he or she should be welcomed and integrated into the existing community.

African countries receive far more refugees than, for example, Europe, but the praxis of immigration policy in African countries shows similar tensions between welcoming immigrants on the one hand and protecting the safety and interests of the citizens of the admitting state on the other. Encounters between members from different communities intensify questions about identity, belonging, and morality, including questions about how to preserve distinctive cultural, religious, or national identities. Such encounters also raise questions about the just distribution of scarce resources on the national level as well as on the level of smaller communities.

The challenges of the everyday encounters between citizens of an African state and African migrants are described in Elina Hankela's book *Ubuntu, Migration, and Ministry: Being Human in a Johannesburg Church* (2014), which is the result of a field study at the Central Methodist Mission in Johannesburg. Hankela tries to understand the encounter between a local church community and African refugees in the context of the concept of Ubuntu. Her research was directed by questions including: What limits and what enables the actualization of Ubuntu in the relationship between the church members and migrants? What do these dynamics expose about being human(e) and about Ubuntu? In 2009, the time of her field study, the church building was host to local congregation members and a shifting population of homeless South African people and largely Zimbabwean migrants. In her analysis of this encounter, Hankela identifies a concurrent existence of both an inclusive and an exclusionary understanding of Ubuntu. The church leaders who showed a positive, welcoming, and supportive attitude towards dwellers from different backgrounds—African refugees as well as South African homeless people—represented an inclusive understanding of Ubuntu. The church leaders' offer of shelter in the church was rooted in both Christian belief and a spirit of Ubuntu:

> The expectations of recognition, respect, care and help in human relationship were justified by references to different sources. Not surprisingly ... Christian faith was an important frame of reference for the notions of care and help, and the 'image of God' motif also loomed behind the demand for respect and recognition. ... Furthermore, besides faith, people's expectations stemmed from cultural expectations – drawn from the very culture(s) wherein *ubuntu* is often said to be a central notion (Hankela 2014, 392).

However, in the day-to-day encounters between church members and migrants, Hankela observed among members of the church as well as among the migrants a number of exclusionary tendencies which were contradictory to the concept of Ubuntu and the official policy of the church leaders. Hankela identified the following reasons for exclusionary tendencies: first and foremost, people were affected by poverty, an ever-growing socio-economic inequality, and by the threat of crime. Such socio-economic factors seem to be a main reason for xenophobic sentiments and a lack of moral ideals like Ubuntu (Hankela 2014, 393). The churchgoers and the migrants existed largely as parallel communities, worshipping at different services, lacking first-hand knowledge about each other, and having little direct personal contact. Reasons for the lack of direct contact were manifold, including such things as prejudice, the misbehaviour of some individuals, and different moral standards, but also material conditions like the uncleanliness of the refugee camp. Facing such troubles didn't make it easy to follow Ubuntu guidelines, as for example, the principle that one must treat a person with Ubuntu regardless of whether they show Ubuntu in return. In general, the 'other' was expected to show Ubuntu in order for one's own group to do the same. Moreover, part of the distancing factors were identity-building concepts like nationality, which functioned as a strong factor of group exclusion at the church. Hankela describes an interesting and complicated dynamic of exclusion on the basis of nationality.[5] For example, South African homeless people viewed as suspect the fact that migrants were also given shelter in the church, and the migrants felt the same about the homeless people. Both marginalised groups had practically no interaction with each other—even though they had a lot in common, considering their equally deprived situations.

All those factors led to rather exclusionary tendencies that they expressed by distancing themselves from each other, calling each other names, stereotyping, and attending separate church services. Also, the fact that church officials sided with the

---

5 At this point we should not forget that former South African president Thabo Mbeki, in his 2005 Heritage Day speech, called for reflection on how 'we can use [the concept of Ubuntu] to define ourselves as South Africans' – here clearly applying the concept of Ubuntu to the entire South African community, that is the nation state. He even demanded that 'Ubuntu [becomes] synonymous with being South African'. Source: http://www.polity.org.za/article/mbeki-heritage-day-celebrations-24092005-2005-09-24 (viewed 20 May 2018)

refugees was viewed with suspicion, and church members felt that they hardly had agency in their own church. Many members of the church community saw the refugees as a threat to their existence as a Christian congregation (Hankela 2014, 394). Hankela's analysis shows that in the lived practice of Ubuntu, in situations where people from different nations and socio-economic backgrounds struggle over scarce resources '... the "reality *ubuntu*" that was negotiated ... was limited by various matters' (Hankela 2014, 392). In general, the study identifies two factors that limit the everyday practice of Ubuntu: the rule of survival restricts the readiness to help and care in the name of Ubuntu, and group identities (particularly nationality, ethnicity, social class, and refugee status) can be tools for exclusion. However, her study shows that Ubuntu can serve in such situations as a guiding principle, which has to be renegotiated day to day, as the encounters between members of the Methodist church community and refugees had to be negotiated anew every day. Hankela shows that 'Being a person through other persons – who belong to a group different from one's own – became possible once there was direct encounter with others' (Hankela 2014, 394). Particularly the section Local Teen Church Youth was able to transcend borders between the different groups. Hankela's observation illustrates two important points, first that the guiding principle of Ubuntu made people able to express solidarity—even under the situation of scarce resources; and second, that the direct encounter, the dialogue, with the 'other' is a precondition to overcome stereotypes and to live our shared humanity. Or as Eze pronounced, in the dialogical process 'the stranger ceases to be an abstract entity to be feared, ostracized or disqualified as part of my humanity' (Eze 2017, 105).

Hankela concludes that, despite all difficulties with practicing Ubuntu in the everyday life of the Refugee Ministry, the concept made sense in this grassroots community:

> It was not only the centerpiece in the leader's vision but also a common undertone in the expectations the interviewees expressed vis-à-vis their situation. In the encounter between

the local church and the refugees and homeless, 'reality ubuntu' was negotiated – and compromised. ... When the practice of *ubuntu* was limited within the boundaries of national, ethnic, religious or other communities among people who shared the same space ... it seemed to restrict the discovery of the humanity of all parties (Hankela 2014, 396).

Conclusion

Based on the description of the concept of Ubuntu by Ramose and Eze, our first question (how migration may be framed in the context of Ubuntu) can now be answered as follows: free movement of human beings (including migration) is not to be taken as a threat or problem for the communities (like nation states) into which refugees immigrate, but as an enrichment of the community. Recognizing the needy refugee in his/her humanness and vulnerability, and welcoming and integrating him or her into the community seem to be categorical imperatives of Ubuntu. A fundamentally positive image of the human being does not allow seeing any individual as a threat, but only as a chance for the development of one's own capacity for being human.

Concerning my second question, practicability, the use of Ubuntu as a guiding principle for shaping immigration policy in a world of nation states and scarce resources has far-reaching political consequences that seem ultimately to require the dissolution of the nation state—although Eze emphasizes that borders need not be done away with. However, Eze does not explain how to reconcile national borders with the cosmopolitan claim of Ubuntu, particularly in respect to practical political consequences.

The classical concept of the nation state is based on two main pillars: a people and a territory. It is thought to be an instrument of national unity, in economic, social, and cultural life. Migration challenges the question of national unity and the governability of nation states. For who is entitled to govern whom in a state (or any other political entity) with a more or less fluid population? Whom does a government represent, if not the voters and their interests, and what should happen if the interests of voters are in conflict with the interests of guests and new members of the community? The idea of fluid populations and borders–as attractive as it might appear at first–poses crucial questions about the structure and function of democracy which needs first of all a 'demos'. Here the concept of Ubuntu appears to leave a number of political questions unanswered.

Seyla Benhabib offers a potentially helpful theory in her book *Another Cosmopolitanism: Hospitality, Sovereignty and Democratic Iterations* (2006). Benhabib proposes a concept of 'porous borders', an approach that recognizes the moral and legal rights of human beings to move across borders, yet simultaneously acknowledges a public authority responsible for the territory of the settled population. Developing Hannah Arendt's notion about 'the right to have rights', Benhabib opposes the idea of open borders on the principle that democracy needs boundaries in order to know which democratic entity is responsible to whom. According to Benhabib it is the *logic of democratic representation* which involves demarcation. Any form of popular sovereignty needs units to remain representative for its population. Citizens must feel that their interests are being represented by the community to which they belong. However, such boundaries don't have to conflict with the human right to move freely. Individuals may leave or join a community as long as they are willing to participate in the creation and maintenance of the sovereign structure.

Benhabib tries to solve the dilemma that immigration policies are enforced against foreigners while they are not included in the process of decision-making regarding naturalization or citizenship policies by insisting that the *demos* has to continuously engage in reflexive acts of self-constitution, where boundaries and membership can be renegotiated.[6] She argues that such a process of democratic iteration will

---

6   This means that the interests of the so-called foreigners have not been given equal consideration and that not all who are affected by a certain decision are included in the process of decision-making).

increasingly incorporate and promote cosmopolitan norms, and maybe someday transcend national boundaries. The European Community and particularly the *European Court of Human Rights* seem to be taking practical steps into this direction.

Apart from the question how democracy could work with fluid borders, migration also gives rise to another important line of questioning that concerns the distribution of scarce resources. For example, in a nation state should the distribution of resources include 'guests' like refugees and immigrants or only citizens of the nation state who build up the community and keep it running? Liberal theorists like Miller or Nagel have found some clear answers to such questions. But what are the Ubuntu answers? Neither Ramose nor Eze answer such questions.

With respect to one of the main reasons for migration, the asymmetrical distribution of resources worldwide, what conclusions can be drawn using the concept of Ubuntu? This point leads us now to the core of the issue of migration: the causes of flight. Nobody likes to be a refugee. Migration was and is for the vast majority of refugees in the past and at present the last option to protect their lives and the lives of their children. In liberal theory, the causes of flight are usually located purely within the state–which in no way does justice either to political, economic, and ecological interdependencies or to the asymmetric power structures of our world (see the critique of Pogge 2002; Young 2006). Flight and migration have various causes rooted in history as well as in the current structure of the world economy which require analysis. A general hospitality towards strangers or migrants does not solve the causes for flight and migration. Thus, how does one use Ubuntu as a guide in determining the causes for flight and assigning responsibility for eliminating those causes? And what consequences do these answers have for migration and migration policy? An ethical concept underlining the ontological relatedness of all human beings, which includes strangers and regards them as an enrichment to the community would be a valuable contribution to global ethics. However, making the assumption that all human beings are interconnected is no substitute for analysis of conflicts of interest between human individuals and communities. Thus, we should not neglect to analyse the reasons for migration and the associated moral responsibility for its causes and remedies. Such an analysis is of importance not only for countries which receive immigrants but also, and primarily, for countries of origin, which suffer both the problems that lead to their population's exodus and the loss of mainly their young and educated citizens.

Ubuntu seems to be a concept that requires serious regard for the dignity of each individual human being, independent of their membership in a certain group, community or state; and thus in practising Ubuntu, one must privilege individual rights to free movement and asylum over the right to national sovereignty. However, current discussions about Ubuntu have not yet addressed important questions regarding the practical consequences and related moral issues of migration for countries of origin and destination countries. Such questions include whether the imperative to preserve a community with intrinsic value takes precedence over an imperative to welcome strangers, and the moral legitimacy of various reasons for refusing or allowing entrance to strangers. Does the responsibility to protect one's community impose limits on accepting strangers? What are the morally legitimate and illegitimate reasons for such limits? Further questions concern the causes of flight and the assignment of responsibility for combatting these causes. We must consider such questions further.

The central issue with this paper which remains is the difficulty to seriously consider Ubuntu from an African paradigm and not restrict it to questions that pit the community and citizen against the nation state as perceived and understood by Western theorists.

Bibliography

Arendt, Hannah. 1978. "We Refugees." In *The Jew as Pariah: Jewish Identity and Politics in the Modern Age.* New York:

Grove Press. Originally published in *The Menorah Journal* 36 (1, January 1943): 69-77.

Arendt, Hannah. 1951. *The Origins of Totalitarianism*. New York: Schocken Books.

Benhabib, Seyla. 2006. *Another Cosmopolitanism: Hospitality, Sovereignty, and Democratic Iterations*. Oxford: Oxford University Press.

Eze, Michael. O. 2010. *Intellectual History in Contemporary South Africa*. New York: Palgrave Macmillan.

Eze, Michael. O. 2017. "I Am Because You Are: Cosmopolitanism in the Age of Xenophobia." *Philosophical Papers* 46 (1, 2 January): 85-109.

Hankela, Elina. 2014. *Ubuntu, Migration, and Ministry: Being Human in a Johannesburg Church*. Leiden: Brill.

Kresse, Kai. 2007. *Philosophising in Mombasa: Knowledge, Islam, and Intellectual Practice on the Swahili Coast*. Edinburgh: Edinburgh University Press.

Miller, David. 2000. *Citizenship and National Identity*, Cambridge: Polity Press.

Miller, David. 2005. "Reasonable Partiality towards Compatriots." *Ethical Theory and Moral Practice* 8 (1-2, April): 63–81.

Miller, David. 1995. *On Nationality*. Oxford: Oxford University Press.

Nagel, Thomas. 2005. "The Problem of Global Justice." *Philosophy & Public Affairs* 33 (2, March): 113–147.

Orbán, Viktor. 2017. Addressing the Hungarian Chamber of Commerce and Industry in Budapest. 28 February 2017. Source: https://www.euractiv.com/section/justice-home-affairs/news/orban-calls-ethnic-homogeneity-a-key-to-success/ (viewed 20 May 2018).

Pogge, Thomas W. 2002. *World Poverty and Human Rights: Cosmopolitan Responsibilities and Reforms*. Cambridge: Polity Press.

Rawls, John. 1999. *The Law of Peoples; with, The Idea of Public Reason Revisited*. Cambridge, Mass.: Harvard University Press

Ramose, Mogobe B. 1999. *African Philosophy Through Ubuntu.* Harare: Mond Books.

Ramose, Mogobe B. 2003. "The Philosophy of *Ubuntu* and *Ubuntu* as a Philosophy." In *The African Philosophy Reader,* 2nd ed., edited by P. H. Coetzee and A. P. J. Roux, 230-38. London: Routledge.

Ramose, Mogobe B. 2014. "Transcending Cosmopolitanism." *Diogenes* 59 (3–4, 1 November): 30–35.

Sandel, Michael. 2005. *Public Philosophy.* Cambridge: Harvard University Press.

Sandel, Michael. 1982. *Liberalism and the Limits of Justice.* Cambridge: Cambridge University Press.

Shutte, Augustine. 2001. *Ubuntu: An Ethic for a New South Africa.* Pietermaritzburg: Cluster Publications.

Young, Iris. M. 2006. "Responsibility and Global Justice: A Social Connection Model." *Social Philosophy and Policy* 23 (1): 102–30.

Chapter 4: UBUNTU, INEQUALITY AND EVERYDAY LIFE: SOME REFLECTIONS ON A MAJOR EXISTENTIAL CHALLENGE

Aloo Osotsi Mojola[1]

The Problem of Inequality in View of Ubuntu

Inequality is a huge challenge to the practice of living out the values of Ubuntu, which include the idea of human solidarity and our common humanity, as well as the promotion of human justice and fairness for all. Inequality is a troublesome reality that affects in a very adverse and inhumane manner the vast majority of humankind, both globally and locally. It is a phenomenon that is entirely manmade. It is a pure human and social construction. It is difficult to believe that any social contract, at its original position would have countenanced the huge disparities and the untenable virtually unbridgeable gaps between the very poor and the very rich, currently characteristic of contemporary everyday reality in the modern world. The renowned political philosopher John Rawls captured very

---

1   The author is a Professor at St Paul's University, Limuru, Kenya and an Honorary Professor, Faculty of Theology, Pretoria University, Pretoria, South Africa.

succinctly what in my view is the deep insight underlying the Ubuntu perspective, (and thus understood from a non-individualistic and communitarian perspective) namely that "Each person possesses an inviolability founded on justice that even the welfare of society as a whole cannot override" (Rawls 1971, 3). Based on the framework of social contract thinking in the manner of Thomas Hobbes, John Locke, Immanuel Kant and the idea of a veil of ignorance, Rawls proposed a way of safeguarding the dignity and worth of every individual in any future society in which all are citizens. He argues that in such a society "All social primary goods are to be distributed equally unless an unequal distribution is to the advantage of everyone" (Rawls 1917, 62). It is unlikely that anyone involved in blindly (i.e. under a veil of ignorance), framing a social contract for a future social order in which he or she were to be a member would will into being, or countenance a society that would produce such monstrosities of injustice as currently characterize present day social reality.[2] The unconscionable suffering of the vast majority of human beings resulting from the manner of distributing or sharing social primary goods in our present world is totally and morally unjustifiable. The Hobbesian nightmare where life for the many is "poor, nasty, brutish and short" (Hobbes 1968, 186) is now more than ever a horrifying reality and an ever present danger encountered on a daily basis. The struggle against social arrangements where humans are daily subjected to a precarious existence, characterized by shame and dishonor, lack of respect or recognition is blatantly reprehensible. Every day and everywhere a vast majority of people are crying for a life of dignity and honor, of self-respect and self-esteem, of being accepted and recognized as human beings.

---

2   Please note that according to John Rawls social primary goods comprise –'liberties, opportunities, income and wealth and the bases of self-respect', and thus also accordingly to Rawls ,the wellbeing of society is based on the condition of the poorest of the poor'.

A typical day in the life of an average subsistence peasant farmer or pastoralist in our African waterless wastelands or our densely populated polluted poverty stricken spaces is characterized by a primordial struggle for survival, a daily rummaging for life's essentials, from water to basic food, in an extremely hostile and unfriendly environment. In recent times devastating famines have almost every other year continued to ravage inhabitants of these vulnerable spaces and places, literally leaving in their wake a ghostly Ezekelian "valley of dry bones."[3] A typical day in our impoverished rural villages does not lack images of women and their young trekking long distances bare foot in search of essential water or firewood. Similarly, a typical day in the life of our wretched slums, such as in the sprawling Nairobi's Kibra or Kayole neighborhoods, or in the life of the numberless unemployed youth or street children of no fixed abode daily spotted in our urban landscape, exposes fellow humans to a daily life without dignity, a life of squalor, daily shame and humiliation, daily pain and daily suffering. Franz Fanon, a revolutionary medical psychiatrist from Martinique, only a few decades ago painted a poignant picture of the colonized in the so-called Third World, describing them as *The Wretched of the Earth*. The situation seems to have grown from worse to worse and more. Henri Lefebvre writes about the "breathtaking degradation of everyday life for large masses of human beings" (Lefebvre 1991, 9) even in such modern developed urban spaces as can be spotted in some corners of France of his time. These masses now more than ever populate the earth in staggering numbers. Such conditions are also being witnessed as well in urban spaces and rural areas in such advanced developed places as those captured in an acclaimed modern sociological tale – *Evicted: Poverty and Profit in the American City* (Desmond 2017).

A Kenyan Newspaper, the *Daily Nation* of 15th March 2017 reported that, "the public wage bill stands at Kshs 627 billion per

---

3   Biblical book of Ezekiel chapter 37.

year, amounting to 50% of the total revenues collected by the government paid to only 700,000 people". This newspaper observed that: "The 627 billion for only 700,000 public officials is the classic case of a man-eat man society: a half of the country's revenue lines the pockets of only two percent of its population." Moreover this does not take into account the spoils that this tiny minority continues to gobble up, to plunder, grab and loot from the national storehouse, including public land, government property, and theft by the billions of moneys budgeted and intended for essential services to the poor, the weak and vulnerable. The growing gap between the top wealthy elite and the bottom poor in Kenya is alarming. The result is shocking poverty and abject health and the related host of social problems. This situation is certainly not limited to Kenya. It has become the norm in a host of African countries, ranging from Angola in the South to Nigeria in the West, to Congo in the Centre, and everywhere in between. This is not however limited to Africa!

The Parade of Dwarfs

Inequality is often experienced in terms of poverty and usually measured by specialists in the field using such tools as the Gini coefficient or the Kuznets[4] ratio, among others. Among the most revealing graphical representations of inequality, I find Jan Pen's 'Parade of Dwarfs'[5] hugely compelling and visually eye opening. Jan Pen, a Dutch economist, in a celebrated economic text *Income Distribution* (Pen 1975), describes a parade that starts with the

---

4   Kate Raworth in her breathtaking book *Doughnut Economics* casts serious doubt on the predictive value of the Kuznetz curve regarding the correlation between progress and the fall of inequality, arguing that it demonstrates "the infamous rise of the one percent accompanied by flat or falling wages for the majority", ibid, p169. Or citing Piketty's words, "Capitalism automatically generates arbitrary and unsustainable inequalities that radically undermine the meritocratic values on which democratic societies are based", cited Raworth, op.cit , p169

5   See YouTube – Jan Pen's Dwarfs and Giants – video. See also Clive Crook's article, "The Height of Inequality" in *The Atlantic Monthly*, Sept 1, 2006).

average person each ordered in terms of height proportional to their income. The shortest in the parade represent the poorest individuals and the tallest in the parade represent the wealthiest individuals. Pen's 'Parade of Dwarfs' visualizes a parade consisting of miles and miles of dwarfs, and punctuated at the end by a gigantic spectacle of a minuscule number of giants of unimaginable proportions and heights. This vivid and unforgettable image imaginatively captures the horrifying reality of inequality in our world showing that "we are all mostly dwarves."[6] Jan Pen draws on something akin to Jonathan Swift's Lilliputian world (Swift 1967), a world peopled by tiny dwarfs invaded by what to us are 'normal' humans but who to the Lilliputian inhabitants appear like huge unimaginable giants. The citizens of Lilliput here represent the vast majority of people on planet earth while the incredibly tiny minority constituting the very wealthy and powerful who dominate and control our world are comparable to the few visiting giants in *Oliver's Travels* who visit Lilliput. Jan Pen's metaphor of the parade of dwarfs is usually represented graphically showing people the size of Lilliputians lined up for miles upon miles and somewhere toward the end of the line a few giants start appearing in the parade. Such a parade of dwarfs with a few giants captures the reality of our world in respect of the challenges of inequality[7].

Poverty and inequality are inextricably linked. Poverty has been notably and powerfully defined as "the absence of acceptable choices across a broad range of important life decisions — a severe lack of freedom to be or to do what one wants" inevitably resulting in "insufficiency and deprivation across many of the facets of a fulfilling life" (Foster 2013, 2). Among the outcomes of poverty the following are usually noted,

---

6 See "Do you realize we're mostly dwarves?" (LVTFan's Blog, January 21, 2011)

7 For a graphical representation of Jan Pen's Parade of Dwarfs see the YouTube video or in Rowan Colbeck's blog, 'The income parade', 8 October 2010

"inadequate resources to buy the basic necessities of life; Frequent bouts of illness and an early death; Literacy and education levels that undermine adequate functioning; and limit one's comprehension of the world and oneself; Living conditions that imperil physical and mental health; Jobs that are at best unfulfilling and at worst dangerous; A pronounced absence of dignity, a lack of respect from others; and Exclusion from community affairs" (Foster 2013, 2). This instructive list of poverty indicators takes us directly to the heart of the matter.

The correlation between the above poverty conditions and the scourge of inequality or between inequality and a whole host of social ills and sufferings has been shown to be rather strong. Richard Wilkinson and Kate Pickett (2009) provide abundant statistical evidence showing a very strong correlation between them. Among the social consequences and misfortunes resulting from inequality they list the following: "high levels of distrust, mental illness (including drug and alcohol addiction), life expectancy and infant mortality, obesity, children's educational performance, teenage births, homicides, imprisonment rates, social mobility" (Wilkinson and Pickett 2009, 47).

The January 2017 Oxfam Briefing paper "An Economy for the 99%" subtitled "It's time to build a human economy that benefits everyone, not just the privileged few" (Oxfam 2017) paints a shocking and grim reality. It reinforces the truth and reality of Pen's parade as a global horror story. The report reminds us that "since 2015, the richest 1% has owned more wealth than the rest of the planet", that "eight men now own the same amount of wealth as the poorest half of the world", that "over the next 20 years, 500 people will hand over $2.1 trillion to their heirs – a sum larger than the GDP of India, a country of 1.3 billion people" (Oxfam 2017). It cites the work of French economist Thomas Piketty who notes concerning the United States, a country admired by many and thought to be an example to aspired to, but where growth in incomes for the bottom half of the population has remained at a standstill contrasted with 300% growth for the top 1% during the last 30 years (Piketty

2015, 24). Vietnam is also cited as an example of a country where the richest man is quoted as earning more per day than the poorest person earns in 10 years (Oxfam 2017). Contributing to this social havoc according to the Oxfam report are the realities of corporations—that prioritize the interest of those at the very top, the exploitation of workers and producers, the evasion of tax or tax fraud, the buying of politicians, what they describe as "super-charged shareholder capitalism" and crony capitalism. Underlying the above are the false assumptions that the market is always right and the role of government should be minimized, that corporations need to maximize profits and returns to shareholders at all costs, that extreme individual wealth is benign and a sign of success and inequality is not relevant, that GDP growth should be the primary goal of policy making, that our economic model is gender-neutral and that our planet's resources are limitless (Oxfam 2017). Oxfam should be commended for exposing this major driver of global ruin and human degradation.

An Ubuntu understanding of Inequality

An Ubuntu approach to understanding inequality focuses on the effect and impact of inequality on human beings and everything that impacts their quality of life as well as their relationships. This includes the human environment and habitat and its implications on human beings, as well as those human activities that often create a momentum of their own beyond human control. Focusing on these with a view to developing human interventions in favor of our future well-being is a necessary imperative for human survival. The primary concern of an Ubuntu approach is human well-being and wholeness, and a prioritization of such key issues as justice, freedom, human agency and human rights. Martha Nussbaum and Amartya Sen's approach to inequality is here viewed as essentially Ubuntu-oriented. Nussbaum refers to this approach as the Capabilities Approach or the Human Development Approach (Nussbaum 2011; see also Sen 1999). Nussbaum formulates the basic question underlying this approach as follows: "What does a life worthy of human dignity require?" She identifies the Central Capabilities at the core of this approach and considers these essential for "a dignified and minimally flourishing life" that any well-ordered society or "a decent political order" must pursue and secure for all her citizens. This is compelling and completely tenable. Included in the list we find the following: *Life* - living out a full life span; *Bodily Health* - a healthy all round lifestyle; *Bodily integrity* - including free movement, free from violent domestic or sexual assault, meeting all essential bodily needs; *Senses, imagination and thought* – ability of using one's senses, to imagine, think, and reason to the full capacity or, 'truly human' way, and taking full advantage of an adequate education, resulting in creative and productive works, etc. *Emotions* – ability to have attachments to things and people, a healthy and balanced expression of one's feelings of love, joy, grief, justified anger, etc.; *Practical reason* – ability reflect and act in a moral and ethical manner; *Affiliation* – ability to live with others, show concern for them, show love and mutual respect, acceptance of the other in a non-discriminatory way, respecting gender, ethnicity, race and religion; *Other species* - care and concern for animals, plants, and the world of nature; *Play* - being able to laugh, to play, to enjoy recreational activities, *Control over one's environment* - active and effective participation in political choices that govern one's life, and ability to hold property on an equal basis with others, having the right to seek employment on an equal basis with others, as well as other fundamental human rights (Nussbaum 2011, 33-34).

Nussbaum and others argue that these capabilities "belong first and foremost to individual persons and only derivatively to groups" i.e. the principle of *"each person as an end"* (Nussbaum 2011, 35). This is a Rawlsian or even Kantian perspective. The individual is placed here before the group. The question naturally arises – Can you have the individual without the group or community? Can the individual survive without the community? Where does the individual come from? How is he or she to understand himself/herself? The Ubuntu[8] perspective understands the individual and the community/group being in a mutual symbiotic relationship, interdependent, inextricably interlinked and inseparable. The individual is a product of the community and depends on the community for her/his survival. Similarly the community is composed of individuals and is only possible through their mutual and intricate relationships and support systems. The aim and raison d'etre of a well ordered, just and truly human society is to empower individual members to actualize as much of the above as is possible given the available resources and means for realizing these. Individuals receive their identity as persons— acceptance, affirmation, support and sustenance from the community. The Nguni proverb '*Umntu ngumuntu ngabantu*' or its variants in other Bantu languages is usually translated as saying, 'A person is a person through other persons.' Archbishop Tutu explains what this means as follows:

> For us, the solitary human being is a contradiction in terms. *Ubuntu* is the essence of being human. It speaks of how my humanity is caught up and bound up inextricably with yours... The completely self-sufficient human being is sub-human...We are made for complementarity. We are created for a delicate network of relationships, of interdependence with our fellow human beings, with the rest of creation...*Ubuntu* speaks of spiritual attributes such as generosity, hospitality, compassion, caring, sharing. You could be affluent in material possessions but still be without *Ubuntu*. This concept speaks of how people are more important than things, than profits, than material possessions. It speaks about the intrinsic worth of persons as not dependent on extraneous things such as status, race, creed, gender, or achievement. In traditional African society, Ubuntu was coveted more than anything else... It was seen as what ultimately distinguished people from animals – the quality of being human and so also

---

8   For more on Ubuntu see A.O.Mojola, "The Bantu concept of Ubuntu in the theology and practice of Bishop Desmond Tutu of South Africa and its implications for deepening the struggle for justice and human rights", forthcoming.

humane. Those who had *ubuntu* were compassionate and gentle, they used their strength on behalf of the weak, and they did not take advantage of others – in short, they *cared*, treating others as what they were: human beings. If you lacked *ubuntu*, in a sense you lacked an indispensable ingredient of being human. You might have had much of the world's goods, and you might have had position and authority, but if you had no *ubuntu*, you did not amount to much. Today, *ubuntu* is still greatly admired, sought after and cultivated…*Ubuntu* teaches us that our worth is intrinsic to who we are. We matter because we are made in the image of God. Ubuntu reminds us that we belong in one family – God's family, the human family. In our African worldview, the greatest good is communal harmony. Anything that subverts or undermines this greatest good is ipso facto wrong, evil (Tutu 2011, 21-24).

John Mbiti, a leading and renowned authority on African religions and philosophy understands this interconnectedness as follows: "I am because we are, and because we are, therefore I am' (Mbiti 1969, 108-109). He explains that "Only in terms of other people does the individual become conscious of his own being, his own duties, his privileges and responsibilities towards himself and towards other people. When he suffers, he does not suffer alone but with the corporate group; when he rejoices, he rejoices not alone but with his kinsmen, his neighbours and his relatives whether dead or living. When he marries, he is not alone, neither does the wife 'belong' to him alone. So also, the children belong to the corporate body of kinsmen, even if they bear only their father's or mother's name. Whatever happens to the individual happens to the whole group, and whatever happens to the whole group happens to the individual" (Mbiti 1969, 108-109).

Amartya Sen, mentioned above, is undoubtedly one of the leading pioneers and proponents of the capability approach to poverty and inequality. Central to his thinking is the idea of freedom and the expansion of freedom as well as individual agency, as necessary to engage and address that multitude of deprivations that currently bedevil the human community.

Interestingly Sen understands development as 'a process of expanding the real freedoms that people enjoy' (Sen 1999, 3) and requiring "the removal of major sources of unfreedom: poverty as well tyranny, poor economic opportunities as well as systematic social deprivation, neglect of public facilities as well as intolerance or overactivity of repressive states" (Sen 1999, 3). Central to poverty and inequality in this view is the focus on 'achievement', 'freedom' and 'functionings'. For Sen achievement is understood as "concerned with what we manage to accomplish," (Sen 1992, 31) and freedom as concerned with "the ability to achieve what we value" (Sen 2009, 208) or "the real opportunity that we have to accomplish what we value" (Sen 1992, 31). Inequality from this perspective is thus understood in terms of capability, where such capability "reflects a person's freedom to choose between alternative lives (functioning combinations)" (Sen 1992, 83). Inequality accordingly implies an inability, or a lack of the wherewithal, to meet one's material or social needs or to realize one's dreams. It implies a deficit involving "incomes, wealths, utilities, liberties, primary goods, capabilities" (Sen 1992, 110). It implies not "having minimally adequate capabilities" (Sen 1992, 111) to pursue one's goals. The 'functionings' referred to above, vary "from the most elementary ones, such as being well-nourished, avoiding escapable morbidity and premature mortality, etc. to quite complex and sophisticated achievements, such as having self-respect, being able to take part in the life of the community, and so on..." (Sen 1992, 5). Inequality thus speaks of powerlessness and an inability to do or to be, to pursue, to actualize, or to realize one's needs and preferences. Sen makes clear that the focus is on "human lives and not just on the resources people have ...proposing a fundamental shift in the focus of attention from the means of living to the actual opportunities a person has..." (Sen 2009, 253). It is no wonder that Sen understands development as "a process of expanding the real freedoms that people enjoy" as indicated above. This is clearly in line with an Ubuntu perspective which focuses on the concrete practice of lived existence rather than on some theoretical ideal.

'The Killing Fields of Inequality'

In his incisive and eye-opening book *The Killing Fields of Inequality* Norwegian sociologist, Göran Therborn makes clear at the outset that "Inequality is a violation of human dignity" and "a d enial of the possibility for everybody's human capabilities to develop" (Therborn 2013,1). He notes among its deadly effects, the following: "premature death, ill-health, humiliation, subjection, discrimination, exclusion from knowledge or from mainstream social life, poverty, powerlessness, stress, insecurity, lack of self-confidence and of pride in oneself, and exclusion from opportunities and life-chances. Inequality is a socio-cultural order, which (for most of us) reduces our capabilities to function as human beings, our health, our self-respect, our sense of self, as well as our resources to act and participate in this world" (Therborn 2013, 1).

Therborn distinguishes three inextricably intertwined and interdependent kinds of inequality, namely: 1. *Vital inequality* "referring to socially constructed unequal life chances of human organisms" that are measurable in terms of mortality rates, life expectancy, health expectancy, among others. 2. *Existential inequality* – factoring in feelings of self-esteem and self-worth as well as of autonomy, human dignity, degrees of freedom, and of rights to self-development. 3. *Resource Inequality*, which takes into account the unequal distribution and access to resources to act and to do. These three inequalities explain the common reality of the "many bodies buried… and the many lives stunted forever by humiliations and degradations…" (Therborn 2013, 49).

Therborn's correctly characterizes inequality as a killer. The consequences of inequality on the quality of life and on everyday life are obvious. He notes that inequality kills through malnutrition. It kills through lack of food and poor eating habits, through stunted and vulnerable lives, through famines, through ignorance and lack of education, through poor immunity, through poor sanitation, through risky life styles, through stress and depression, through unemployment, among other factors. In his book Therborn notes for example that:

> Inequality kills in many ways. It starts already in the uterus, before the baby is born —a baby [born] to a poor mother, or an undernourished mother. It is not only bad nutrition, because it is the same phenomenon, in a smaller proportion, in the rich countries, that babies of poorer class or lower class mothers tend to be underdeveloped as fetuses and they are born underweight, and in some countries like India, seriously underweight. And this has lifelong consequences, when we are talking about probability here. There are always individuals that can be lucky, but already, this difference in fetus development at birth slows and tends to truncate your development as a child, your motor development and cognitive development. And secondly it increases the risk of a certain type of diabetes and a certain type of heart disease at late middle age or early old age [that] predisposes you to an earlier death. So this is one way in which inequality kills; unequal uterine development (Therborn 2013, 49).

There is no doubt that inequality affects and impacts every area of our lives – from the cradle to the grave. It affects our thought life. It affects our everyday life and determines how we die.[9]

Alienation and Everyday Life

Inequality is the stuff of everyday life and is unavoidably implicated in the reality of alienation and obstacles to full human self-realization. Clearly the everyday life is the space where alienation plays itself out. Henri Lefebvre has captured this well: "Everyday life is profoundly related to all activities, and encompasses them with all their differences and their conflicts; it is their meeting place, their bond, their common ground. And it is in everyday life that the sum total of relations which make

---

9   Subtitle of Keith Payne's book *The Broken Ladder*, 2017.

the human - and every human being – as a whole takes its shape and its form. In it are expressed and fulfilled those relations which bring into play the totality of the real, albeit in a certain manner which is always partial and incomplete: friendship, comradeship, love, the need to communicate, play, etc." (Lefebvre 1991, 97). It is in everyday life and activities that the reality of alienation is experienced. Alienation is at the heart of the everyday. The everyday is characterized both by the reality of inequality and the reality of alienation. Alienation is often experienced in terms of lack of self-esteem, lack of self-worth, a sense of meaninglessness, a lack of opportunities for self-fulfilment and self-actualization. It is experienced in terms of a heightened sense of aloneness and disconnection from community. To be alienated literally means feeling like an alien, feeling like a stranger to oneself, to one's community and indeed to humanity as a whole. It could be argued that alienation is not just subjective feeling but rather objective reality. It is a reflection of social, economic and political circumstances in which one is situated. The individual only happens to be the locus of this disjunction of the subjective and the objective, i.e. alienation. Alienation has been understood from a Marxist perspective as "… an action through which (or a state in which) a person, a group, an institution, or a society becomes (or remains) alien 1) to the results or products of its own activity (and to the activity itself) and/or 2) to the nature in which it lives, and/or 3) to other human beings, and – in addition and through any or all of 1) to 3) also 4) to itself (to its own historically created human possibilities)" (Bottomore 1983, 9-10). Alienation has also been understood more broadly as alienation of humans from nature, from their fellow human beings, from the work of their hands and minds, from themselves (Schachtel) or as powerlessness, meaninglessness, social isolation, normlessness and self-estrangement (M.Seeman) (Bottomore 1983, 14). A number of foreign words in German such as, *Entfremdung* (being a stranger to onelf), *Seinvergessenhet* (a sense of forgetting oneself or not understanding oneself) and *Heimatlosigkeit* (a sense of homelessness) among others have been employed by philosophers such Martin Heidegger to capture the challenge of alienation in everyday life. Such philosophers and writers including Jean Paul Sartre, Albert Camus among others understood alienation as leading to a kind of inauthentic existence as opposed to an authentic existence. Inauthentic existence implies that one is not oneself, and that one's choices are not one's own, or that one's life is not what is willed by oneself, but rather a consequence of circumstances beyond one's control. Inauthentic existence implies a powerlessness to make autonomous choices, or to decide and live out in pursuit of one's freely chosen preferences or options. Inauthentic existence implies hopelessness, normlessness, meaninglessness. The challenge of de-alienation and of inequality and of poverty is the supreme challenge of our time, of human existence, of human survival, and of human emancipation or social transformation. It is essentially the central challenge of social thought. There is however a sense in which the idea of Ubuntu and of human solidarity and community somehow destabilizes these and makes life tolerable through laughter and joy, and dance and celebration of the life's little accomplishments and achievements, through mutual sharing and mutual acceptance and affirmation of the other, through a common life in community and mutual support in times of grief and happiness. The idea of an Ubuntu world view and value system reinforces the practice of life lived on these terms. It makes human life meaningful and worth living.

The Everyday as a Site of Struggle and Resistance

Inequality is an existential threat and daily challenge unavoidably embedded in our everyday life. It is characteristic of the human life cycle for the vast majority. It stares us in the face when we wake up and when we lie down to sleep. It perhaps even dominates the content of our dreams and thought life. Inequality creates a world where one is daily confronted with the struggle to survive, to stay alive; a world where one is stuck in a

127

straitjacket between a rock and a hard place. This world is characterized as noted above with daily deprivations, a hand to mouth subsistence, constant physical and mental illness, a low life expectancy, low literacy and educational levels for both parents and their children, high rate of teenage pregnancies and births, high imprisonment rates, stigmatization, among others. This is a world without hope, without jobs, without dignity, without self-respect or self-esteem, and for many without a sense of meaning or direction.

This reality makes daily life defined by inequality a site of struggle and resistance, a site of battles to stay alive. Our contemporary world for the vast majority is so characterized with daily efforts to move from inauthentic to authentic existence and to move away from the sense of meaninglessness and lack of self-confidence. The primary priority is the struggle to create a world where emancipatory choices and transformative lifestyles for the everyday are possible for the majority. This calls for nothing short of a new world order— a revolutionary transformation of the present world order. This is a tall order, improbable but possible. Our hope lies in this struggle, engaged on a daily basis, by all means possible, in a search for a new, more humane world, a new political and economic social arrangement characterized by justice and peace, freedom and fairness. The struggle entails taking up lifestyles and strategies that seek daily to undermine the structures of inequality and the values that prop it up. The struggle entails deliberately confronting and engaging the ideology of power and of empire and the power structures as well as networks that spread death and misery, and make a living from these. What is the place of Ubuntu in all these? What is the role of Ubuntu in engaging these harsh realities of human existence?

Ubuntu and the Everyday

Undoubtedly it is in the daily struggles of the everyday that Ubuntu is severely tested and challenged. In these daily struggles where lives have been reduced to the barest, where the focus for the masses is the struggle for survival, where human dignity and self-worth is defined by the powerful elite and the wealthy as inextricably linked to the materialistic ideals of property, power and prestige – in this commonplace human scenario the common people in the context of Ubuntu understand human value as anchored on the relational in the context of community, on being affirmed by the neighbor, and by members of the immediate family and the extended family, and the wider community. The common people are empowered by the values of Ubuntu which in essence subvert the dominant materialistic narrative. Ubuntu zeroes in on the values of human community and solidarity, and understands the project of humanity as only possible when anchored on a radical understanding of our common humanity and on our dire need for one another in community. Mwalimu Julius Kambarage Nyerere's failed Ujamaa project in Tanzania was a laudable and audacious experiment that sought to confront the social challenges and evils of inequality in the name of Ubuntu/Utu[10]. Ubuntu understands humanity as sustainable in the long run only in community and in solidarity, and in the context of peace and harmony. Ubuntu understands humans as interconnected, interdependent and interlinked. "No man is an island". "I am because we are". My existence is dependent on that of others. The prevailing and hegemonic metanarrative is totally opposed to the Ubuntu metanarrative. It is greedy and egocentric, exploitative and oppressive, murderous and life-threatening; and moreover subversive of the values that maintain and sustain human community and solidarity. The reigning metanarrative is ecologically and environmentally insensitive and unsustainable. It is destructive of the environment and the conditions necessary for the preservation of life in general and the future of humanity in particular.

---

10   Aloo Osotsi Mojola, "Remembering Mwalimu Nyerere – the power of his moral vision and a redefinition of his legacy", forthcoming.

Despite the existential challenges imposed by the magnitude of the realities of inequality, both global and local, an Ubuntu value system and life style arguably remains the only viable and sustainable basis for a human life that is tolerable and worth living. It makes life meaningful and provides life's meaning in the celebration of the other, through the gifts and values of laughter and joy, common friendship and comradeship, love and mutual sharing, and through the breaking of barriers of all types - family, clan, ethnic, racial, political, ideological, religious, et al. An Ubuntu value system and life style makes life worth living as we recognize and affirm our common bonds, our common humanity, our common sisterhood and brotherhood. Ubuntu encourages sharing ourselves and our gifts, sharing our resources, being our brother's keeper. The Ubuntu value system and lifestyle strives for equality, yet celebrates diversity and difference. It celebrates our differing gifts and talents and understands them as gifts for the maintenance and sustenance of community. It is in the practice of Ubuntu that our people have conquered numerous challenges and obstacles in the way of their struggle for survival and in the affirmation of their humanity as a people and as individuals.

These challenges are enormous. Promotion of the Ubuntu value system and life style in the contemporary inhuman maze of inequality, alienation, poverty and a multitude of human deprivations is not an easy journey. Yet we must immediately embark on this labyrinthine journey and struggle and continue on the same. *A luta continua*!

Bibliography

Atkinson, Anthony B. 2015. *Inequality – What can be done.* Cambridge, Mass: Harvard University Press.

Bottomore, Tom, ed. 1983. *A Dictionary of Marxist Thought*, Cambridge, Mass. Harvard University Press.

Bouchey, Heather, J. Bradford DeLong and Marshall Steinbaum, eds. 2017. *After Piketty – The Agenda for Economics and Inequality.* Cambridge, Mass: Harvard University Press.

Bourguignon, Francois. 2015. *The Globalization of Inequality.* Princeton and Oxford: Princeton University Press.

Johnston, David Cay, ed. 2014. *Divided – The Perils of our Growing Inequality.* New York: The New Press.

Chaney, David. 2002. *Cultural Change and Everyday Life.* Basingstoke, UK: Palgrave.

de Certeau, Michel. 1984 [1988]. *The Practice of Everyday Life.* Translated by Steven Randall. London: University of California Press.

Dabla-Norris, Era, Kalpana Kochhar, Nujin Suphaphiphat, Frantisek Ricka and Evridiki Tsounta. 2015. *Causes and Consequences of Income Inequality: A Global Perspective.* Washington, DC: World Bank.

Deaton, Angus. 2013. *The Great Escape – health, wealth and the origins of inequality.* Princeton and Oxford: Princeton University Press.

Di Muzio, Tim. 2015. *The 1% and the Rest of Us – A Political Economy of Dominant Ownership.* London: Zed Books.

Dorling, Danny. 2014. *Inequality and the 1%.* London: Verso.

Duchrow, Ulrich and Franz J. Hinkelammert. 2004. *Property for people, not for profit – alternatives to the global tyranny of capital.* London, New York: Zed Books.

Fanon, Frantz. 1961. *The Wretched of the Earth.* London: Penguin Books.

Fisher, William F. and Thomas Ponniah, eds. 2003. *Another World Is Possible.* London: Zed Books.

Foster, James, Suman Seth, Michael Lokshin, Zurab Sajaia. 2013. *A Unified Approach to Measuring Poverty and Inequality – Theory and Practice.* Washington, DC: World Bank.

Gardiner, Michael. 2000. *Critiques of Everyday Life.* London: Routledge.

Gray, John. 2002. *False Dawn – The Delusions of Global Capitalism.* London: Granta Books.

Highmore, Ben. 2002. *Everyday Life and Cultural Theory: An Introduction.* London: Routledge.

Hobbes, Thomas. 1968 [1651]. *Leviathan*. London: Penguin Books.

Iliffe, John. 1987. *The African Poor – A History*. Cambridge, UK: Cambridge University Press.

Lefebvre, Henri. 1991 [1947]. *Critique of Everyday Life*. Translated by Verso. New York: Verso.

Lines, Thomas. 2008. *Making Poverty – A History*. London: Zed Books.

Milanovic, Branko. 2016. *Global Inequality – A new Approach for the Age of Globalization*. Harvard, Mass: Belknap Press of Harvard University Press.

Mojola, Aloo Osotsi. Forthcoming. "The Bantu concept of Ubuntu in the theology and practice of Bishop Desmond Tutu of South Africa and its implications for deepening the struggle for justice and human rights."

Mojola, Aloo Osotsi. Forthcoming. "Remembering Mwalimu Nyerere–the power of his moral vision and a redefinition of his legacy."

Nussbaum, Martha. 2011. *Creating Capabilities – the Human Development Approach*. Cambridge, Mass: Belknap Press of Harvard University Press.

Oxfam. 2017. "An Economy for the 99%." *Oxfam Briefing Paper*, January 2017. https://d1tn3vj7xz9fdh.cloudfront.net/s3fs-public/file_attachments/bp-economy-for-99-percent-160117-en.pdf.

Piketty, Thomas. 2013. *Capital in the Twenty-First Century*. Cambridge, Mass: Belknap Press of Harvard University Press

Piketty, Thomas. 2015. *The Economics of Inequality*. Cambridge, Mass: Belknap Press of Harvard University Press.

Piketty, Thomas. 2016. *Chronicles – On Our Troubled Times*. London: Penguin Random House.

Rawls, John. 1973. *A Theory of Justice*. Oxford: Oxford University Press.

Raworth, Kate. 2017. *Doughnut Economics – Seven Ways to Think Like a 21ˢᵗ – Century Economist.* London: Penguin Random House, UK.

Roberts, John. 2006. *Philosophizing the Everyday – Revolutionary Praxis and the Fate of Cultural Theory.* London: Pluto Press.

Rothkopf, David. 2008. *Superclass – How the rich ruined our world.* London: Abacus.

Savage, Mike. 2015. *Social Class in the 21ˢᵗ Century,* London: Penguin Books.

Sen, Amartya. 1981. *Poverty and Famines – An Essay on Entitlement and Deprivation.* Oxford, UK: Oxford University Press.

Sen, Amartya. 1992. *Inequality Reexamined.* Oxford, UK: Clarendon Press.

Sen, Amartya. 1999. *Development as Freedom.* Oxford, UK: Oxford University Press.

Sen, Amartya. 2009. *The Idea of Justice.* London, Penguin Books.

Smiley, Tavis and Cornel West. 2012. *The Rich and the Rest of us – A poverty Manifesto.* New York: Smiley Books.

Stiglitz, Joseph. 2015. *The Great Divide.* London: Penguin Books.

Therborn, Goran. 2013. *The Killing Fields of Inequality.* Cambridge, UK: Polity Press.

Wilkinson, Richard and Kate Pickett. 2010. *The Spirit Level – Why Equality is Better for Everyone.* London: Penguin Books.

Chapter 5: "THE HISTORICAL DIMENSION OF UBUNTU IN EVERYDAY LIFE"

Niels Weidtmann

The 'Genetic' Aspect of Ubuntu[1]

The concept of Ubuntu has attracted the attention of philosophers for a couple of different reasons. Among them, the fact that the concept of Ubuntu is common to many different peoples of Sub-Saharan Africa is certainly a prominent one. Another reason may be found in its being present in everyday life. The notion of Ubuntu does not refer to a highly abstract and philosophical concept only, but rather seems to highlight a human characteristic expressed in many modes of behaviour in the everyday. As is well known, thanks to the increasing literature published on the concept of Ubuntu, "ntu" literally means something like "life force" or the "principle of life", while "ubu" refers to the commonality or universality of something – or, as Ramose puts it, "ubu evokes the idea of being in general" (Ramose 2002, 324). Ubuntu thus literally means something like the commonality and ubiquity of life force or the principle of life (for a discussion of this meaning see Weidtmann in press). However, it is usually interpreted to pinpoint the particular

---

1   By 'genetic' I am not referring to genes but to genesis. Genesis not in a theological sense though but in the general sense meaning something like 'coming into being'.

importance ascribed to the community in African societies and to emphasise that it is the relationship to the community, which makes someone a person (Gyekye and Wiredu 1992). Shutte, Ramose, and others have pointed to a couple of proverbs that express the meaning of Ubuntu. The most prominent one in this context certainly is "umuntu ngumuntu ngabantu" – or, in the language of the Northern Sotho from which Ramose draws on, "Motho ke motho ka batho" (Samkange and Samkange 1980, Shutte 1990, Ramose 2002). This proverb is usually translated to mean "a person is a person through other persons" (Samkange and Samkange 1980). The phrase easily explains why Ubuntu can be found in everyday life. Human beings do have a social character and thus it is hardly surprising that their social relationships pervade the entirety of their lives. However, the saying that "a person is a person through other persons" not only points to human sociality, but beyond that hints at the meaning of sociality by stating that someone becomes a person only through her relationship with others. Sociality is constitutive of personhood and, therefore, it is an essential need rather than just a given characteristic of human beings. Thus, Ubuntu must not simply be equated with the mere existence of social bonds. Metz, for example, takes Ubuntu to mean the "capacity for communing" or the "essential ability to love others" (Metz 2011, 544). The understanding of Ubuntu as an expression of a human capacity helps to counter a simple equation of Ubuntu with social bonds and allows people to refer to Ubuntu in the context of human dignity, as Metz does. In fact, human dignity must not depend on the actual existence of social bonds as can easily be acknowledged with regard to an imprisoned person who is forcefully cut off from all her social relationships, but nevertheless keeps her human dignity. However, this understanding still falls short of realising the 'genetic' aspect of Ubuntu. By referring to the *'genetic' aspect* of Ubuntu I want to point to the fact that Ubuntu is not simply given but has to come into being through experience. This may be more obvious with respect to a phenomenon like love. Love just like friendship is not about a capacity nor is it about the mere existence of any social bonds. Love is experiential. Once you do experience it, however, it does change everything – yourself, the other, the relationship. In very much the same sense the notion of Ubuntu points to the fact that personhood becomes constituted by engaging in social relations and developing social bonds. In fact, this is what happens in everyday life.

Let us take another glance at the example of friendship. We know very well that good friendship can have a notable impact on our personalities. By experiencing friendship, we feel proximity to other people and maybe also close affinity with them, both of which may help us to gain growing self-confidence and to engage with others confidently. In short, it gives us confidence in and about the world around us, making it a better place. Friendship also makes it easier to accept advice, to share ideas and goods, and not to take oneself too seriously. Overall, friendship in most cases helps in making us happy. All of these points to the fact that friendship is not just about relating to somebody else, but it is also about personal growth of the individual in question. However, friendship bond is not something immutable. It is constantly re-constituted and negotiated if friendship has to be sustained. Thus, Ubuntu like friendship is not something we simply evoke, but rather it is an experience that has to be renewed time and again.

Other examples for cases in which we can find this 'genetic' aspect of Ubuntu in everyday life are music and dance. Both music and dance bring people together and help people establish intense relationships. Although music may be played on one's own as well, it usually is performed together with others integrating different musical instruments. In the latter case, it is again quite obvious that the interplay with others has great impact on a single musician. The musician communicates with all other musicians through her instrument. However, not only does she have to synchronise her own playing with that of the others, her playing very much relies on the interplay between the sounds created by all other musicians. Her performance actually gets its musical meaning only by the harmony of this interplay. The flutist, to name just one example, therefore owes her musical personality to the relationship which she has with all other musicians when playing together. The same holds true for dancing. Dancing is an apt example of Ubuntu in the everyday, not only because people gather and have fun performing together, but because it clearly demonstrates that the performance somehow demands a communicative interaction with others. The dancer has to adapt her movements to the music as well as to the movements of other dancers. Not every movement of the body makes up a dance but only those movements that correspond and harmonise with the music and the movements of all other dancers. Additionally, the dancer not only adapts her movements to the situation, but to some extent she is instructed by the music as well as by the movements of other dancers and reacts to the commands given to her by the entire situation.

With respect to the importance of the family and the community in everyday life, it can be shown that the impact which these social groups have on their members relies on communicative acts and the constant re-constitution of social bonds. For anyone coming from Europe or the so-called "Western" world, it must be striking to realise how strong family bonds can be in most African societies. The importance of the greater community and the impact it has on an individual life has been emphasised in several studies on the organisation of African societies. In fact, the communal relationships actually are at the heart of Ubuntu. However, what I have just outlined for the phenomenon of friendship, music, and dance holds true for the family and community as well. Communal bonds are not simply a given fact characterising each individual human being but have to be performed and lived, i.e. they have to be renewed, re-formed, and re-constituted constantly (Weidtmann in press). Thus family bonds go beyond biological connections.

Ubuntu and Ethnic Communality

While it is clear that Ubuntu's understanding of personhood cannot be reduced to biological relationship, it is nevertheless difficult to make the same case for ethnic affiliation. I wish to argue that the ethnic category is central in any philosophical discussion of African communality in general and of Ubuntu in particular. Most literatures on the important role that communality plays in African societies will invariably make reference to the family, clan, or ethnic group (Appiah 1992; Bujo 1993; Gyekye 1995 and 1997; Ramose 2002; Wiredu 1996 and 2009). This also is the case whenever one tries to understand the meaning of Ubuntu (Samkange and Samkange 1980). Why is that? Is it by accident, maybe because ethnic groups in the past have been important in African societies and thus many examples of ethnic communality got passed on while examples of other forms of communality may have been lost through the passage of time? Or is it because Ubuntu has stronger affinity to ethnic than to the other communal formations? If the first answer were correct, i.e. linking Ubuntu to any kind of communality, then Ubuntu could be equated to the notion of friendship. If however, as I try to argue, the second answer is right, then we do have to find out why Ubuntu has a stronger affinity to ethnic than to the other communal formations. My answer to this question will focus on what I call the historical dimension of sociality which is much more present in the family, clan, and ethnic community than in any other communal formation and which is of particular importance to the concept of Ubuntu, in my view. However, before I explicitly turn to this historical dimension I will briefly discuss two points that – in one way or the other – may hint at Ubuntu's strong affinity to ethnic affiliation.

To begin with, the privileging of ethnic affiliation may have been one of the reasons why the *Truth and Reconciliation Commission* (TRC), which President Nelson Rolihlahla Mandela set up in 1996 in the name of Ubuntu has not really succeeded in reconciling South African society. It is, I suppose, the 'genetic' aspect of Ubuntu, i.e. its quest for a visible sociality and the constant re-constitution and renewing of community bonds, which made Ubuntu more appealing in stabilising the process of reconciliation in South African society after the end of Apartheid in 1994. Mandela was hoping that the work of the TRC would help to strengthen social cohesion within South African society. While this has widely been praised internationally there have been many critics from within South African society (Gobodo-Madikizela 2003 and Bell and Ntsebeza 2001). The critique, I suppose, is due to Ubuntu's affinity to ethnic communality rather than national unity. In fact, the different peoples of South Africa are still struggling for social cohesion.

Secondly, let me briefly look at another point which may support the assumption that there still is an aspect of Ubuntu that has not yet clearly been articulated in any of the philosophical studies published on this concept in recent years. The idea of humanity and in particular the idea of communality which is ascribed to Ubuntu sometimes has been taken to be oppose to the Western concept of individualism, which is assumed to form the basis of a highly competitive society. That, however, may not be entirely correct. It is possible to argue that communality also has some presence and significance in Western societies very much in the same way that elements of individualism do have some presence in African societies. Heinz Kimmerle and many others have argued that the communal aspect may be more pronounced in African societies than in Western societies but that nevertheless individualism and communalism should not be played off against each other (Bujo 1993; Gyekye 1997; Kimmerle 1983 and 2007). It may be in reaction to this discussion that Ubuntu has been interpreted by Metz and others to mean nothing other than the capacity for friendship or love (Metz 2011). However, while both, friendship and love certainly are a part of the Ubuntu concept, I do not think that these virtues are able to describe Ubuntu entirely. If Ubuntu was only about the important role of friendship in a society, it would not be anything particular or exceptional. After all, all these values can be found in any cultural context. To name just one, Aristotle takes friendship to be the guarantor of any democratic polity since it is friendship which allows accepting a plurality of different opinions (*doxai*) (Aristotle 1995, 1155a). While each opinion has its own right, none of them must be taken to form the reason of state. It is friendship which forms the political community of the ancient Greek *polis*. Not to be misunderstood here: I am not saying that Ubuntu necessarily has to be a concept particular to African societies in order to be a precious concept. To the contrary, Ubuntu may well become a universal concept that will be learnt by other peoples and that will sometimes be transferred to different cultural contexts. However, it will be learnt and transferred to other cultural contexts only if it means something that is not yet fully grasped by such phenomena as friendship, hospitality, and love. In other words, the analysis of the concept of Ubuntu may lay open some connotations of values like friendship, love, and hospitality that have not yet been fully realised in non-African societies. Which connotations these are we might learn by looking more closely at the relationship between Ubuntu and ethnic communality.

The historical Dimension of Ubuntu

As we have seen, in some cases the concept of Ubuntu has travelled from its traditional base to more contemporary situations. Examples already mentioned are the TRC and Metz' attempt to argue for a moral theory based on Ubuntu. However, in doing so, the original meaning of Ubuntu may change or get modified. In fact, it is not all that important whether the original meaning is retained in Ubuntu's current applications to social, political, and philosophical questions. Concepts do change over time anyway. With respect to the question, though, whether the traditional focus of communality on family, clans, and ethnic groups is relevant to the idea of personhood and thus to the meaning of Ubuntu, it may be necessary to refer back to its original meaning. So, what is the difference between strong social bonds within a family, clan, or ethnic group and likewise intense and lively social relations across clans and groups? My first guess would be that members of the same clan are more likely to know each other better than are people of different clans. However, this does not necessarily have to be the case. But even if it is not, members of the same clan still share the same forefathers, i.e. the same ancestry. In fact, community in African societies often is, at the very least, meant to include the ancestors and sometimes even the unborn. Interestingly, ancestors do not only represent the past or even the origin of a community but they take part in community life in the way that their beliefs and desires, which either have been passed on by oral tradition or are carried out by the living, are taken into consideration whenever important decisions are to be made. This, I suppose, may be important because it allows for a complex understanding of the clan as transcending the biological connection of its individual members. It is therefore not the biological descent but rather the presence of the past in the life of the community that justifies the primacy of ethnic communities. The link to the past in communal life adds another dimension to contemporary communal life by giving it a clear sense of history and heritage and thereby providing some orientation for the future. It is this historical dimension that is the source of sustenance for communal as well as individual life. Thus the participation of the individual person in the communal life of her family, her clan, or the respective ethnic group has an important impact on her personhood not only because of the reciprocity of social relations, as it is true in any kind of social relationship, but equally because of the historical trajectory of the community which represents something like a metaphysical hold on her life. By recognising the presence of the past in her/his community, an individual is likely to recognise that she/he is an integral part of that community, which involves the community's past and future. The individual life therefore is lived and performed in ways that by far exceed the limits of individual experience. This may explain why the individual members of a community traditionally have been obliged to support the life of the community, and why the elderly is shown particularly greater respect. In fact, traditionally those who have contributed the most to the life of their community are accorded the highest reputation.

To reiterate, I do not think that biological descent is responsible for the survival of clan or ethnic communities. Rather, it is the recognition of the historical dimension of communal life that helps to enrich personal life and create an awareness of this underlying dimension. In fact, in the history of many African nations, especially in the post-colonial era and in the immediate aftermath of independence, the possibility of forging a common historical destiny was so real that the bridge between the pre-colonial past and the post-colonial future seemed to have been shared by all peoples living together in the newly formed nations for some time. The idea of a common destiny in some cases was deliberately promoted by some of the leaders of these nations. Outstanding personalities like Nkrumah, Nyerere, Senghor, and – thirty years later, but in a comparable historical situation – Mandela - all seemed to have been able to unify the people of their nations.

By the historical dimension underlying and bearing communal life I do not mean a foundational principle or value system, static and unchanging. Instead the underlying dimension is that which an individual carries with her/him, as part of her/his history and heritage. As Mudimbe writes we all carry our past with us (Mudimbe 1988). Nevertheless, this sense of communal history gives meaning to life and therefore may be described as offering a hold on us in a metaphysical sense as mentioned above. In any case, the experience I want to draw attention to is that of experiencing one's own life as being borne by the underlying dimension of the past and future, not only with respect to the individual, but also to a historical life experience of which the individual life is only a part. The experience is also about recognising that the individual life owes itself to the totality of life as a whole – to a communal stream.

My thesis thus is that the meaning of Ubuntu, i.e. that "a person is a person through other persons", does not simply refer to the importance of community over individuality, but rather the awareness that individual life is inextricably bound up with ones past as well as one's future. As a lived experience it may be called a metaphysical dimension of life. The 'genetic' aspect of Ubuntu outlined above is due to the need of actually performing this experience. It requires some sensibility for that which grounds and sustains life and therefore it may be associated with the capacity to sense the historical dimension of life as it is represented by the community. Since this capacity has an affective character, we might associate it with the sense of hearing in contrast to that of vision. Kimmerle even has suggested what he calls a "methodology of listening" with respect to the intercultural encounter with African cultures (Kimmerle 1991, 8). However, it is not just the need to listen to what the other person says and means that characterises Ubuntu but rather the ability to experience one's contemporary being as borne and enabled by a historical dimension. The moment is therefore experienced as representing this underlying historical dimension.

We have seen that the underlying historical dimension stands for the past and future of any particular situation of a person's life. In this respect it might be called the dimension of descent or, in order to avoid any biological connotation, the dimension of belonging. The relationship of descent and belonging is not restricted to that of an individual person to her community, but can be found at all levels of life. The sustaining dimension of life may also be found in nature or anywhere else depending on the particular situation of a person's life. Thus, Ubuntu is about experiencing the multi-dimensionality of life.

Ubuntu in Music and Art
Let me finally return to Ubuntu in daily life and give a few examples of what I think might be understood as the search for an underlying dimension of descent. Music is particularly

interesting in an intercultural context since it allows an aesthetic understanding even in cases where rational forms of understanding may be difficult. Music thus demonstrates that intercultural relationships, just as with any human relationship, cannot be restricted to the intellectual level, but include very lively aesthetic as well as bodily dimensions. However, even though music most often facilitates intercultural understanding this does not necessarily have to be the case. One can easily imagine that some particular kind of music may sound unfamiliar and somewhat irritating. In the long run, listening to it may become a pain, and the bodily feeling of pain does not vanish only because one rationally decides to be tolerant. I even suppose that in most cases, regardless of whether it is about music or anything else, tolerance is based on rational thought only to a minor extent. Luckily music more often than not facilitates intercultural understanding than hinders it.

In African societies music has always been and still is very prominent. In fact, African music has influenced not only modern jazz and soul but today is almost omnipresent in international pop-music. It is often played in a group and accompanied by dancing and singing. Singing and music may also accompany labour. Music helps to structure life and it builds community by bringing people together. However, this is not the only aspect of music that is akin to Ubuntu. Music sometimes allows us to hear an underlying dimension to which it is connected and which renders it meaningful, because it is not in every case that it is constituted by the ideas and the interplay of the musicians. The first example of this interplay is the playing of a drum (Weidtmann 1998a). While there are all different kinds of drums, they all share certain characteristics (Simon 1983). For instance, drums produce individual sounds, which are clearly different from one another. First of all, the drum is a rhythmic instrument rather than a melodic instrument. Also the sound of the drum is rather dark and grave and somehow earthy. Some drums even are said to talk. Finnegan, for example, argues that in an African orchestra the chief drummer may directly interact with dancers: "The chief drummer maintains a running commentary on the dance, controls the line dancers with great precision, calls particular persons by name to dance solo, tells them what dance to do, corrects them as they do it, and sends them back into line with comment on the performance. He does this by making his drum talk, even above the sound of four or five other drums in the orchestra" (Finnegan 1970, 497). Thus, the drummer not only provides a rhythm that comes to his mind, but he adapts this rhythm to the particular situation. Moreover, the drummer not only reacts to the sound of other instruments and to the movements of dancers but he even responds to something else which seems to lie underneath the concrete situation and that can be said to constitute its particular atmosphere. The drummer somehow listens to this atmosphere and tunes the rhythm he is playing accordingly. However, the drummer may not sense the atmosphere of a particular situation right away, but he must pick it up in the course of playing. The drummer himself has to get into his playing. Drumming is more than the skilful handling of an instrument; it is also a form of communication with the environment as well as with the people listening. Listening to the drum, one therefore not only has to listen to the sound, but one also has to try to follow the way in which the drum itself is listening and corresponding to its environment. Therefore, it is not surprising that often it is alleged that in some old rhythms the ancestors would call to the living. Drumming is a form of communication at different levels, sensing underlying dimensions, and trying to make these dimensions audible. This may also explain why the narration of a traditional Griot used to not only be accompanied, but also preceded by music. The narrative which the Griot is telling has to be understood on the basis of resounding dimensions of communal wisdom. These resounding dimensions of communal wisdom are commemorated and made explicit by music.

Mufuta reminds us of an old legend about the origin of drumming as it has been passed down by the people of the Luba (cit. Bimwenyi-Kweshi 1982, 119): A man comes to God the father and asks him for a profession. God hands him a drum and he strings a thread from the drum and tightens it at the man's heart. Every time God moves that thread the man rises and starts to play the drum. By playing the drum he brings the wisdom of God to his fellow human beings. This legend highlights the power of the drum. The drum allows its listeners to hear and physically feel the dimensions underlying and bearing everyday life. It makes these dimensions resound in one's body. This idea is illustrated in the following picture: The body of the drum usually is formed out of wood, i.e. plant material, while the drumhead is made of skin, i.e. animal tissue. The drum's opening is directed towards earth; in the picture I am suggesting this would be the dimension where the drum receives its sound from. Finally, the drum is beaten by men who, in playing the drum, may sense the different dimensions underlying and bearing humanity, i.e. the dimensions of animals, plants, and inanimate materials.

All of this demonstrates how music may help us experience the multi-dimensionality of life which I suggested makes up the core of the Ubuntu concept. Let me mention just one more example with respect to the everyday experience of Ubuntu in music. This example is about the Amadinda music of the people of Baganda from Uganda (Kubik 1983; Weidtmann 1998a). Amadinda music is played on a balaphone. Unlike the drum, the balaphone is a rather melodic instrument. In Amadinda music, the balaphone is played by three musicians together. The first, called the "Omunazi", starts to play a short melody, and keeps repeating it over time. Then the second player, the "Omwawuzi", comes in with yet another melody the rhythm of which is interlocked to that of the first melody. Because these two melodies interfere and tend to override each other, the listener has a problem in following even one of them. However, at times the listener may hear a new melody arising from the two melodies at play. After some time, it is this new melody that the third musician, the so-called "Omukoonezi", starts to enforce by playing his part. The new melody is not created by the interplay of Omunazi and Omwawuzi alone but rather the listener of the music has to search for it or, to be precise here, has to listen for it in order to grasp the meaning of the music. The Omukoonezi enforces what he and all other listeners already hear.

Ubuntu and Orality

If Ubuntu is indeed about the sensibility for the multi-dimensionality of life in general and for the historical dimension in particular, as I am arguing for in this chapter, one might turn to the oral tradition of most Sub-Saharan African societies in order to recognise some structural similarities here. In the case of oral tradition, anything from the past that persists has to be remembered by somebody (Weidtmann 1998b). That means that it actually has to be present in current life, but should not be forgotten for some time because there is little chance of recovering it at a later point in time. So, how are traditions sustained and rendered visible? Either they are learnt just like any other knowledge. That probably is true for those parts of the tradition which are useful in everyday life and which therefore simply form part of the stock of knowledge of a society. Alternatively, traditions are apparent, not in the same way as is everyday knowledge, but rather in the form of shared beliefs and desires, which are constitutive of the society's social life and its self-conception. The self-conception does change in time but usually it does not cut off all connections to the past. Rather, the self-conception of a society reflects the way this society interprets, dismisses, or takes up its own past. This latter way, in which the past may be present in oral tradition, is somehow structurally similar to the concept of Ubuntu, as I have outlined already. In fact, in an oral tradition it is very important to keep alive the memory common to one's own community.

The relationship between the power that a word has in oral traditions and the concept of Ubuntu which points to the sensibility for the principle of life underlying one's own life is expressed in Francis Bebey's novel *Agatha Moudio's Son*:

The spoken word means life, life which goes on, which man must respect at all times, because it is the only thing here below that never fades. Men who can write lose this profound respect for life. They know that their thoughts will not be debased with the passage of time: they know that what they say or think today will be the same tomorrow, no matter who lives after them: the written word remains and gives a permanent shape to their thoughts. In this way, the spoken word, the natural manifestation of life, is replaced by a completely conventional invention of men, the written word. It is then easy to understand how life itself loses some of its importance [...] (Bebey 2007, 16).

Orality also links sagacity to Ubuntu, as I have outlined elsewhere (Weidtmann 1998b). When Odera Oruka started collecting wise sayings and identifying philosophical sages in 1974, he wanted to bridge the gap between traditional and modern philosophy. While modern philosophy relies on written texts, the African tradition for the most part has been an oral one. Therefore, it obviously has been difficult to pass on extended philosophical thought. Thus, Oruka argues, philosophy had to be transmitted in short sayings. According to this argumentation, then, wise sayings represent philosophical insights in condensed form. According to Oruka, however, the elderly people who remember the sayings and who are recognised for this wisdom and, therefore, are often asked for advice in all kinds of existential problems may be, but do not necessarily have to be philosophers. Rather, he argues, in order to count as a philosopher, a sage has to critically reflect on the sayings and to be able to argue for or against them. While all this sounds pretty plausible, it nevertheless seems questionable whether sagacity can be understood just in the same way as modern philosophy is understood. At least modern philosophy is hardly ever exercised in the context of counselling. This, however, obviously has been and still is the case with sagacity as, for instance, Heinz Kimmerle has pointed out (Kimmerle 1991, 91). The question then is what function do wise sayings have in the course of counselling? While it certainly always is interesting to hear what some wise women and men once thought about life, it is hard to imagine how this should help a person asking for advice in a very concrete life situation. It is my view that we need to take the oral character of sagacity into account in order to understand the function of the wise sayings in the context of counselling. It should be remembered that in oral traditions only those sayings passed on over generations will be remembered. Certainly those sayings remembered better are those which seem to be relevant to the people passing them on. After some time, therefore, only those sayings that represent common beliefs and desires are remembered. Consequently, the wise sayings have the capacity for providing the traditional basis of communal beliefs. Therefore, in the context of counselling they may remind the person in need of help of the foundational basis of these sayings and, thus, of the self-understanding of the community. By doing so, the sayings can help relate the existential problems a person may have in a concrete life situation to the dimension of the community. The sages do not explain or teach philosophical insights to the consulter but present several sayings transmitted over time and then give the consulter the chance to understand his actual situation against the background of the community's traditions.

Here again we face an example in which people try to relate a particular situation to the greater context to which it belongs. However, it does not help the person in need at all to simply state that her life is part of the communal life. She has to actually experience or feel the relationship of her situation to the communal life, and she may do so by relating her problem to the sayings.

Concluding Remarks: Ubuntu in Communal Life

From what has been said so far it should be clear that I am suggesting not simply equating Ubuntu with the importance of communality. While communality is at the heart of Ubuntu, there is yet some other aspects characteristic to Ubuntu. Let me highlight just three of them:

First, Ubuntu has a historical dimension. To say that "a person is a person through other persons" does not simply refer to the importance of social relations, but reminds the individual person that she owes her life to others and that by living, she carries forward the lives others have lived before her. It's her turn to live, but it's not her life alone or, to be even more precise, life in principle is not exclusively hers. Since she owes her own life to life in principle, even her own life is not exclusively hers. The community is of particular importance in this respect, because it is the community which represents the past as well as the future of the life that the individual person is living.

Second, Ramose points out that Ubuntu refers to the embeddedness of man not only in the community, but in the universe as a whole (Ramose 2002). I suggest that Ubuntu actually refers to a multitude of different dimensions. Ubuntu definitely includes the belonging of a person to her community. However, there is more to Ubuntu. Just as a person belongs to the community, the community itself is embedded in a historical lifeworld[2] which not only includes the community of the living persons, but their ancestors and even unborn babies. History and tradition are of great importance to any community. The historical lifeworld in turn is part of the universe. There are many different dimensions nested one into another. Thus we undermine the universality of Ubuntu when we restrict it to a narrow understanding of the community in African societies.

Third, Ubuntu does not refer to a static, but a 'genetic' concept. It is not an ontological concept which simply affirms a static understanding of the African being as rooted in community as opposed to individual experience *per se*. Rather, I suggest that Ubuntu relies on the actual experience of 'belonging' – belonging of a person to the community, or put differently

---

2   The notion of a "lifeworld" was introduced by Edmund Husserl to draw attention to the experiential character of any historical world (Husserl 1962).

belonging through active experience and engagement with a historical lifeworld and the universe. The relationship itself is not the focus here, but the actual experience of that relationship. This difference between imagined and fixed relationship on the one hand and the actual and current experience of this relationship on the other, is of great importance; because only when a person actually experiences her belonging to a greater context will she realise that the specificity of her own life only gains true meaning by reference to the greater context. The realisation of meaning is something that has to be experienced and cannot simply be stated or known through rational analysis. It is not enough to know that the meaning of a particular situation may be grounded in the greater context. In order not only to know about the meaning, but to believe the meaning, one has to experience or even feel it. Meaning always has an existential character. If I feel that my life is meaningless, it does not help that someone else proves to me the fact that indeed my life is meaningful with respect to, let's say, my family or the community. If I do not feel this meaning, if I do not experience my life to be meaningful with respect to my family, then the proof someone else gives to me does not mean anything.

To summarise all of these, I would like to suggest that Ubuntu refers to the experience that a particular situation is in fact always embedded in a greater context comprising the past as well as the future of the situation and that the meaning of a particular situation is constituted through its belonging to a context. The particular situation is borne by the greater context to which it belongs. However, this context is no simple fact but it is able to contextualise the situation only when the situation is experienced as taking part in the greater context. Ubuntu, therefore, is about experiencing the greater context or the underlying dimension being represented in the particular situation.

Ubuntu philosophy may be the realisation of the 'multi-dimensionality' of reality and thereby the attainment of a deeper understanding of reality, rather than the exploration of an abstract universal aspect of reality as it manifests itself in the *logos* that Western philosophy tends toward. To be clear here, I do not think that these two approaches to reality, i.e. Ubuntu which goes for the multi-dimensionality of reality, and Western philosophy which tries to explore the ever unifying *logos*, contradict each other. Rather they might learn from one another and complement each other. This is why I think Ubuntu is so invaluable for philosophy in general.

Bibliography

Appiah, Kwame A. 1992. *In my father's house. Africa in the philosophy of culture*. Oxford: UP.

Aristotle. 1995. *Nikomachische Ethik*. Philosophische Schriften Bd. 3. Translated by Eugen Rolfes and adapted by Günther Bien. Hamburg: Meiner.

Bebey, Francis. 2007 [1971]. *Agatha Moudio's son*. Translated by Joyce A. Hutchinson, Cambridge: African Writers series. London: Heinemann.

Bell, Terry and Dumisa Buhle Ntsebeza. 2001. *Unfinished business: South Africa, Apartheid and the Truth*. Cape Town: Redworks.

Bimwenyi-Kweshi, Oscar. 1982. *Alle Dinge erzählen von Gott. Grundlegung afrikanischer Theologie*. Freiburg: Herder.

Bujo, Bénézet. 1993. *Die ethische Dimension der Gemeinschaft. Das Afrikanische Modell im Nord-Süd-Dialog*. Freiburg: Herder.

Hobsbawm, Eric and Terence Ranger, eds. 1993. *The invention of tradition*. Cambridge: Cambridge UP.

Finnegan, Ruth H. 2012 [1970]. *Oral literature in Africa*. Open Book Publishers. Oxford: Oxford UP.

Gobodo-Madikizela, Pumla. 2003. *A human being died that night: a story of forgiveness*. Cape Town: David Phillip Publishers.

Gyekye, Kwame. 1995. *An essay on African philosophical thought. The Akan conceptual scheme*. Philadelphia: Temple UP.

Gyekye, Kwame. 1997. *Tradition and modernity. Philosophical reflections on the African experience*. Oxford: Oxford UP.

Gyekye, Kwame and Kwasi Wiredu. 1992. *Person and Community.* Ghanaian Philosophical Studies, I. Washington, D.C.: The Council for Research in Values and Philosophy.

Husserl, Edmund. 1962. *Die Krisis der europäischen Wissenschaften und die transzendentale Phänomenologie.* Husserliana VI, 2. Auflage, Den Haag: Nijhoff.

Kimmerle, Heinz. 1983. *Entwurf einer Philosophie des Wir. Schule des alternativen Denkens.* Bochum: Germinal.

Kimmerle, Heinz. 1991. *Philosophie in Afrika – Afrikanische Philosophie.* Frankfurt/M.: Campus.

Kimmerle, Heinz. 2007. "Ubuntu and Communalism in African Philosophy and Art." In *Prophecies and Protest – Ubuntu in Glocal Management,* edited by Henk van den Heuvel, Mzamo Mangaliso and Lisa van de Bunt. West Lafayette: Purdue UP.

Kubik, Gerhard. 1983. "Die Amadinda-Musik von Buganda." In *Musik in Afrika,* edited by Artur Simon, 139-165. Berlin: Museum für Völkerkunde Berlin.

Metz, Thaddeus. 2011. "*Ubuntu* as a moral theory and human rights in South Africa." *African Human Rights Law Journal* 11: 532-559.

Mudimbe, Valentin Y. 1988. *The invention of Africa. Gnosis, philosophy, and the order of knowledge.* Bloomington: Indiana UP.

Ramose, Mabogo B. 2002. *African philosophy through ubuntu.* Revised edition. Harare: Mond Books Publishers.

Ranger, Terence. 1993. "The invention of tradition in colonial Africa." In *The invention of tradition,* edited by Eric Hobsbawm and Terence Ranger. Cambridge: Cambridge UP.

Samkange, Stanlake J.T. and Tommie M. Samkange. 1980. *Hunhuism or ubuntuism: a Zimbabwe indigenous political philosophy.* Salisbury: Graham Publishers.

Shutte, Augustine. 1990. "Umuntu ngumuntu ngabantu." *Philosophy and Theology* 5 (1): 39-54.

Simon, Artur, ed. 1983. *Musik in Afrika*. Berlin: Museum für Völkerkunde Berlin.

Wiredu, Kwasi. 1996. *Cultural Universals and Particulars. An African Perspective*. Bloomington: Indiana UP.

Wiredu, Kwasi. 2009 [1980]. *Philosophy and an African culture*. Cambridge: Cambridge UP.

Weidtmann, Niels. 1998a. *Der Weltcharakter der Kulturen in der interkulturellen Welt. Eine Auseinandersetzung mit Hermeneutik und Strukturphänomenologie am Beispiel Afrika*. Dissertation, Würzburg: MF.

Weidtmann, Niels. 1998b. "Kann Schriftlichkeit fehlen? Afrikanische Weisheitslehren im interkulturellen Dialog." *Polylog. Zeitschrift für interkulturelles Philosophieren* 1: 73-84.

Weidtmann, Niels. In press. "The philosophy of Ubuntu and the notion of 'vital force'." In *Ubuntu and the Reconstitution of Community*, edited by James Ogude. Bloomington: Indiana UP.

Chapter 6: PARTICIPATORY COMMUNICATION IN CONSTRUCTING CONJUGAL LOVE IN AFRICA: CASE OF THE BAGANDA AND THE MA'DI [1]

Dominica Dipio

Introduction: Africa's Communitarian Principle

Participation is an indelible part of the everyday in the African context. In the African context, it is impossible to imagine a qualitatively rewarding life outside participation, right from the everyday to the highly ritualized and religious experiences. One's humanness is gauged by the level of involvement in the life of the community in all its aspects, including the intimate sphere of conjugal relationship. In this chapter, I explore the levels of participation by members of the community in formatting more lasting marriage relationships

1   I am grateful to the CAPREx-ALBORADA Fund for facilitating my "Mother-centred Africa from the Lens of Folktales" research. The information from this research has enriched this paper. I also thank Dr Merit Kabugo of the School of Languages Literature and Communication, Makerere University, and Mr Henry Akra Ayiasi of Uganda Management Institute for the key information they gave on Buganda and Ma'di courtship and marriage procedures respectively.

between couples. I focus on the processes of constructing conjugal relationships in two ethnic groups in Uganda – the Nilotic Ma'di and the Bantu Baganda; and what these processes reveal about the philosophies of the communities. The Baganda are a traditionally centralized society, while the Ma'di are a segmentry community. Although structured relatively differently, the basic ideological logic of the communities is patriarchy. Thus, the gendered relationships around courtship and marriage are similar. In both societies, women appear to have greater agency in choosing the man of their choice. But is this really the case? My analysis shows the dynamic power relations and how, in the words of Foucault (1980a), power conceals itself.

I also analyse the dynamic relationship between the individual and the community in as intimate a matter as conjugal relationship in a communitarian African context. Although "superficially" marriage is a relationship between two people, undercurrent there are deep and broad networks of connectedness and participation to form and sustain the relationship. The everyday spirit of connectedness is manifested in "thicker" profiles around marriage occasions. There is little that is private and personal in the phase of courtship as it involves various levels of mediation and participation by community members. The entire process of courtship and marriage, especially in the past, emphasized the relationship between communities within which the key individuals are ostensibly free to make their choices within the broad frame of patriarchal logic. The tension between individual freedoms within the ethos of the community, as Gyekye explains is intricate. The two can never be independent of each other, but constantly co-exist. "The interaction between the individual and community (or group) is therefore considered basic to the development of the individual's personality as well as to the overall success and well-being of the community" (1996, 50). Thus, although it is the individual, as an autonomous, responsible, and rational being (Gyekye 1997, 54) who may take the initiative to begin a relationship, the community is as much an interested party in the successful working of this relationship and marriage.

Moemeka's (2000) five principles, in defining the traditional communitarian societies, are important for explaining the participatory nature of relationship in African societies. In the first place was the experience of the community (the collective will of its members) as supreme over the individual. The system of socialization and social practices emphasized this hierarchy of supremacy. The view Moemeka expresses here is similar to that of Mbiti (1969) and Menkiti (1984) who both emphasize the radical view that in the African context, the communal takes precedence over the individual. Secondly, respect for authority, invested in elders who were responsible for both the temporal and spiritual life of the community was held in high regard. Embedded in this was the respect for seniority. However, as guardians and leaders, elders were not above the collective will of the community. The African perspective of the community is not simply an additive aggregate of people. The 'we' in the African sense is a fusion of the individual with the rest of the members in a 'collectivist' sense, leading to 'organic' identity, where one's identity cannot be autonomous of other members of the community. One's personhood moves from the society to the individual, not vice versa. In the African perspective, "priority is given to the duties which individuals owe to the collectivity, and their rights, whatever these may be, are seen as secondary to their exercise of their duties" (Gyekye 1997,180).

Among the Ma'di, this collective identity of the community is expressed in the concept of *e'i* (literally translated as "the home") that bears its ethics. Thirdly, while the communitarian principle allowed for every member to have a say in the affairs of the community, respect was attributed to old age, perceived as the "seat of wisdom." Elders, perceived as people with greater experience and wisdom, often had the last say, and their words carried greater weight. Fourthly, although the community was supreme, the individual was, nonetheless, a useful member of the community; and hence, it has a responsibility to protect him/her against anti-social behaviours. The community, in turn, saw its survival in the wellbeing of its individual members. In this regard, it was important to the community, what choices, such as of marriage partners, its individual members made. Family lineages and heritages were important to the community, especially in matters of marriage. And finally, the life of the community was encased in religion and spirituality: religion and spirituality were what bound the community together (Faniran 2008). These five principles that represent the African communitarian worldview are interwoven and linked to each other. They also demonstrate a similar interconnectivity between the individual and the community. Gyekye is among those scholars who give equal status to the individual and community, for, "individuality is not obliterated by membership in a human community" (1997, 40). According to him, the individual has a dual moral responsibility: for self as an entity, "and for others as co-members of the community with whom she shares certain basic needs and interests" (Gyekye 2010, n.p.). In a communitarian society, the members are bound by the "ethical values of compassion, solidarity, reciprocity, cooperation, interdependence, and social well-being" (Gyekye 2010, n.p.). Participation and involvement are moral mandates that guide social relationships in traditional African communities, caught up in reciprocity. In matters of marriage, this logic of participation made for greater stability in relationships that often created bonds of friendship among communities. Thus, meaningful existence is around participation and relationships. Participation is even more pronounced in relationships that lead to marriage because of the significant position marriage holds in African worldview.

I analyse courtship and marriage as part and parcel of the everyday. The everyday refers to the ordinary life of individuals in social contexts. It is power from below, as distinct from power from above the hegemonic order (De Certeau 1984; Foucault 1980a). Although marriage is a key rite (moment) of passage in formally structured society, the socialisation process leading to it is part of the everyday activities. Two categories of activities are involved in courtship and marriage: one is part of the ordinary socialisation of the genders, and the other is a specific rite associated with this passage. However, the "rite" aspect "sits" on the everyday that preceded it. In this context, I consider courtship and marriage as parts of the everyday: ordinarily, every member of the society is, in the domestic sphere, socialised towards it. In the following section, I focus on the theoretical perspectives relevant in this analysis.

Theories of the Everyday

I adapt the ideas in Michel de Certeau's (1984) well-cited book, *The Theory of Everyday Practice*, and aspects of Michel Foucault's *Discipline and Punishment* (1977) and *Power/Knowledge* (1980) that focus on the complex and non-linear nature of power in the everyday in my analysis of the courtship and marriage cultures of the Baganda and the Ma'di. To a great extent, the two theorists lean on each other in their understanding of power in the everyday. It is difficult to speak of the everyday outside power relations. Both de Certeau and Foucault draw attention to the dynamic, non-linear and productive nature of power. Both underline that power and control are never complete; the strategies of those in control have blind spots which the subordinate groups take advantage of to evade absolute control. In the context of this chapter, with patriarchy as the organising structure of the two communities I analyse the hegemonic order. Power from below is often invisible in its ordinariness, just as power from above can be invisible when tempered by the ideological apparatuses embedded in culture like the family, school and religion. De Certeau sees society as divided into two groups: those who wield power (the ruling class whom he refers to as producers of culture), and the ordinary people (he refers to as users/consumers of culture). The producers of culture have the disciplinary machinery at their disposal to control the other social groups. However, the subordinate classes are not simply passive recipient and consumers of power. They have a complex way of conforming to the rules in order to evade them. The central argument in his theory is how the ordinary people, who are actually the marginalized majority, through their everyday actions of appropriation and evasion subtly resist power. Ordinary people, in the everyday, beyond subservience to power, engaged in 'silent production' of culture in their locations on the margins of society. What the subordinate classes practice in the everyday, to cope with power are tactical maneuvers.

The two keywords in de Certeau's theory are "strategy" and "tactic." He sees strategy as the structures and institutions of power set in place to discipline and gain from the subordinate groups; while tactics are the practices employed by ordinary individuals to evade, manipulate and survive power's quest for absolute control. "A strategy assumes a place that can be circumscribed as proper (*propre*) and thus serve as a basis for generating relations with an exterior distinct from it (competitors, adversaries, 'clienteles,' 'targets,' or 'objects' of research)" (De Certeau 1984, xix). Strategy is the dominant and organising order of reality. Tactics on the other hand disrupts and challenges the strategy by "poaching" on and gradually "eroding" it. Hence, in the everyday the practice of ordinary persons is embedded a kind of politics of resistance. The dominated members in society, de Certeau argues, are not by any means passive or docile. Referring to them as "consumers" of culture only conceals how their everyday life "invents itself by poaching in countless ways on the property of others" (1984, xii-xiii). Tactics are, thus, employed as and when the need arises, they are fragmentary, on the borderline of the hegemonic power structure, and have no permanent structures. Because it is neither permanent nor stable, "a tactic depends on time – it is always on the watch for opportunities that must be seized 'on the wing.' Whatever it wins, it does not keep. It must constantly manipulate events in order to turn them into 'opportunities.' The weak must continually turn to their own ends forces alien to them" (De Certeau 1984, xix). Tactics are the clever tricks or devices the weak use to create niches for themselves within dominant power structures; such as using (poaching) official hours of work to do personal work, as a form of resistance. Kentel explains de Certeau's concept of tactics thus:

> Tactics, on the other hand, are practices that are developed totally different from strategies. Tactics are not implied in certain institutional or spatial borders. They have no explicit borders. Tactics, leak into strategies and they are like poaching or eroding power mechanisms. They have techniques but they have no intentions of capturing or defeating strategies. Tactics, which depend on reasonable utilization of time, are practices that come together and disrupt rapidly. Resistance acts that are developed against strategies of the power lack permanent positions. When circumstances require, tactics develop as crucial practices that are interferences to strategies or power mechanisms (Kentel 2011, 7; quoted in Yilmaz 2012, 67).

In this chapter, I focus on unpacking the patriarchal strategies and tactical activities of the participants in courtship and marriage practices of the Baganda and the Ma'di. How do the weak – women – in this context, erode and evade patriarchal power to carve for themselves spaces of power within patriarchy? How do they comply without giving up everything to power? Because the ordinary, everyday person does not come through as "expert" or an authoritative figure, she is easy to bypassed as insignificant. This, according to de Certeau, is where her tactics to evade the control of patriarchy becomes invisible. She can poach on and undermine power without being noticed. In his reading of de Certeau, Yilmaz (2012) explains the workings of tactics in everyday practices, where individuals are not passive "consumers," but active agents interacting with power and producing new forms of resistance where,

> ...new schemes of practices of especially individuals who are apart from hegemonic power groups, classes, and communities become more significant. Cultural codes, practices, texts, and actually all cultural products created by

hegemonic power groups lead all people to act, think, produce, consume and exist within determined borders of power. Within this existence, "the different ones" can also produce new forms of resistance against this predetermined way of living (Yilmaz 2012, 68).

The new forms of resistance individuals produce do not usually draw attention to themselves, as they must continue to exist within the hegemonic power structure. On the surface they continue to appear compliant to power, while "eroding" it undercurrent. In terms of gendered power relations within patriarchy I examine, particularly, the role of the *Ssenga* (in Buganda) and the female elders as mediators in the courtship and marriage actions. The *Ssenga* is a controversial character who on one hand advances the agenda of patriarchy, but at another level, resists it by surrounding herself with "female secrets" that are inaccessible to men. Her influence over her nieces is equally complex: she teaches them to remain complaint to patriarchy; but also outlines for them certain boundaries a husband must not cross in relation to them. (see Tamale 2005) Apparently, within the strategy of patriarchy, there are limited spaces of freedom for the "weak" to occupy and apply their tactics.

I also invoke Michel Foucault's idea of bio-power (theory of mastery over the body) and panopticon architecture (a theory of how wielders of power control and shape the behaviour of the subordinates) to understand the relationship between hegemonic and everyday powers. Foucault sees power as more "dense and pervasive than a set of laws or a state apparatus" (1980a, 158). While he acknowledges the power of the state, he shifts his view beyond "to a whole series of power networks that invest the body, sexuality, the family, kinship, knowledge, technology and so forth" (1980a, 122). In his theory of panopticon, he argues that power/control is gained through knowledge and surveillance. Power and knowledge are therefore inextricable. He makes this point in *Discipline and Punishment*:

Knowledge linked to power, not only assumes the authority of 'the truth' but has the power to make itself true. All knowledge, once applied in the real world, has effects, and in that sense at least, 'becomes true.' Knowledge, once used to regulate the conduct of others, entails constraint, regulation and the disciplining of practice. Thus, there is no power relation without the correlative constitution of a field of knowledge, nor any knowledge that does not presuppose and constitute at the same time, power relations (Foucault 1977, 27).

This concept is important in my reading of how power/knowledge is negotiated and shared in the gendered actions around courtship and marriage practices within institutionalised patriarchy. Although in her responsibilities the *Ssenga* executes the schemes of patriarchy, as de Certeau puts it, she does not surrender everything to power. Besides its repressing and censoring role, power also "produces domains of objects and rituals of truth" that the community believes in (1977, 194). The *Ssenga's* ability to "produce truth" and transmit it to the "novices" in her care, is where part of her power lies. She is seen and sought after as an exceptional source of knowledge on matters of marriage and domestic affairs in general. One who has knowledge has power.

The panopticon, which Foucault integrates in his theory of surveillance and control, is an architectural design located in institutions like schools, prisons, and factories, to facilitate surveillance/knowledge/and control of people. The knowledge that one is constantly under surveillance leads to self-surveillance and self-regulation. In the context of this paper, the rules, taboos, dos and don'ts of society act like panopticons in regulating and forming character. These rules eventually become internalised; and without coercion, the subordinates are self-regulated in ensuring that they follow them. In *The History of Sexuality*, Foucault coined the term, 'bio-power' to refer to how power is subtly manifested in the everyday. "Its success is proportional to its ability to hide its own mechanisms" (Foucault 1980b, 86). Bio-power is a subtle regime of self-disciplining, where the objective of the hegemony is to train bodies, minds and souls that are self-regulated. In the words of Foucault, "to discipline the body, optimize its capabilities, extort its forces, increase its usefulness and docility, integrate it into systems of efficient and economic controls" (1980b, 139). Individuals become so "fabricated" into the social order that they eventually participate in their own repression and disciplining (Foucault 1977). In this process, dominant power conceals itself by appealing to the desires of the subjects to do what is apparently in their interest, making power appear non-repressive.

Foucault sees the interaction between power and resistance as a continuous process of "retreats," "re-organization" and "battles" (1980b, 56). He sees power as everywhere, not concentrated in a few, but rather diffused in everyday discourses and forms of knowledge. It is always shifting and subject to negotiations. There are multiple centers of power and truth that acquire value according to the status of those who pronounce the truth. His caution is that, we should not look at power in terms of: "it 'excludes.' it 'represses,' it 'censors,' it 'abstracts,' it 'masks,' it 'conceals,'" but also in terms of its capacity to produce and reproduce reality (in Rabinow 1984, 205).

Courtships and Marriages in Africa

In Africa, the traditional indicator of maturity, adulthood and responsibility was marriage. Ordinarily, marriage was not optional: it was the expectation of the community that its members grow into married men and women and carry out the responsibilities associated with this status. Because of the importance of this stage, the community took great interest in the decisions individuals made to get married. The dynamic relationship between the individual and the community is also evident in this stage of one's development. Interconnectedness, solidarity and reciprocity that are key components of African humanism (Ubuntu) are richly experienced at this stage (Tutu 1999; Nussbaum 2003).

There were different types of marriage in traditional Africa, such as arranged marriage constructed by parents of children, who may not even be born yet. Or a baby girl, still to be born, who may be booked to cement a relationship of friendship and reciprocity between two families. When the children grow up, the marriage is formalised (Faniran 2008, 128-129). Respect for a father's authority as an elder obliged the children to obey. Marriage may also be 'forced' for several reasons, such as where a pact between two families have already been made, or where bride-wealth had already been paid before the woman's consent; or when the woman became pregnant outside wedlock. Among the Ma'di, chiefs could also 'force' women to marry them without undergoing the process of courtship. All they did was to claim the woman they fancied by placing beads around her neck, as a sign of their interest which could not be turned down even if the woman in question was already betrothed (Ovuru 2017). A bride may also be 'stolen' in case of competitive courtship that dragged on for long, and the bride was slow in making a decision. Marriage may also be through elopement. This was often done to offset payment of pride-wealth in case the beloved spouse could not afford it; or when the parents did not approve of the marriage. This last case is clearly a form of resistance to the status quo, in challenge to parents' disapproval and patriarchy's expectation of female honour and virginity before marriage. A girl may get herself pregnant as a form of resistance, to bail her beloved out of the hefty demand for bride price that he cannot afford. The value of a pregnant woman in this case is less, because she is seen as dishonourable (see Dipio 2014, 90-96). In this instance, the "weak" tactically evade patriarchy without dramatizing themselves as outright rebels as they remain bound by the rules of the status quo (De Certeau 1984, 35-7). However, the commonest form of marriage among the Ma'di, in the past and today, is the consensual one; while in traditional Buganda, the "architectural" hand of the parents, represented by the paternal aunt – *Ssenga* who acted as a middle-woman to the parents and the groom – had the upper hand, although this is not quite the case today. What is similar to both ethnic groups is that whether the process is apparently consensual or not, the "drama" is played within the frames of patriarchy and the principles of communitarianism. Different members participated in the process from courtship to the actual marriage and the birth of a child, for no marriage was considered successful without the expected fruit of a child (Faniran 2008,129).

The Process of "Consensual" Marriage

In this section, I describe the major processes of traditional courtships of the Ma'di and the Baganda that lead to marriage. I start with the Ma'di process that is apparently built on consensual relationship between two young people, although this is carefully performed within the panopticon scheme of patriarchal logic. The individual participants know that they must operate within the internalised rules of patriarchy (see Foucault 1977). Thus, early in the relationship, a young man or woman informed a senior member of the family, either the father or an aunt. The elder then set an inquiry in motion, to know more about the family background of the family their son or daughter intends to marry into (Faniran 2008, 130-131). The inquiry checked for a number of core qualities in the lineages of the intending parties.

For both for the Baganda and the Ma'di, the following were some of the issues investigated in the background check:

1. Verifying blood relationships and its "degrees" in the family lineages. Where the relationship was close, the family and the community intervened to stop the courtship.[2]
2. Relatives also cared about the kind of families the parties came from. This is what the Ma'di refer to as *ovi*. Does the family have good *ovi* or bad one? Bad *ovi* is usually described widely to include witchcraft, selfishness, meanness, unkindness,

---

2   This is markedly different from the pastoralist Bahima in Uganda and Rwanda who encouraged marriages among cousins, to ensure that wealth circulated among relatives.

associated with thieving. Families with good *ovi* are associated with generosity, kindness, and honesty. The background checks thus cared about the moral quality or virtues of families – the good or bad "name" of the family. These are values that define the principles of African humanism (Ubuntu). These are the values that make one a human being – a person. The individual must undergo these through the process of socialisation before he or she is branded a person, as Ramose (1999, 81) explains.

3. The "scan" then moved to the individual, both at the level of moral and physical attributes. Someone who came from a pedigree of hardworking and prosperous families was/is highly desirable. It was assumed that the individual would continue the dominant traits of his/her family line. The quality of hard work associated with one's future prosperity was so important to both the young man and woman that families where young men were lazy, idlers, and louts, even if they were charmers, were flagged "red" and avoided. One could foresee trouble and poverty in the way of such a union. In Africa higher premium was placed on the young woman to be married into the family as she was the one involved in forming the character/morality, feeding and creating wealth for the sustenance of the family in the everyday (Amadiume 1987, 39).

4. Another important check was on longevity and health related issues. These were both physical and psychological illnesses such as epilepsies, leprosy, violence, suicidal tendencies, depression and madness associated with the lineages. Families where there were frequent and "unnatural" or violent deaths of both adults and children were avoided. These were families that the Ma'di refer to as having *ali* or *leke*. *Leke* is a negative trait that is a result of the sins/acts/behaviour of a lineage member that was/is believed to be transferred from one generation to the next, and was/is manifested in some of the illnesses mentioned above. Intimate relationships were avoided with families believed to be under the spell of *ali* or *leke*.[3]

---

3 Actually, causes of frequent deaths among children may result from a disease like sickle sell anaemia rather than a result of *ali* or some crime

5. Physical attributes were important, although these were
   rated low in the hierarchy of desirable qualities for
   marriageability. Although a woman was expected to be
   beautiful, her beauty was not just physical. It embodied
   beauty of body, mind (intelligent), good character
   (morality) and hard work (industry/enterprise); and this
   was stressed throughout her locations as a daughter, wife
   and mother during her socialisation in the everyday
   (Amadiume 1987, 94). The Ma'di proverb, *zaa ronyi ni abu
   a imwa* (the pretty girl has a foul mouth), is a caution to
   suitors that external beauty alone is not a great value in
   marriage. When it comes to men, physical beauty was/is
   even further down the scale of the desirable qualities.
   African folktales are replete with stories of ugly men, such
   as hunchbacks who emerge as successful in marriage
   contest for the chief's beautiful daughter. This is because
   such men demonstrate the desirable qualities of a mature
   man; and physical beauty is certainly not one of these
   qualities. Wit, intelligence and industry were highly valued
   qualities in men. Abasi Kiyimba (2005, 261), in his research
   on Buganda proverbs explains how good looks is not a
   value to search for among the celebrated virtues of a man
   such as hard work, entrepreneurship, intelligence and wit.
   While a woman's physical beauty is cherished, it is
   ridiculous to focus on a man's handsomeness as a value to
   assess his marriageability.

The elders in the extended family, perceived as
knowledgeable and wise, made it their duty to intervene in
guiding the courtship and marriage relationships among its
individual members because they were inextricably connected
with them. Should anything turn unpleasant with the marriage,
the entire community was affected in different ways. This is
Ubuntu, as a lived experience of connectedness and wholeness

---

committed by an ancestor. But such scientific evidences were not
available to explain such deaths. Nonetheless, this logic ensured child-
deaths were minimized as people avoided marriages into such families
with high infant mortality risks.

of a community, and feeling one's humanity is caught up in another person's, and sense of belonging "in a bundle of life" (Tutu 1999, 34). Thus, the importance of minimizing possible future challenges even before the marriage happened. The community's ability to do such background checks along the lines outlined above indicates that marriages were largely endogamous – among different clans within the ethnic group (Amadiume 1987, 70-71). These various checks made marriages more durable and less violent as years of marriage relationships would have constructed more solid friendships among and between the communities.[4]

Key Participants in the Courtship Processes

The age in which a young man and a young woman got married differed from community to community. Among the Baganda marriage, especially for girls happened in early teenage. Some of the reasons for this were to guard against incest and premarital pregnancies. To avoid such possibilities, that were immanent, early marriages were encouraged. Patriarchy's institutional panic and effort to control the sexuality of its members and to benefit from it was seen in establishing taboos such as incest and female honour around virginity. In the words of Foucault, children's bodies (sexuality) thus come under control and surveillance and become punishable when they do not comply. And so, "surveillance and control, engenders at the same time an intensification of each individual's desire, for, in and over his body" (1980, 56-57). This makes the body a locus for conflict and control between the owner and the parents/family. The "strategy" of patriarchy in this regard, was to get the children

---

4   The expression, 'we marry' or 'we do not marry' with such and such clans was common among the Ma'di. This shows that marriages were mostly endogenous, and the communities were fairly familiar with each other. The fact that there were many checks and efforts at control constantly indicate the possibility of resistance from the 'weak' below.

married off as soon as they reached "maturity" (puberty). For girls, this was soon after menarche. Boys too married in their teen, at the onset of puberty, when the voice breaks. For the girl, early marriage ensured she was a virgin.[5] There was greater risk of losing virginity if one married long after puberty. In tandem with the strategy of patriarchy that sought to materially and socially gain from the marriage, rewards were associated with one's daughter being a virgin (see Vaughan 2007). Parents prided themselves in the virginity of their daughters. The biggest embarrassment and shame for the mother and aunt would be the discovery of their daughter's premarital sexual activity (Kabugo 2017).

In traditional Buganda the courtship process was heavily mediated and managed by the parents, represented by the paternal aunt–*Ssenga*. The baton to assess a young man's suitability to marry one's daughter was in the hands of the *Ssenga* who wielded, and still wields, a great deal of authority in this. She became the voice of her niece who remains silent throughout the entire process of traditional courtship. While the young man would get to know his intended a little earlier, when he paid a visit to the young woman's aunt, who spoke on her behalf, the young woman got to know her fiancé when the decision for their marriage had been settled by the parental figures. The one who had the final word on this matter was the aunt, who represented the patriarch. Tamale (2005) describes the *Ssenga* as a representation of "one of the most powerful cultural inscribers of women's bodies among the Baganda." This complex institution "facilitates and reinforces patriarchal power, while at the same time subverting and parodying it" (Tamale 2005, 12). The *Ssenga*, as an institution, emerged out of a strong patriarchal

---

5   In the past as marriages happened quite early, both were expected to be virgins. This is why the *Ssenga* and the grandfather had the responsibility to mentor their nieces and nephews respectively, among he Baganda. Similarly among he Ma'di, where morality was monitored by the occult spirituality of the punitive *Tumi* that does not discriminate between the genders, both were expected to be virgins by the time of their marriage.

institution where women are ordinarily subordinated to men. In reference to Tamale's research the not so clear origin of the *Ssenga* institution, coming into existence as a survival plan to evade and offset male violence in the domestic sphere, aligns well with de Certeau's theory of how the weak (women/wives) use tactics to live relatively comfortably with patriarchy (Tamale 2005, 15-16; De Certeau 1984, xii-xiii). The relationship between the *Ssenga* is a complex one. She poaches on patriarchy to create some controversial spaces of control for women: she tutors her nieces in the skills and attitudes that would lead to happier and less violent marriages. At another level, Foucault's concept of panopticon comes into play here. What appears to be *Ssenga's* power is actually a mandate handed over by patriarchy to surveil and control the bodies and minds of the young women under her tutelage so that they are easy to control by their husbands. This, however, is packaged by the *Ssenga* ideology as "female power" to control their husbands through their "subservience". Subservience is double edged in this regard. As Tamale puts it, this includes "sexual placation" that is used as tactic of "counteracting domestic violence" (2005, 16). In line with Foucault's (1980, 124) theory of bio-power, the *Ssenga's* role is to create docile bodies and minds that are subservient and pleasure giving, but this is also meant to manipulate and control the man who continues to retain his position of authority over her. The *Ssenga's* tutorial to her niece, "Be a nice, humble wife, but turn into a *malaya* (prostitute) in your bedroom!" (Tamale 2005, 27) in order to control and keep the husband shows how the *Ssenga* uses her position tactfully as an advocate and challenger of patriarchal control at the same time. To become a "prostitute" in one's bedroom means to throw off all coyness and to give maximum sexual pleasure for one's husband. This, the *Ssenga* teaches, is one way of sustaining a marriage.

One of the key lessons the *Ssenga* gave/gives was/is on the practice of 'visiting the bush' (*okukyalira nsiko*). This practice pre-menarche females performed, of stretching or elongating the labia minora, was a significant phase of preparing the body for marriage. While the immediate motive of this practice was to sexually satisfy the man, it was packaged as having surplus pleasure for the woman as well. This was presented as one of the cardinal keys to sustaining mutually pleasurable and happier marriage, and so it was compulsory. It became an important cultural identity and aesthetic markers of a marriageable Muganda woman (Tamale 2005, 27; also see Larsen 2010, Martinez Perez & Namulondo 2010, Martinez Perez 2015).[6] During this intense period of socialisation, the niece went to live with her aunt. This is an exclusive "women only" ritual that shrouds the *Ssenga* and her knowledge with aura of mystery and power. It is, thus, a space of "power and knowledge." Even as she instructs her pupils to be subservient to the status quo, she also empowers them on how to have some degree of independence, and on the limits of tolerance to abusive relationships (Tamale 2005, 17). As expressed in the Baganda proverb, "She who says, 'Oh misery!' will die in her married state; she who says, 'I cannot bear it' will leave,'" there is, indeed, room to leave a satisfactory marriage. For the woman, one such reason was/is dissatisfaction with her sex life. The position of the *Ssenga* as the chief custodian of female sexuality has carved her an authoritative position in Buganda (Tamale 2005, 20). She, like no other woman, has the licence to use rich metaphoric language to speak about sexuality, a subject surrounded by taboos and inhibitions in Africa. In this regard, the *Ssenga*, has the two types of power that Foucault (1980, 34) writes about in *Power/Knowledge*: "the power of knowledge of the truth and the power to disseminate this knowledge." In the cultural logic, the aunt is a better tutor than the mother because she shares the

---

6   The elongation of the labia minora is practiced by other Bantu ethnicities like in Zambia, Malawi and Rwanda. In all these communities, the main reason for the practice is the enhancement of sexual pleasure, mainly for the man. In a research conducted by Martinez Perez & Namulongo (2010) on the value of this practice, over 70% of men in Wakiso District (Uganda) appreciate this practice as enhancer of sexual desire for both parties.

same clan with her niece. She transmitted the unique idiosyncrasies of her clan, together with its secrets, to her niece. The *Ssenga* was the third party in the relationship from the beginning to the end. She became a confidant to the intending couple. She remained close and supervised the relationship up to the time the marriage was consummated. She bore witness to the marriage consummation by being physically present at the moment of coitus. On the part of the young man, it was the grandfather, rather than the father who mentored him into manhood. The grandfather, believed to be, steeped in the knowledge, skills and secrets of the clan, was as well the best mentor for the young man. He supervised the entire process and ensured that his grandson was ready for the new status and role he was ascending to (Kabugo 2017). In her principal responsibility as one who grooms females to become good and desirable wives, any culpability in this area would be blamed on her, and "a husband who was dissatisfied with his bride's behavior, particularly her 'bedroom etiquette,' would blame it on the laxity of her *Ssenga*, even returning the bride to the *Ssenga* for 'proper' training" (Tamale 2005, 17). In turn, the *Ssenga* who mediated her niece's courtship could go so far as to undress the suitor to certify his fitness to sexually satisfy her niece. Similarly, on the nuptial night, she had the license to demonstrate and assist the young couples to perform satisfactory coitus, since this was expected to be their first experience (Kabugo 2017).

Among the Ma'di, women appeared to enjoy greater liberties during courtship. Ordinarily, she chose her husband from the many suitors who courted her. The initial meeting could be a casual one on the road, at a water point, in the market or in a dance arena, but the actual courtship took place at her father's home, to ensure some degree of surveillance. To date, well-groomed women speak fondly of how long their courtships were. They say this to distinguish themselves from contemporary young women who are courted "on the road" or in disco halls and bars, and for much shorter duration. Different forms of surveillance trailed the entire process of traditional courtship.

For instance, the suitor never visited his intended alone. He always came in the company of at least one peer, just as the young woman also had her peers around her. The principal one was the go-between (*maju*), or spokesperson for the young man. He mediated the communication between the suitor and the woman. Similarly, if the woman wanted to send a massage to her suitor, she did so through one of her close friends, or through the *maju*. Indeed, she communicated more often with the *maju* than with her intended. The *maju* moved more frequently between the two parties, carrying messages and love tokens (*asi lete*) as indicator of commitment. The *maju* was usually a poetic and eloquent charmer who trumpeted the virtues and abilities of the suitor he represented. His role was to persuade the young woman to prefer his friend. The *maju's* importance, to date, is seen in his being included among the people who receive gifts during bride-price settlement. He was/is appreciated for his skills of persuasion and pleasantries. Even after marriage, he continues to play his role as a close friend to the couple and intervenes in times of conflict between the couple.

Among the Ma'di the family itself facilitated the process of courtship in the everyday. The young woman was exempted from many of her usual daily chores to give her ample time to attend to the several suitors who visited her. "The big granary in the family compound was where men 'perched' to wait to be invited in a hut for more intimate conversations. A female with desirable qualities would attract up to three suitors in a day, and the young woman spent the better part of the afternoon receiving and seeing off suitors. It was up to her to choose to see a suitor or not" (Drania 2015). The seriousness with which the institution of marriage was treated ensured that courtship was prolonged to allow for better knowledge of the other, and for compatibility. A woman's worth was also measured by how long it took to court her. In the cultural aesthetics of courtship, it was her responsibility to make it "difficult" for the suitor's team to win her. As Childs (2010, 124) found out in her research on traditional courtship of the Japanese, "Courtship was often a long, drawn-out matter, with convention requiring men to plead their case patiently while women resisted." Pleasure resided in resisting the suitor and making it difficult for him to get the woman he loved. The logic was, the longer it took, the more valuable the memory of the experience for both parties. Also, this was believed to create stronger bonds after the marriage, among the key players involved. Often, the brothers of the young woman put obstacles in the suitor's way to test his qualities, such as abilities to solve problems, negotiate and control temper. It was in the interest of every member of the family/community that this process went well; for the decisions the individuals made or were made on their behalves would affect the entire extended family.

Both among the Baganda and the Ma'di the *Ssenga* and the *maju*, respectively, mediated the communication between the suitor and his intended. This was a strategy to minimize the possibility of direct contact and to ensure no pre-marital sex and pregnancies happened outside marriage. However, this by no means eradicated premarital sex or pregnancies altogether. As de Certeau (1984) theorises, in the very operations of "strategy" is embedded the possibility of resistance and non-compliance of the subordinates. Although the body was under surveillance and trained to be self-controlled, it could rebel against the forces of repression. Among the Ma'di, the value of self-control in matters of sexuality was expressed in the final stage of courtship, *owu roka*. This was a test, particularly, for the suitor who was allowed to spend a couple of days in the family of his intended. His integrity and honour were put under test before he was allowed to marry from the family. This rite involved the young man sleeping in the same hut with his intended, for a couple of days without sexual contact with her. *Owu roka* literally means using the other's arm as a pillow. For the first time, the bodies were close to each other, but without crossing illicit boundaries. The point of this rite was to test the discipline, trustworthiness, and self-control or restraint of, especially, the suitor. The parties knew that sex before marriage was prohibited. Participating in this ritual also assured the elders and the parties that they had internalised the values of the community, and they could be trusted to practice it outside direct surveillance. The successful completion of this rite led to the settlement of bride price. The performance of *owu roka* coheres with Foucault's theory of bio-power, which is the principle of auto-regulation of the body to conform to the sexual norms and values of the community. As the individuals performed this rite, they did not experience it as repression, but rather mastery and triumph over the body. Quoting from Pylypa (1998, 21-22)

> "Biopower", Foucault asserted, operates on our very bodies, regulating them through self-disciplinary practices which we each adopt, thereby subjugating ourselves…. Individuals thus voluntarily control themselves by self-imposing conformity to cultural norms through self-surveillance and self-disciplinary practices, especially those of the body such as the self-regulation of hygiene, health, and sexuality.

This is an indication that power does not always represent itself as repressive in the everyday. Indeed, it is more effective when power produces knowledge and desire in the subjects who is self-motivate to conform to the values of the society for her own good (Foucault 1980b, 59). This makes participants of the rites of both *owu roka* and *okukyalira nsiko* self-motivated.

The Logic of Bride Price and Gift Exchange

Today, payment of bride price is a hotly contested discourse categorised among those practices that lead to the oppression of women in the domestic sphere (Turner 2009). This is because of the degradation of the practice that is now attuned to the logic of capitalism. From this perspective, the arguments for the abolition of pride-price sounds valid. The traditional logic, however, was more of gift exchange to cement social relationships among communities. Today, what appears as "traditional" is a deviation of what used to be. Among the Ma'di, for instance, the items used as bride price were largely symbolic. Although these items have retained their traditional, symbolic names, the contents have changed. For this reason, I will use the present tense. The settlement was done in three phases. In the first phase were gifts for the women in the bride's family. These are mostly tokens of appreciation for women's caregiving and "servant" roles. They are offered by the suitor and his entourage of 10-20 people who are formally hosted by the bride's family.[7] The gift they offer for the mother figure is *losira li*. The *losira* was the traditional papyrus mat used both as bed and seat for women. Literally, *losira li* is to roll up (fold up) the mat after use. The mother has been rolling and unfurling the *losira* for her daughter to sleep on as she grew up. This token is a symbol of appreciation for bringing up her child well. Folding up the *losira* means henceforth, the bride has no bed in her mother's house. In some cultures like the Baganda, the bride's "bed" is symbolically burned to underline that she no longer has a permanent bed in her mother's house, as she transits to her new, life-long home. She is, nonetheless, welcome to return as a visitor (Kabugo 2017). However, implicit in this symbolic drama of the permanence of marriage is patriarchy's awareness and anxiety of the possibility that the marriage could break. The public performance impresses on the bride to work hard to ensure the marriage works, not only in her interest, but that of the community/family.

Other gifts characterised as *idja* (firewood), *fura ebe* (the flour used for preparing food and beer), and *lebuga nzi* (removing the

---

7   In the case of elopement marriage, the bride's 'brothers' in the extended family visited the groom's home to 'look for' their sister. The groom's family paid a 'fine' called *irima*, which literally means, 'to be made to sit'. The bride's brothers usually played tough and refused to sit down, unless a fine was paid to make them have a conversation with the groom's family. Such a penalty happened when the marriage did not follow the honourable process of settling the bride price before the woman moved to her husband's home. This fine served as a form of 'discipline and punishment'.

baby strap from the back) are all offered for women in appreciation of their maternal roles as producers of food and bearers of children. Since the bride who has been involved in the gender specific role of collecting firewood is leaving, her family needs to be relieved of the stress her absence will cause. The *lebuga* is the strap a mother used for carrying a baby on her back as she performs her domestic chores. The *lebuga* was traditionally made of bark-cloth. The pressure of the strap made impressions on the body of the carrier. Unstrapping the *lebuga* from the mother's back symbolises letting go of the "child," as well as relieving the mother of the burden of "childcare." Henceforth, the responsibility is removed from the mother's "back" as the child enters adulthood through marriage.

The Bride Price

Marriage brings together families (communities) that were hitherto strangers. Settlement of bride price happens after some degree of rapport and confidence has been established between the two communities. It is characterised by long sessions of negotiations, conducted by skilled men, following ritualised patterns. Once again, the items offered here are of symbolic nature, such as: four meters of cloth laid on the ground, on which other symbolic items will be placed. This included a tin of paraffin and matchbox (light), cigarettes, and a box of soap. These are all items that might be used in the course of the negotiation that may drag into the night. Between 3 and 6 traditional Ma'di hoes were given. As a blacksmithing community, iron was one of the sources of wealth among the Ma'di. Their hoe, that served as a legal tender was a lump of iron that could be smelted into other iron implements like knives, axes, spear blades and arrows.[8]

---

8   Because the community no longer engage in blacksmithing, 18 ordinary hoes or their equivalent in money have now replaced the Ma'di hoes. The hoes are shared among the paternal relatives of the bride and used for cultivation.

Three cows, a bull and ten goats were offered and shared with the extended family of the bride. Cattle were important sources of wealth and bride price was a significant source of wealth in the community. A family with many daughters was considered potentially wealthy. The bride price each daughter would fetch increased the size of the family kraal and its prosperity. The value of women as wealth creators is expressed in the Ma'di proverb, *zaa ni leti* (a girl is a way); which means, girls create connections and bail communities out of poverty (see Amadiume 1987, 39). The groom's family also provided construction materials for a kraal – to provide shelter and security for the animals they had gifted. One hundred arrows and three spears were given to the bride's family, to protect the homestead and the resources in it. A token allowance in (today in cash) called *ogu loro* (cushion for the back) was given for the elders to "massage" their backs for participating in the, often, long and tedious negotiations. Today other optional gifts may be offered for the bride's mother and father, for the maidens in the family in appreciation for their services during the marriage ceremony. This gift, *aja uwe* (wiping the dust off the knees), refers to the politeness exhibited by the maidens who usually kneel when they serve guests. The bride's maternal uncle, invested with utmost honour, is one of those who receive a gift. His dignity derives from his connection to one's mother. The inclusive nature of African culture ensures that uncles and aunts are more foregrounded in the marriages of their nieces and nephews than the actual parents. Because marriage is an affair that involves families, gifts that are acquired through bride price are shared out with relatives. It was unheard of for a nuclear family to receive and keep a bride price all for itself (see Dipio 2008). The go-between is not forgotten for the role he plays during courtship. As the best friend and spokesman of the groom, he used his garb for eloquence and courtly manners to persuade the bride to marry. The gift offered him is symbolically referred to as *odo, peke* or *idi*. These refer to any of the dry portions travellers carry as handy foods on long journeys. In the past, they included: roasted sweet peas, peanut/sesame butter, dry meat or fish that are nutritious and rich in protein and soluble oils. Finally, a pair of sheep – male and female – are important ritual items that conclude the main items used for bride price. The groom's party offers this to the bride's family. The pair of sheep – a symbolic gift that expresses the desire for peace and lasting relationship – seals the harmonious relationship between the two families.

Among the Baganda there are symbolic gestures of exchange between the two clans initiating a marriage relationship. One of them is the exchange of coffee beans between the father of the bride and the groom. A coffee bean is single and double at the same time, as it is always paired. The father and the groom eat the pair in a rite that cements their unity and being part of each other. Once a father has shared a coffee bean with an intending man, the marriage between the bride and the groom is as good as sealed in the eye of the community. It is an indicator that the young man has been "born" as a son into the family of the bride. This is expressed in the Luganda proverb, "Who brings forth a daughter also gets a son." Secondly, the relationship between the groom and his brother in law is of particular importance, and it is marked by a distinct gesture. A senior brother in law demands a gift of a cock from the groom before he can "allow" him to marry his sister. Clearly such a token gift is meant to cement friendship and brotherhood between the two men, differently related to the woman in question. Crafting friendship is the core value here. In the past, this gesture was so important that a brother would not consider his sister "married" to a man who did not offer him the gift of a cock. Indeed, in the case of many suitors seeking his sister's hand in marriage, he would not take seriously, a man who failed to offer him a cock, even if that man had already shared a coffee bean with the bride's father. The point being made here is that, for the young man to be "born" into the bride's family, he needs warm interpersonal relationships with as many family members as possible. In the different stages of courtship, the three people who represent the different categories of family membership and interests are the father, the aunt and the brother. The suitor must pay keen attention to his relationships with these constituencies if he is to win the bride (Interview with Kabugo 2017).

Unlike the Ma'di, there are no animals involved in Baganda "bride price" settlement. Most of the items brought by the groom's family are foods and drinks that are used for the celebrations. The local beer, to date, is mandatory among the various traditional marriage foods. This is one food item the entire community, the living and the dead, partakes in. Generous portions of libation are poured for the latter on this occasion (Kabugo 2017). What would make the groom win the bride are tests, set by the bride's family. These tests are teasers and jigsaw puzzles that are challenging to solve. They range from solving riddles, to bringing to the family an item that is rare to find, or reciting one's genealogy up to a certain generation. They tested one's wit, intelligence, tenacity, self-control and problem solving abilities. It is not just an individual who solved the problem, but the entire clan put their "heads" together to provide the needed solution, so that they could win the bride. In the past, as long as they failed the test, they would not take the bride. The language that is used in such a space is specialized: proverbial and highly poetic. The tests create the opportunity for the two parties to engage and assess each other. The best men in the art of speech and intellectual gymnastics are chosen to represent either side. In the end, the two sides bond and construct warm relationships, and end up having fun. The whole process of courtship and marriage, in both communities, is constructed on layers of participation.

The Bride's Transition to her New Family

A traditional dance party would be thrown in the bride's natal home to celebrate the sealing of the marriage. The songs sung eulogise the virtues and beauty of the bride and the "signature" characteristics of the women in her clan. Amidst the general celebrations the paternal aunts and married women in the bride's extended family give her final counsel before she leaves for her new home. They take turns to point out her strengths, which she could turn to her advantage for "survival" in the marriage, as well as point out her weaknesses that could be her downfall if she does not work on them. Her failure would be a shame and disappointment for the entire clan. The point constantly driven home is that she is not just an individual, but a member of a clan. She is urged to carry the banner of the virtues of her clan to the family she is getting married into. In this ritual of "departure," the woman who is seen as a subordinate within patriarchy is ambiguously placed. She does not only adapt to the values of the new community, but also influences it as she becomes directly responsible for the overall education of the children in the family. She goes to her new home as an agent and shaper of culture. The hold of patriarchy over her is never complete (De Certeau 1984). In Buganda, the "tactics" the bride is made to perform before the womenfolk, as an assurance that she will succeed in her marriage is the "ritual of tears". Kabugo's explains:

> If a bride did not shed tears at this stage of the marriage process, it was considered a bad omen – an indicator that the marriage might not work. In case of a 'hard-hearted' bride, the elderly women who came to give her 'final' advice slapped her as they exaggeratedly pointed out her weaknesses. This was a moment when the aunties gave her 'hard talk' for the last time. This was their last opportunity to correct her and demand of her to change her undesirable behaviour. They might even abuse and slap her as they told her to leave her unbecoming ways. As far as the family was concerned, they were marrying off a 'perfect' woman to represent them 'out there'. A good woman was one who has the sensitivity to be touched to tears (Interview with Kabugo 2017).

"Tears" are controversial in this context. They do not simply show the woman's subservience or weakness. They can also be used as tactics to undermine or trick power, in order to "get away with it." In this regard, it becomes a weapon in the woman's possession to manipulate her husband who is located in a superior position in relation to her. It is one of the ways to turn her weakness into power. As de Certeau argues, "Many everyday practices...are tactical in character. And so are, more generally, many 'ways of operating': victories of the 'weak' over the 'strong'... clever tricks, knowing how to get away with things...." (1984, xix) What appears like cruelty is actually the older women's way of teaching their daughter the tricks of surviving marriage in patriarchal societies, where a wife is placed on the margins of the society. A woman who can cry is constructed as good and humble, and so the system can be off-guard with her.

In Ma'di past marriage, a retinue of young and unmarried women finally escorted the bride to her new home after the parents and elders gave their blessings. Up to twelve maidens (depending on the means of the groom's family) accompanied the bride, carrying the gifts, mostly kitchen and household wares that her family gave her. The escorts had specific roles: to give their clan member company as she settled in the new home where she is still a visitor. They also helped her in the domestic chores since many visitors came to see the new bride. As they served the guests, the bride and her maids took this opportunity to display the good qualities of the women from their clan, such as industriousness, generosity and cheerfulness – considered desirable qualities in a woman. This was a kind of advertisement – a performance of impressive and impressionable qualities. The behaviour of the maids spoke for the entire clan, and so the bride was usually careful in selecting who should accompany her to her marital home.[9] It was the custom, for a newly married bride to 'spoil' with hospitable services, the guests who come to see her. To dramatize her kindness, she would go to the extent of preparing warm water, even, for the extended family to bathe in

---

9 In many Ma'di and Nilotic folktales, a deformed, ugly or disease-ridden sister who wants to accompany her sister to her bridal home is always sternly prevented from joining the group of beautiful girls who accompany the bride.

the evening. Such service was her kind of "honeymoon." She served the community instead of withdrawing into a private "hide-out" with the groom, as the case is in today's westernized marriages. These services were labour intensive, which explains the participation of the maids as her aids. They fetched water, firewood, ground grains, and cooked quantities of foods. Depending on the family's capabilities, the visit would last between two to four weeks. This was adequate time for planting the seed of new relationships between some of the maidens and the eagerly observant young men who often accompanied them in their outdoor chores and participated in pleasantries with them. The young women also took the period to assess the character of the family their clan member has been married into. If they evaluated it as a good family/clan, they would, themselves, be encouraged to marry into the same clan (Interview with Koma 2015).

The bride was traditionally welcomed to her new home by dance party. This went on for a couple of days. The bride was expected to dance with groups of people who came to celebrate her. "Seeing the feet of the bride" was both literal and symbolic. She was assessed on how well she danced. Skilful movement of the feet is characteristic of Ma'di dancing. A wife's agility in the dance arena was used to judge her other abilities as a wife. Okot p'Bitek vividly expresses this in *Song of Lawino* when his main character describes the meaning of being a good dancer in the context of the Acoli:

> A girl whose waist is stiff
> Is a clumsy girl
> That is the lazy girl
> Who fears grinding the *kabir* millet (1972, 21).

In many African communities high premium is put on pre-marital virginity, especially of women. Beneath patriarchy's emphasis on virginity is, indeed, its panic that sexuality is a terrain difficult to bring under control. Different strategies, such as early marriages, taboos and beliefs all helped the members to internalise these values and become self-regulated. Among the Ma'di, for instance, there was no need for the virginity proof of public display of the "stained sheet" on the nuptial night.[10] In line with Foucault's theory of bio-power (1980), the members of the community were expected to be self-disciplined and regulated, lest they suffered the wrath of the *Tumi*.[11] Lies were most offensive to the *Tumi* spirituality.

In traditional Buganda, on the contrary, the "stained sheet" testimony was practised. On the nuptial night, the *embaga* dance was performed to receive the bride in her new family. This is a special dance with coded messages for the bride. The *Ssenga* who was always seated next to the bride explained to the niece the meaning of the rhythmic movements of the dancers, the tone, tempo and texture of the drums that are all related to the impending first coital experience that awaits her. Using the mediation of dance, the *Ssenga* revised the lessons she had taught her over time. The climatic moment was the "text" on the nuptial sheet. Her pride resided in her niece being found a virgin. The morning after, the nuptial sheet, with three possible texts was given to the *Ssenga* to be taken to the bride's mother, either with gift of a goat (if she was found a virgin) or without (if she was not a virgin). It was the most painful moment for a mother if the aunt returned home without a goat. A sheet stained with the virginal blood was cherished and kept by the mother as a relic of

---

10 Among Bantu communities like the Baganda, the display of stained bed sheet following the first coitus was mandatory as it brought honour to the womenfolk of the bride's clan, especially to her mother and the *Ssenga*. It also attracted gifts for the bride's mother and paternal aunt for having groomed the bride well. It was consequently a sad experience when there was no clear evidence of virginal bloodstain.

11 The *Tumi* was an occult power instituted in every homestead that guarded and protected the values of the members of the same lineage. The Ma'di refer to it as the invisible policeman of the home. Whoever committed an offence and failed to confess it to the elders in the homestead was struck (to death) by it. The *Tumi* cherished truthfulness. Illicit activities like premarital sex, murder, and theft were offensive to it. But if one came forward and confessed an offence, the *Tumi* would spare such a person. Thus, truth remains one of the cardinal values in the community.

honour for her and her daughter. However, for various reasons, a sheet may not be stained, even if the young woman was a virgin. If the young woman lost her virginity before marriage (may be through rape), and she confessed this to her suitor before marriage, and the groom did not mind marrying her in spite of this, the gracious groom may send the unstained sheet to the mother with a goat, to cover up for his wife who has confessed what happened in her past. The third text was a sheet with a hole in the middle. This was the most disgraceful text a mother would get. It was an insult to her and the family that failed to raise a "good" girl. It showed lack of integrity on the part of the bride who came out as a liar: presenting herself as a virgin when she was not! In this strata women are clearly the "weak" who have to prove themselves as worthy of marriage honours. Nonetheless, they were not passive, even in this regard. They found ways to manipulate the situation to their advantage. If what patriarchy wanted was a virgin, they found ways of "packaging" the bride as such. The Cameroonian filmmaker, Dikongue-Pipa, represents in his film, *Muna* Moto, how women respond to society's obsessive pressure on them to be virgins before marriage. In line with de Certeau's theory of tactics, women use their knowledge in herbs to repair their lost virginity. Thus, control can never be complete. Further, although it was/is desirable that marriages be permanent and lifelong, and to ensure this the entire community got at times intimately involved in constructing it, embedded in the same system is the awareness of the fragility of marriage. Although the patriarchal strategy of bride price payment makes it difficult for marriages to break, there were, and still are, cases where women left their marriages and returned to their natal homes, and at times, bride price are returned. However, the thick network of social relationships created between the two clans does not break, as marriage is not simply about two people. The Baganda express this desire for the continuity in clan relationship in the following proverb: "Your woman runs away, but she does not defame you."

Conclusion: Change and Traces of the Past in the Present

Most of the practices around courtship and marriage described above have either disappeared, are in the process of disappearing, or have greatly transformed. Traces of communitarianism, nonetheless, continue in contemporary courtship and marriage ceremonies. Today, courtship is more of an individual engagement between two people who often meet in cultural contexts that are different from the traditional ones. More often than not, sex and cohabitation go hand in hand during courtship. The nuclear and extended families get involved at a much later stage, unlike in traditional communities where the bigger part of marriage related interactions were done by the parents and the children merely followed the decisions of their parents, as was the case in Buganda. Among other things, the "clinical" background check ensured incest was avoided. Today, there are many cases of incest as seen in frequent media reports. According to the 2014 Action for Development (ACFODE) report,[12] among sexual offences in Uganda, incest has the second highest frequency after aggravated defilement. In the past, the fear of this taboo also encouraged early marriages. These are indicators of how complex the domain of sexuality is. When it came to the issue of payment of bride price, it was the collective home (the extended family), under the leadership of the paternal uncle, who ensured that the family – *ei* – paid the bride price. This meant that wealth, in terms of cattle, was collective: it belonged to the extended family, and this circulated among them. Today, wealth or property is more individual. A family or

---

12 ACFODE, (2014). "Analysis of Cases of Sexual Violence Reported in Major Print Media in Uganda". *http://acfode.org/wp-content/uploads/* 2016/03/sexual-offences-5.pdf. Accessed 14 Dec. 2017. Also see Uganda Radio Network (2007). "65-Year-Old Widow Fined Ushs 20,000 for Incest", May 31: 10:59.

an individual son in the family may pay the entire bride price for his own wife. This is a situation one Ma'di elder singled out as the reason for the kind of selfishness that tarnishes the values of Ubuntu. The older generation laments the passing of the unity and solidarity in the community with regard to marriage:

> Today Marriage has lost value. It has become too individualistic. A young man may bring a young woman home without involving the extended family. In the past, the extended family paid the bride price. Today, individuals boast of the millions they pay for their wives' bride price as a show of their financial sufficiency. This has destroyed the strong social network among cousins and extended families. This trend has eroded our cultural value of marriage (Interview with Anziri 2016).

Today there are different types of families, ranging from the more conventional nuclear and extended ones, to single parent, absentee parents, adoptive, never married, same-sex families. All of these present their own challenges. Change in traditional practices is a factor that cannot be ignored. However, today practices like bridal showers are aligned to the need to have an expert mentor on matters of marriage, similar to the manner that the traditional *Ssenga* used to do. Today, in Uganda, young women seek the services of 'professional' *Ssengas* either face-to-face or through the media. That modern Ugandan women, regardless of ethnicity, can pay for such services shows how important the knowledge they acquire is in empowering them to negotiate with dominant power in the domestic sphere (see Tamale 2005). The tactics they learn from the *Ssenga* serves as the "weapon of the weak" – an alternative power that, in the word of de Certeau, erodes or manipulates dominant power without appearing overly rebellious. This is cultural continuity and adaptation to change at the same time. This, also, shows that the search for a kind of "traditional" community, even in the context of city dwellers, remains an indelible part of African identity, expressed in the philosophy of Ubuntu in the everyday.

Bibliography

Amadiume, Ifi. 1987. *Male Daughters and Female Husbands.* London: Zed Books.

Bagnol, Brigitte & Mariano Esmeralda. 2011. "Politics of Naming Sexual Practices." In *African Sexualities,* edited by Sylvia Tamale, 271-287. Pambazuka Press.

Childs, H. Margaret. 2010. "Coercive Courtship Strategies and Gendered Goals in Classical Japanese Literature." *Japanese Language and Literature* 44 (2): 119-148.

de Certeau, Michel. 1984. *The Practice of Everyday Life.* Berkeley: University of California Press.

Dipio, Dominica. 2008. "Symbolic Actions and Performance in Conflict Resolution Rituals of the Ma'di of Uganda." In *Performing Community,* edited by D. Dipio, L. Johannessen and S. Sillars, 87-110. Oslo: Novus.

Dipio, Dominica. 2008. *In Their Own Voices,* vol. 1. 44 minutes. Muk-Nufu Production, Literature Department Makerere: Kampala.

Faniran O. Joseph. 2008. *Foundations of African Communication.* Abuja: Spectrum Books.

Foucault, Michel. 1977. *Discipline and Punish: The Birth of the Prison.* Translated by Alan Sheridan. New York: Random House.

Foucault, Michel. 1980a. *Power/Knowledge: Selected Interviews and Other Writings, 1972-1977.* Translated by Collin Gordon, Leo Marshall, John Mepham, Kate Soper. New York: Pantheon Books.

Foucault, Michel 1980b. *The History of Sexuality. Volume I: An Introduction.* Translated by Robert Hurley. New York: Vintage.

Gyekye, Kwame. 1996. *African Cultural Values: An Introduction.* Accra, Ghana: Sankofa Publication Company.

Gyekye, Kwame. 1997. *Tradition and Modernity: Philosophical Reflections on the African Experience.* Oxford: Oxford University Press.

Gyekye, Kwame. 2010. "African Ethics." Accessed 25th Dec. 2017. https://plato.stanford.edu/entries/african-ethics

Kiyimba, Abasi. 2005. "Gendering Social Destiny in the Proverbs of the Baganda: Reflections on Boys and Girls." *Journal of African Cultural Studies* 17 (2): 253-270.

Larsen, Josefine. 2010. "The Social Vagina: Labia Elongation and Social Capital among Women in Rwanda." *Culture, Health and Sexuality* 12 (7): 813-826.

Mbiti, John. 1969. *African Religions and Philosophy*. Nairobi: Heinemann.

Menkiti, Ifeanyi. 1984. "Person and Community in African Traditional Thought." In *African Philosophy: An Introduction*, 3rd edition, edited by Richard A. Wright, Lanham. Maryland University Press of America, Inc.

Moemeka, A. Andrew. 2000. *Development Communication in Action: Building Understanding and Creating Participation*. New York: University Press of America, Inc.

Nussbaum, Barbara. 2003. "*Ubuntu:* Reflections of a South African on Our Common Humanity." *Reflections* 4(4): 21–26.

Nzegwu, Nkiru. 2011. "'Osunality' (or African Eroticism)." In *African Sexualities*, edited by Sylvia Tamale, 253-270. Pambazuka Press.

Okot, p'Bitek. 1972. *Song of Lawino*. Nairobi: East African Educational Publishers.

Perez, M. Guillermo, and Harriet Namulondo. 2011. "Elongation of Labia Minora in Uganda: Including Baganda Men in a Risk Reduction Education Programme." *Culture, Health and Sexuality* 13 (1): 45-57. DOI:10.1080/13691058.2010.518772.

Pylypa, Jen. 1998. "Power and Bodily Practice: Applying the Work of Foucault to an Anthropology of the Body." *Arizona Anthropologist* 13: 21-36.

Rabinow, Paul, ed. 1984. *The Foulcault Reader: An introduction to Foulcault's Thought*. New York: Pantheon Books.

Ramose, Mogobe. 1999. *African Philosophy through Ubuntu*. Harare: Mond Books.

Tamale, Sylvia. 2005. "Eroticism, Sensuality and "Women's Secrets" among the Baganda: A Critical Analysis". *Feminist Africa: Sexual Cultures*, Issue (5): 9-36.

Turner, Atuki. 2009. "Matrimonial and Family: Harmful Tradition." https://www.dandc.eu/en/article/womens-rights-unganda-view-bride-price-burden

Tutu, Desmond. 1999. *No Future without Forgiveness*. London: Rider.

Vaughan, Genevieve. 2007. *Women and the Gift economy: A radically Different Worldview is Different*. Toronto: Inanna Publications and Education.

Yilmaz, G. Gaye. 2013. "Tactics in Daily Life Practices and Different Forms of Resistance: The Case of Turks in Germany." *Procedia: Social and Behavioral Sciences* 82: 66-73. doi:10.1016/j.sbspro.2013.06.226

Chapter 7: TRANSITIONAL JUSTICE FROM BELOW? LEARNING FROM 'EVERYDAY' LIVED EXPERIENCES IN SOUTHERN AFRICA

Cori Wielenga

Introduction

Transitional justice mechanisms, as with the liberal peacebuilding framework more broadly, are increasingly being critiqued for not having had enough local ownership and legitimacy, and have had little relevance for those outside urban centres (Bell 2009; Lambourne 2009). In various contexts where transitional justice mechanisms have been implemented, the normative framework on which transitional justice rests has come into question, whether because it 'failed to recognise' local norms or failed to address the broader socioeconomic context (Subotic 2015).

This chapter situates itself within the larger debate around the 'local turn' in peacebuilding, which includes local agency and ownership, but as Leonardsson and Rudd (2015) point out, has often been more visible as a rhetorical tool than in actually shaping peace interventions. They identify two arms of the 'local turn' literature in peacebuilding, the one focusing more on 'peace from below' and the other on an emancipatory approach to the local as peacebuilding (2015, 834). This chapter speaks to both these arms, with its emphasis on the 'everyday' lived experience of communities and what these tell us about justice.

Keeping in mind Randazzo's (2016) concern with 'the local turn', including the danger of 'picking and choosing' forms of everyday agency that fit the normative lens we bring to a study, this chapter nevertheless privileges the "real everyday lives and needs" (Richmond 2009) of people in rural communities in southern Africa in relation to conflict and its resolution. It does this within the broader interest of transitional justice interventions in response to mass violence. Transitional justice is often defined as a set of judicial and non-judicial measures implemented by different countries in order to address the legacies of mass violence (Boraine 2006). These measures include criminal prosecutions, truth commissions, reparations programs, and various institutional reforms (Bell 2009). On the African continent, the most renowned example is that of South Africa's Truth and Reconciliation Commission, but Liberia, Sierra Leone and Kenya are but a few of the other contexts in which truth commissions operated. Rwanda's 'hybrid' *gacaca* courts which integrated a 'traditional' practice into a national justice process is also often cited amongst the examples of key transitional justice interventions on the continent.

Apart from these examples, which are, although criticised, nevertheless seen to have at least had some degree of effectiveness in meeting their stated objectives, there are many others that were planned but have never been actualised, such as is the case in Burundi and the Democratic Republic of Congo.

Transitional justice mechanisms are, in most instances, implemented in the capital cities of a country and seem to have more impact on the political elites than on the 'everyday' lives of people. Considering that 60-90% of African societies are rural, evidence is emerging that large portions of African populations are simply completely disconnected from these kinds of major interventions in which the international community is pouring enormous amounts of money. Further, many of those outside of the urban centres also do not have access to the formal state-sponsored justice system.

In the absence of the formal justice system or meaningful transitional justice interventions, the question that emerges is, how do people in rural communities meet their justice needs? What can we learn from the everyday conflict resolution practices of people in rural communities in Africa?

This research draws from data collected by a research team at the Centre for the Study of Governance Innovation at the University of Pretoria. To date, we have undertaken research through survey questionnaires, interviews, focus groups, and the more ethnographic approach of immersion, in communities in Mozambique, Zimbabwe, Burundi and Namibia[1].

Our research suggests that most of the practices related to meeting community's justice needs are deeply embedded in the collective memory of a given community that have evolved and adapted over time and reflect everyday realities that are unique to that community. This includes moral, social, political, economic, spiritual and cultural spheres. Broadly, these practices seem to have an intrinsic role not so much in punishing an offender or compensating a victim, but in maintaining the *social harmony* of a society for the purpose of its survival, as will be explored further in this chapter.

These everyday realities, I suggest in this chapter, reflect something of the African worldview of Ubuntu. These practices

---

1   This chapter is based on a research project on Ubuntu that was funded by the Templeton Foundation and a research project on 'Justice during transitions' that was funded by the Council for the Development of Social Science Research in Africa (CODESRIA). Fieldwork for this latter project, in Zimbabwe, Mozambique, Burundi and Namibia was undertaken by Ruth Murambadoro, Zefanias Matsimbe, Patrick Hajiyanda, and Erika Dahlmanns, respectively. I participated in the Namibian fieldwork directly which is one of the reasons I lean quite heavily on this case in this chapter. Dr Chris Nshimbi and I, as leaders of the research team, are in the process of publishing a book volume on these findings. This chapter focuses on a particular aspect of the research rather than broadly comparing findings from the field.

reflect a deeply cosmological understanding of personhood, and the embeddedness of an individual in their community in the broadest and deepest sense. 'Community' here includes those who have passed, those who are still to be born, the spirit world, and in some cases also the natural world. What is argued in this chapter is that justice in these contexts cannot be understood, nor can justice needs be met, without understanding the everyday norms, values and worldviews in which conflicts and their resolutions emerge.

Ubuntu and the Everyday

What exactly the term 'Ubuntu' refers to remains a debate, with some arguing that it is intrinsically part of a shared African identity and others suggesting that it is a term that has been instrumentalised for political purposes (Gade 2017). Praeg (2014, 11) suggests that one of the reasons why Ubuntu is difficult to define is because its "meaning has always been and will continue to be a function of the combination of local needs and global expectations", specifically local needs for cultural identity and the global demand for the expansion of human rights, "by essentially infusing the meaning of these rights with local understandings". Praeg (2014, 11) further suggests that the current Ubuntu discourse, particularly in South Africa, is a means by which Africans can critically engage with Western ideas through an African lens. Or as Masolo (1994, 1) more strongly writes, "as an African philosophy, unhu/Ubuntu is about resistance to the Western philosophical discourses that deny Africa its contribution to world knowledge and civilisation."

But beyond being evoked in political discourse, Ubuntu also needs to be understood as it is 'lived' in communities across the African continent. In order to better grasp how Ubuntu is understood in practice, Gade (2012, 488) asked this of South Africans of African descent and organised their responses in two clusters. In the first cluster, Ubuntu was described as the moral quality of a person. In the second cluster, Ubuntu was described as a phenomenon (philosophy, ethic or worldview) according to which people are interconnected. From a review of the literature, Gade (2012) concluded that older writings referred to Ubuntu more as a moral quality and that it was only since the second half of the 1990s that Ubuntu started to be defined as a philosophy. Desmond Tutu, who is often associated with the popular growth of the concept, emphasised the moral side of Ubuntu, describing a person with Ubuntu as being 'generous, hospitable, friendly, caring and compassionate' (Gade 2012, 491).

Roederer and Moellendorf (in Gade 2012, 486) suggest that '(t)he Nguni word 'Ubuntu' represents notions of universal human interdependence, solidarity and communalism which can be traced to small-scale communities in pre-colonial Africa, and which underlie virtually every indigenous African culture'. In South Africa, the term Ubuntu is often commonly associated with the Nguni proverb *Umuntu ngumuntu ngabantu* (which Tutu in the mid-1990s translated to mean 'a person is a person through other people') and stresses the way in which, within African philosophy, interdependence and community are emphasised over individualism (Gaylard 2004). Gade (2012), however, stresses that Ubuntu was first connected with this Nguni proverb during South Africa's transition to democracy in the 1990s, possibly as an argument against segregation ideology.

Terms with similar meanings can be found all over sub-Saharan Africa, however, the precise meaning of these terms have not been established, and therefore cannot be assumed to have the same meaning (Gade 2012, 486). De Tejaba (1979, in Ramose 2002) is often quoted for having said that the philosophy of Ubuntu 'goes from the Nubian desert to the Cape of Good Hope and from Senegal to Zanzibar'. Kamwangamalu (1999, 25) suggests that the terms *umundu* in Kikuyu, *umuntu* in Kimeru (Kenya), *bumuntu* in kiSukuma and kiHaya (Tanzania), *vumuntu* in shiTsonga and shiTswa (Mozambique), *bomoto* in Bobangi and *gimuntu* in kiKongo (Democratic Republic of Congo), and *gimuntu* in giKwese (Angola) are all variants of 'ubuntu'.

Discussions concerning the meaning of Ubuntu immediately take one to discussions about African philosophy, African humanism and African identity. Bell (2002, 40) suggests that African humanism is rooted in traditional values of mutual respect for one's fellow kinsman and a sense of position and place in the larger order of things, including one's social order, the natural order, and the cosmic order. African humanism is often understood in comparison to Western individualism, and as the South African writer, Es'kia Mphahlele, argues, in contrast to this, the African begins with the community and then determines what the individual's place and role should be in relation to the community (Mphahlele 2002, 147).

John and Jean Comaroff (2001, 267), in speaking of conceptions of identity, remind us that we cannot speak of '*the* African conception' of personhood, and that we cannot simply juxtapose so-called Western and African conceptions of identity, assuming one to be about the autonomous individual and the other about a collective sense of identity. Similarly, I am not proposing a homogenous 'African justice' which is at once shared across the continent and different from any other conceptions of justice. Not only is justice understood and practiced in many different ways across the African continent, but there are many (indigenous) communities across the globe that share characteristics of African justice practices.

Even so, our findings and the literature suggest that there are certain conceptions of personhood that are central to African ways of being which have implications for justice during transitions. These conceptions of personhood are characterised by the fact that they are relational, and that communities are composed of complex networks of relationships. Englund and Nyamnjoh (2004, 9), describe how in postcolonial African states people accommodate multiple identities and speak of a 'relational aesthetic of recognition'. Rather than recognising distinct communities of differences, they suggest we recognise the relationships that unite groups of people, and to acknowledge these relations not only as something inserted into communities after they emerge, but as intrinsic to the very emergence of the communities.

These networks or webs of relationships are not only between people, but point to the cosmological, or metaphysical. They include the relationships between the living, the not yet living and the living dead (Benyera 2014). Some would even include the relationship to the ecological (Murove 2004). The intrinsic importance of the intersection of the physical and metaphysical are most visible in the cleansing rituals that characterize most African systems of justice (see for example, Baines 2010). Even were a conflict to be resolved between individuals through the formal state system, on returning to their community, these individuals would need to engage in a cleansing ritual that involves the whole community in the cosmological sense (Allen 2007; Baines 2010; Masoga 1999; Honwana 1997).

This practice is not unique to rural communities. Mobility between urban and rural spaces is a characteristic of most African societies, to the extent that Nyamnjoh and Brudvig (2014) argue that we need to interrogate notions of 'urban' and 'rural' altogether. Although the focus of this chapter is on rural communities, many people living in urban centres have a rural 'home' they return to, where they engage in these cleansing rituals in order to restore the balance or social harmony between themselves and their community of origin.

Justice is thus not about individual accountability, nor about any kind of social contract between an individual and the state. It is not about the rights and duties of a citizen (as in the case of the continental European civilian law system), or to protect an individual from the state (as in the case of the British common law system) (Joireman 2001). It is about restoring social harmony and the balance in the web of relationships that are integral to the survival of the community.

The concept of Ubuntu captures something of this web of relationships, or the interdependence or 'interconnectedness-towards-wholeness' (Krog 2008) that characterises many African societies. Madlingozi (2015) describes Ubuntu as the ontological and epistemological philosophy of the Bantu people that demands the affirmation of the dignity and humanity of every being as a way of ensuring being - becoming and communal harmony. It is this emphasis on harmony that emerged in our fieldwork in Burundi, Mozambique, Namibia and Zimbabwe.

Introducing the Cases

This chapter draws its findings from the fieldwork undertaken in Burundi, Mozambique Namibia and Zimbabwe, which hold distinctly different cultural, political and colonial backgrounds. Significantly, Zimbabwe was colonised by the British, Burundi by the Belgians, Mozambique by the Portuguese and Namibia by Germany, and later South Africa. These colonial histories shaped the formal justice systems that emerged in each respective context, and the degrees to which the informal justice systems were integrated.

Each country has experienced periods of mass violence, and extended periods of low-level conflict which have been of both of a political and interpersonal nature. These continuums of violence can often be traced to the colonial period, intensifying with struggles for independence, and followed by continual violence at varying levels of intensity from independence to date. In Zimbabwe, the liberation struggle (1965-79), which culminated in independence in 1980, was followed shortly after by intense levels of violence in Matabeleland (1980-87), followed by the violence of land reform and then election violence, which has continued in the form of low-level violence between political parties until today. Burundi gained its independence in 1961, and following the violence of the colonial period, entered a succession of intense conflicts in 1965, 1969, 1971, 1972 (described as the genocide of Hutu intellectuals), 1988 and 1993, which became a thirteen-year civil war. Even after the Arusha Peace and Reconciliation Accords were signed, low-level violence has continued in Burundi, particularly at election time. In Mozambique, a ten-year liberation struggle resulted in independence in 1975, but was followed shortly afterwards by a lengthy civil war, from 1977 until 1992. However, low level conflict has continued since that time. Namibia's struggle for independence was not with the German coloniser who had committed the Herero genocide in 1907, but with South Africa, who had taken over the administration of Namibia in 1920. In 1948, when the National Party came to power in South Africa, the same apartheid policies that were practiced in South Africa were brought to Namibia. The struggle for independence began in 1966 but was only achieved in 1988.

In all four cases, although perhaps the least so in Namibia, it is clear that there has never been a period of sustained peace, or a 'post-conflict' period. There is also evidence emerging from the fieldwork that, in many communities, interpersonal and political conflicts have often overlapped, with people using the pretext of political conflict to settle personal grievances, or where personal grievances have conflated with political ones, escalating conflict within communities. For example, much of the conflict in Burundi has been between neighbours, about land (which is crucial for survival), but this has quickly escalated to conflict between warring parties or between ethnic groups. Alternatively, conflict on the political level for a piece of the power pie, has translated into conflicts between neighbours who had been living peacefully for decades.

Each country has developed different responses to these various levels of conflict. Responses to intense levels of conflict (armed conflict between organised groups) have often been influenced by what mediation process was followed, and which donor countries have had a role to play. In Mozambique, the focus has been on political reconciliation and the development of the country, without any transitional justice mechanism being implemented, and a *de facto* amnesty for all parties to the conflict. In Zimbabwe, the British government initially implemented official amnesties, and later this was also the response to mass violence by the post-independent government. Only recently, under international pressure, and pressure from the opposition

203

political party and NGOs is there an attempt to establish a reconciliation commission to deal with the effects of mass violence. In Burundi, the mediation process was strongly influenced by South African mediators, as well as the major donors, namely, the United Nations, European Union and Belgium. This has led to the inclusion of transitional justice mechanisms in the peace agreement, although the proposed truth commission and special tribunal were never implemented. In Namibia, amnesty was issued for all those who fought on either side of the liberation war. Attempts to hold the German government responsible for the genocide of the Herero have not yet been successful.

Significantly, in each case, in the absence of transitional justice mechanisms to deal with periods of intense conflict and where the vast majority of citizens are unable to access the formal justice system to resolve day-to-day conflicts, the informal justice system has played a central role in meeting people's justice needs.

Everyday Justice

Although there are differences in the informal justice practices of each case, they all follow similar principles, which include the role of community leaders and elders, clear hierarchical structures, easy accessibility for the community (with these practices taking place under a tree, for example), affordability, protection of the communities' heritage, values, and identity, decision making through negotiation and consensus and a strong spiritual component evident in the use of cleansing rituals that are deeply embedded in the fabric of a given community. In each case there has been some adaptation of the practices to meet contemporary realities. In all of them, maintaining social harmony remains a central purpose of the practices.

In all four cases, the elders or chiefs play an important role as mediators not only of the conflict but of a multiplicity of complex relationships. This includes the relationship between a community and their ancestors, the relationship between a community and local government, and the relationship between a community and the 'world out there'.

As in precolonial times, in Zimbabwe the structure of the local court system is made up of the family court, village court and the chief's court, and these courts are located near the residence of the village chief with sessions conducted under a tree or in village halls. In Burundi, uniquely, a fairly homogenous set of practices for conflict resolution have become institutionalised in the form of the *Bashingantahe*, wise elders in the community that people would turn to if their conflicts could not be resolved by family members or religious leaders. These leaders do not inherit their position but are elected into it by members of the community (although this differs between communities in more recent times). In the community studied in Mozambique, the traditional authorities are organised into three levels: at the lowest level is a leader chosen by the community who is in charge of ten households; they report to the leader holding traditional power at the level of the family, who in turn report to the traditional chief. In most of these communities, people living together in one village belong to the same extended family. In Namibia, in the communities that were researched, community courts had stopped functioning for some time but were revived as a result of government intervention but operated almost entirely without the state, and within the framework of customary law.

Practically, in all four countries, a dual or parallel justice system exists. Informal justice systems operate alongside, and on the fringes of, the formal justice system. In all four cases, the informal justice systems are recognised, largely through two Acts: one is the act related to customary law and the other is the act related to traditional authorities. To differing degrees in each country, traditional authorities have some level of state legitimacy in fulfilling the role of arbitrator in conflicts, and to some degree, customary law is recognised by the state as offering legitimate procedural guidance to conflicts brought to the appointed authorities. However, the jurisdiction of traditional authorities is limited to civil and not criminal cases.

In the three southern African cases, traditional authorities operate through what is called community courts, which present a hybrid of tradition-based practices and the kinds of practices found in the formal justice system. For example, in many of these courts, all proceedings must be recorded and documents are sent to the capital city for review. In Namibia, at the start of a session, people are sworn in with the same oath as used in the formal justice system. At the same time, within a court session, people in conflict might be advised to visit a *sangoma*[2] for healing or a goat might be slaughtered and eaten together as a sign of reconciliation between the parties.

A reflection on the cases brought to the community court reveals what kinds of justice needs communities have. Cases might include theft of a cow or disputes over land. But we also observed cases that would never be brought to a formal court system. For example, a husband came to the court with the complaint that his wife drinks at the *shebeen* all day instead of taking care of her family. Several people in the community brought to the courts attention the fact that an elderly woman was disrupting the community by swearing and screaming at people, and spreading false rumours. In another case, someone was accused of having placed a curse on someone else while they were possessed by a demon during a Pentecostal prayer meeting.

The response to these cases on the part of traditional authorities includes a broad range of interventions, from talk therapy, to transmitting advice and wisdom, to drawing from the Bible, to drawing from other spiritual practices. At times, compensation is requested. In the past, before state intervention, at times, punishment in the form of beatings or whippings may have been meted out, and still occur in some contexts. The central concern with every intervention, though, is the restoring of social harmony.

---

2   *Sangoma* is the word used in South Africa and Namibia to describe a traditional healer.

One traditional leader said it so well when he said, "They come in crying and we talk and talk and talk until they smile again." This can take hours. This may mean repeated sessions with the same people. It may mean many different people in the community becoming involved. It may require a series of rituals and ceremonies that bring about cleansing, healing and reconciliation. Reconciliation is not only between conflicting parties but with the whole community, including the ancestors and the spirit world.

One cannot understand the functioning of these community courts without understanding what harmony means in and for these communities. Many of the communities we visited were extremely poor, and people were struggling tooth and nail to survive. There were many conflicts as a result of poverty and hardship, as well as due to political and national conflicts. Thus, harmony was by no means intrinsic to the community.

However, our findings suggest that the community courts had the function of reviving a spirit of togetherness and harmony in their respective communities. For example, in one Herero community in rural Namibia, we heard the story of how the community had disintegrated due to a complete lack of leadership during a succession dispute between chiefs. The community had no access to the formal justice system and community courts had not yet been established. One of the community leaders we spoke to described that time as a "nightmare." "People had no respect, they were beating and insulting each other, they were drinking, they had no respect as Herero." Then the community courts were established and order started returning to the community. The community leader said the court became a 'stop sign', but it was more than this. It reminded people of who they were as Herero, where they came from, of their customary law and of the way they should be as a community. It became a place where reconciliation took place and relationships could be restored. Our sense was that these courts were a place where a sense of Ubuntu was being evoked, where community members were reminded of it again.

Part of understanding justice as harmony, and understanding these systems that operate above, below and alongside the formal systems, is understanding the difference between human rights and human dignity. These draw from completely different ways of being in the world. Customary law emphasises human dignity, in which "injustice arises when one person is unresponsive to the personal character and activity of another's being ... this also explains the idea that the perpetrator of injustice is much worse off than the victim" (Batley, forthcoming). A cosmological understanding of personhood emphasises the interdependence of people with one another, their environment and the spirit world. An offence thus effects the whole cosmological order, and offenders are divorced from the cosmological order until they are restored again, through the relevant ritual or practice of a given community.

This was evident in various cases across countries. Again, drawing from Namibia's community courts, we heard of numerous cases in which offenders would beg the one that they had offended not to take them to the police where they would possibly be sent to jail and have a criminal record. But those that had been offended, too, expressed preferring the community court, as their offender was often someone they knew or would interact with on a daily basis. It made more sense for the relationship to be repaired and to receive compensation from the offender, than to have the offender sent to jail. If he were to be sent to jail he would lose his job and no longer be able to provide for his family. Taking care of the family would become the responsibility of the whole community, placing an additional burden on everyone. The one offended would not receive any compensation. When returning to the community after a period in jail, because everyone lives in such close proximity to one another, the relationships would need to be repaired in any case, and with a criminal record the offender might never be able to find work again. It is thus to everyone's benefit, including the community leaders, and every member of the community, to ensure no one goes to jail but that conflicts are resolved within the community. It is therefore far better that the offender retains his job, cares for his own family and pays compensation to the one he offended.

What was found in all these communities, across four different countries, is that community courts were part of the everyday life of the communities. Traditional authorities were able to intervene because they themselves were deeply embedded in the everyday. Although we were not able to gather a lot of data on this, tentatively, we were finding that even organised armed violence at a national level was understood and responded to in this same everyday way.

Conclusion

As mentioned in the introduction, informal justice systems embody a collection of practices that are deeply embedded in the collective memory of a given community that have evolved and adapted over time and have a broad range of functions, including moral, social, political, economic, spiritual and cultural. Their purpose is to maintain the *harmony* in the community. As Honwana describes in the Mozambican context,

> if the relationships between human beings and their ancestors, between them and the environment, and among themselves are balanced and harmonious, health ensues. However, if they are disrupted in any way, the wellbeing of the community is jeopardised. There is a complex set of rules and practices that govern the maintenance of well being and fecundity in the community (1997, 297).

Our sense is that what is happening in these communities would be difficult to understand without really understanding an African worldview. These practices reflect a deeply cosmological understanding of personhood, the embeddedness of an individual in their community in the broadest and deepest sense.

Although there is quite some research on detailed case studies by anthropologists on specific practices in specific communities, very little work has been done comparatively, across cases. Even less work has been done to translate the deep case study work to the policy level. Frameworks on transitional justice suggest integrating informal justice practices as a way to address mass violence. They often suggest 'bumping up' these practices up to a national level in order to become integrated into a national, state response to mass violence. But this reflect a misunderstanding of these practices function, and how deeply embedded they are in the everyday lives of a community.

One of the questions emerging from the research is whether episodes of mass violence can really be understood as being separate from the everyday. In the lived reality of communities, it seems as if there is a complex conflation of conflicts specific to a particular community and national, political conflicts. There is evidence for that in almost every episode of mass violence throughout the continent.

In contrast, the dominant transitional justice framework assumes that mass violence has a start and end date and can be understood in this contained way. It assumes that a mechanism can be implemented for a given duration of time that addresses this finite period of violence. It assumes that once the transitional justice mechanism has completed its task, the transition period is over and the formal justice system can take up its task again.

But on the margins of both the formal transitional justice mechanism and the formal state system, a different set of processes is operating. Most people are part of these processes outside of the formal system. Most people hardly ever come into contact with the formal system, whether during a transition or outside of it.

Observing the everyday lives of everyday people suggests they are operating according to other systems altogether. Yet our knowledge about these other systems is minimal. Rhetorically, at least, it has become 'trendy' to tap into these, because at some level everyone understands that they hold legitimacy for people. But we are still a very long way from understanding how these practices function and the ways in which they are embedded in communities.

What is necessary for a more meaningful integration of the formal and informal justice systems is a deep understanding of the everyday realities of people on their own terms, and from within the framework of an African worldview. Particularly as the evidence suggests that these practices can bring about the kind of reconciliation transitional justice mechanisms aspire to but largely fail in.

Bibliography

Allen, Tim. 2007. "The International Criminal Court and the invention of traditional justice in Northern Uganda." *Politique Africaine* 3(107): 208.

Baines, Erin. 2010. "Spirits and social reconstruction after mass violence: Rethinking transitional justice." *African Affairs* 109(436): 409-430.

Batley, Mike. (forthcoming). "Integrating policy and practice: An example from South Africa." In *Justice during transitions: Developing policies that reflect African realities*, edited by Cori Wielenga and Christopher C. Nshimbi. Dakar: Codesria.

Bell, Richard H. 2002. *Understanding African Philosophy: A Cross-cultural Approach to Classical and Contemporary Issues*. London: Routledge.

Bell, Christine. 2009. "Transitional Justice, Interdisciplinarity and the State of the 'Field' or 'Non-Field'." *International Journal of Transitional Justice* 3(1): 5–27.

Benyera, Everisto. 2014. "Exploring Zimbabwe's Traditional Transitional Justice Mechanisms." *Journal of Social Science* 41(3), pp. 335–344.

Boraine, Alexander L. 2006. "Transitional justice: a holistic interpretation." *Journal of International Affairs* 60(1): 17–30.

Comaroff, John L. and Jean Comaroff. 2001. "On Personhood: an Anthropological Perspective from Africa." *Social Identities* 7(2): 267-283.

Englund, Harri and Francis B. Nyamnjoh. 2004. *Rights and the politics of recognition.* London: Zed Books.

Gade, Christian B. N. 2012. "What is Ubuntu? Different Interpretations among South Africans of African Descent." *South African Journal of Philosophy* 31(3): 484-503

Gade, Christian B. N. 2017. *Discourse on African Philosophy: A New Perspective on Ubuntu and Transitional Justice in South Africa.* Rowman and Littlefield.

Gaylard, Rob. 2004. ""Welcome to the World of our Humanity": (African) Humanism, Ubuntu and Black South African Writing." *JLS/TLW* 20(3/4): 265-282.

Honwana, Alcinda M. 1997. "Healing for Peace: Traditional Healers and Post-War Reconstruction in Southern Mozambique." *Peace and Conflict: Journal of Peace Psychology* 3(3): 293–305.

Joireman, Sandra F. 2001. "Inherited legal systems and effective rule of law: Africa and the colonial legacy." *The Journal of Modern African Studies* 39(4): 571–596.

Krog, Antjie. 2008. ""This thing called reconciliation…'forgiveness as part of an interconnectedness-towards-wholeness." *South African Journal of Philosophy* 27(4): 353-366.

Lambourne, Wendy. 2009. "Transitional Justice and Peacebuilding after Mass Violence." *International Journal of Transitional Justice* 3(1): 28–48.

Leonardsson, Hanna and Gustav Rudd. 2015. "The 'local turn' in peacebuilding: a literature review of effective and emancipatory local peacebuilding." *Third World Quarterly* 36(5): 825-839.

Madlingozi, T. 2015. "Transitional justice as epistemicide: On Steve Biko's pluralist co-existence 'after' conflict." Seminar held at the Wits Institute for Social and Economic Research, Witwatersrand University, 7 July.

Masoga, Mogomme A. 1999. "Seeds of violence and vengeance, South Africa and Symbolic ritual cleansing." *Affiliations* 6(1): 213-224.

Masolo, D.A. 1994. *African Philosophy in search of identity*. Indiana: Indiana University Press.

Mphahlele, E. 2002. *Es'kia*. Edited by James Ogude, Sam Raditlhalo, Ndavhe Ramakuela, Marcus Ramogale and Peter N. Thuynsma. Cape Town: Kwela Books, Johannesburg: Stainbank & Associates.

Murove, Munyaradzi F. 2004. "An African Commitment to Ecological Conservation: The Shona Concepts of Ukama and Ubuntu Munyaradzi Felix." *Mankind Quarterly* 45(2): 195-215.

Nyamnjoh, Francis B. and Ingrid Brudvig. 2014. "Conviviality and the boundaries of citizenship in Africa." In *The Routledge Handbook of Cities of the South*, edited by S. Oldfield and S. Parnell, 341-355. New York: Routledge.

Praeg, Leonhard. 2014. *A Report on Ubuntu*. Pietermaritzburg: University of KwaZulu-Natal Press.

Ramose, Mogobe B. 2010. "The death of democracy and the resurrection of timocracy." *Journal of Moral Education* 39(3): 291-303.

Randazzo, Elisa. 2016. "The paradoxes of the 'everyday': scrutinising the local turn in peace building." *Third World Quarterly*, 37(8): 1351-1370.

Richmond, Oliver P. 2009. "Becoming Liberal, Unbecoming Liberalism: Liberal-Local Hybridity via the Everyday as a Response to the Paradoxes of Liberal Peacebuilding." *Journal of Intervention and Statebuilding*, 3(3): 324-34.

Subotic, Jelena. 2015. "Truth, justice, and reconciliation on the ground: normative divergence in the Western Balkans." *Journal of International Relations and Development* 18(3): 361–382.

Chapter 8: EXPRESSIONS OF RESISTANCE: UBUNTU, BLACK CONSCIOUSNESS AND WOMEN IN SOUTH AFRICA'S STUDENT MOVEMENTS

Unifier Dyer

Black Consciousness is a political philosophy indigenous to the African continent that appropriates Ubuntu as a fundamental tool of resistance against domination, effacing of history, culture and identity, and indoctrination. In his major work, *I Write What I Like* Stephen Bantu Biko draws from diasporic ideas and ideologies but emphasizes Ubuntu as the foundation upon which African life is imagined, shaped and built. This chapter argues that Black Consciousness is in many ways a call for the revival of Ubuntu. The return to Ubuntu is also about indigenous thought, practice and knowledge resuscitation and a closer focus on beginning with what already exists in African thought and reading the world from this vantage point.

At a time when many of the world's institutions of higher learning are being influenced by a wave of alt right ideology South Africa has faced its own educational challenges. While our colonial ancestors turn over in their graves students have had their concrete memory removed from sight and rattled the gates of their institutional legacies. Greater access to the institution by the marginalized majority is demanded and its educational frameworks are being tested to their thinkable limits. At the forefront of the student movements in South Africa under the growing lexicon of: #FeesMustFall and #RhodesMustFall, is #BlackGirlMagic and collectives such as For Black Girls Only, iQhiya (isiXhosa for head scarf or wrap /symbol of strength and burden) and Feminist Stokvel (investment, saving club). Behind these are women who in their time do not accept what Mamphele Ramphele calls 'honorary male status'. Women are again adopting Black Consciousness and positioning themselves at the centre of emerging and existing struggles even as they are voices that are often times effaced, rendering them insignificant and silenced, ensuring they have no audience. Through Black Consciousness women are highlighting the element of community and care, collective voicing and militancy.

Fallism

Leading the October 2015 #FeesMustFall and August #RhodesMustFall movements were women in a complex web that incorporated voices of the marginalized. In this space womxn[1] were not a homogenous group that worked as one seamless collective but rather the very make-up of what has collectively been termed the Fallist movement[2] came from non-aligned individuals who chose not to be represented by Student Representative Council bodies (Economic Freedom Front, ANC-aligned Progressive Youth Alliance). Instead they rallied mainly through social media and WhatsApp groups, what Patricia Hill Collins calls "networked social movements", and were represented by no specific leader (Collins and Bilge 2006, 141). When there were media tactics to single out individuals

---

1   Non-gendered name used by those who resist and push back against woman.

2   Nationwide student protests took form in their institutions relating to the particular issues they were concerned with. The umbrella term coined is Fallism and included demands that student wanted met such as #OutsourcingMustFall (2016), #FeesMustFall, and #RhodesMustFall.

there was strong resistance and a move to make room for diverse modes of resistance.

What was common were the demands that echoed in each of these movements. The calls were to end the outsourcing of university workers who were contracted by the university and denied all the benefits of full employment that faculty and administration enjoyed; free, quality, decolonized education for all students, and greater inclusion of Black students and Faculty in especially former white and privileged universities. Historically-black universities have protested year after year since 1994 for quality student housing and accommodation, fully equipped facilities and an end to financial exclusion but these calls have overwhelmingly fallen on deaf ears. It was not until former-white universities which had growing numbers of Black students (many of whom came from better economic standing but were still disempowered and underrepresented in positions of power) that students gained an audience (Godsell and Chikane 2006, 60).

In August 2015 Black students from the University of Cape Town (a former white university which under apartheid excluded Black learners on the basis of race) marched for the removal of the statue of British colonialist Cecil John Rhodes who died in 1902, with his racist ideology intact, and still in the public domain in 2015— disturbingly celebrated through an erected monument. #RhodesMustFall came from a need to protest by South Africa's institutionally, structurally and economically disenfranchised Black majority. This majority Black was at the University of Cape Town, still largely a minority within the gates of the institution. This is a paradoxical position. These students eventually went head on with the university management which was protected largely by the state police and later private security. Despite this, students succeeding in having the statue removed from the campus premises—their everyday premises.

In October of 2016 students at the University of the Witwatersrand (WITS) organized the first of many protests that would spread countrywide under #FeesMustFall calling on university management and government to do away with the 6% fee increase. After #NationalShutdown former President Jacob Zuma announced a 0% increase on national television after backing down from addressing students from across the country at the Union Buildings, the official seat of the government in Pretoria. Students were however not entirely satisfied with the announcement since their objective was to completely do away with higher education fees for all South African students. The 2017 Commission of Inquiry into Higher Education and Training released by the government to address the issue of how to fund free education is still modeled on loan system and has substituted the National Student Financial Aid government loans for Income- Contingency Loans from commercial banks. Free education has been limited to technical and vocational education at Technical Vocational Education and Training (TVET) which were established after all former Technikons were turned into universities and a vacuum in vocational training emerged.

And yet, free education was but one nodal point in the list of demands students made. Complimenting it was quality, decolonized education. Students introduced vocabulary and concepts such as decolonization and intersectionality, drew from thinkers including, but not limited to, Stephen Bantu Biko, Frantz Fanon, Audre Lorde and Ngugi Wa Thiong'o, aligned with schools of thought such as Black Consciousness and Pan-Africanism, and named university spaces Azania House (UCT) or Solomon Mahlangu House (WITS). The conversations were not always met with the same kind of rigorous critique the concepts were presented. Voices that gave great power to the decolonial move were young womxn whose early pronouncements were empowering.

Black Consciousness and the Spirit of Ubuntu

One of the greatest challenges to humanity has been the violence of man. Stephen Bantu Biko was able to highlight this at the height of Apartheid in South Africa when Black students were facing among other things a crisis in education where they were required under Christian National Education to be taught an inferior form of education, Bantu Education under the Bantu Education Act of 1953. Resistance to this culminated in the Soweto Student Uprisings on June 16, 1976 largely led by Black Consciousness leaders. As a politically and culturally conscious philosophy Black Consciousness emphasized knowledge creation drawn from and centered within Black life. Black here was not defined in racial terms but rather implied a self-making and self-definition that was necessary for all oppressed people who sought to liberate themselves from Apartheid not simply politically but psychologically too. Biko thus saw the link between liberation and Ubuntu as necessary. Essentially a concept such as Ubuntu was fundamental to the kind of world Biko envisioned for post-Apartheid South Africa. He drew from a common memory evidence of a functional and ideal society which he could not recognize in the Apartheid system. Biko drew from a past in which Apartheid did not exist but not from a present in which Ubuntu did not exist. Principally Biko was re-imagining into being an ideal that had aspects of it already in existence— ever changing, sometimes hidden and certainly suppressed.

Steve Biko goes to length on the African philosophy of Ubuntu without directly using the term but articulates the concept with clarity. He outlines four facets to the African concept of Ubuntu namely, shared or collective concern, the ancestral, music, and land. In his analysis of African culture Biko describes Ubuntu as fundamentally "Man-centered." In other words, in a man-centered culture the issue is not what man is by definition but rather how man behaves. Biko says that in such a culture the greatest emphasis is on communication premised on a level of intimacy. Constant communication is said to be woven into all aspects of life, necessarily involving sharing all manner of information often among peer groups. To elaborate he observes that "house visiting was always a feature of the elderly folk's way of life." So regular was this act that, "no reason was needed as a basis of visits. It was all part of our deep concern for each other" (Biko 1978, 46). This has to do with what Biko says is at the heart of *our* culture— communication. This communication extends to the ancestral, coated in religious tones. For Biko ancestors are the connection between the living and God, and they are consulted in all aspects of life. No special occasion is needed to commune with them nor is there a designated place of worship. Worship according to Biko causes a rift between life and religion, something that does not generally feature in African spiritual practice. In addition to this there exists a concept of morality and interconnectedness that explains the collapse of everyday living and spaces of communion with the ancestors. Biko equated the ancestors to Christian saints, adding that they are also a continuation of who they were as living persons. There is thus no separation between those living and those dead and they are referred to with the same and even greater respect or reverence than a person. Of this he says then, "we believed in the inherent goodness of man- hence we took it for granted that all people at death joined the community of saints and therefore merited our respect" (Biko 1978, 103). For Biko, the ancestors continue to be part of the community as involved participants, calling on and called upon.

The emphases Biko places on the characteristic of shared concern within African culture is directly linked to human engagement as a unit that progresses only when each member is cared for not as a burden on the collective but as a mark of the upward movement of the community. Biko thus pronounces, "we are prepared to have a much slower progress in an effort to make sure that all of us are marching to the same time" (Biko 1978, 46). This rhythmic metaphor is grounded in actual music which according to Biko was a collective expression of a common experience, in which rhythm communicated the mood and movement of the group in unison. He tells us that "nothing dramatizes the eagerness of the African to communicate with each other more than their love for song and rhythm" (Biko 1978, 46). African music for Biko defined moments of collective resistance and support, where together people carried the burden of their suffering. This leads him to remark: "music and rhythm were not luxuries but part and parcel of our way of communication. Any suffering we experienced was made much more real by song and rhythm" (Biko 1978, 47). Indeed, this is a theme that resounds throughout much of Black Consciousness poetry. To the issue of land Biko places great emphases in tandem with nationalist movements. For him it is a task of re-appropriating an identity through the name Azania as well as revisiting terms of property ownership that echo practices of joint proprietorship. The use and settlement on land had at its center Man and therefore the needs of the community. This was tied to the issue of poverty which was not an individual burden to be carried by one family but rather, through extending invitations a household could receive the assistance of 'extended family', neighbors and the community. Here again the element of sharing is central. Evident in this thinking is that sharing is a signifying break from individualism.

Biko falls within a group of African thinkers and political leaders who were proponents of Black Power, communitarianism, Pan-Africanism, Negritude and Nationalism. These anti-colonial leaders were from a generation that sought to combine Western ideology with indigenous thought to fashion a strongly independent African vision. When considering the direct link Black Consciousness has to Ubuntu one is drawn to read Biko alongside Tanzania's first President, Julius Nyerere and his socialist informed political philosophy, *Ujamaa*. They both introduced indigenous African philosophies into the politics of the nation state. Biko was also strongly influenced by such thinkers as Fanon and Aimé Césaire, but also the Civil Rights movement leaders.

It is curious to see the idioms that Biko uses to talk about African culture. Biko says that African thought follows an approach of "situation-experiencing" and substantiates his point by referencing Zambia's first president Kenneth Kaunda who makes a distinction between on the one hand, western thesis and antithesis logic, scientific methodology and its binary approach, and on the other hand African pre-scientific collaboration between the rational and non-rational. Kaunda appropriates such a juxtaposition to isolate Western and African thought from one another and thus make an argument for African expression similar to first President of Senegal, Léopold Sédar Senghor's idea of an emotional African self. Such an account faces the pitfall of imagining a self against a Western framework. There is that distinctively Negritude tone to this understanding and one can detect a grain of what Pauline Hountonji calls ethnophilosophy. The parlance of Negritude comes forth in Biko's thoughts here:

> In spite of my belief in the strong need for scientific experimentation I cannot help feeling that more time also should be spent in teaching man and man to live together and that perhaps the *African personality* with its attitude to laying less stress on power and more stress on man is well on the way to solving our confrontation problems (Biko 1978, 49).

It is the idea that there is an African personality which echoes Senghor but is also a remark on Ubuntu which is never quite annunciated. The closeness of the two may have one mistake Ubuntu for sharing some relation to Nativism or Negritude but this would be erroneous and reductive or simplistic.

When examined Ubuntu is the overarching moral institution upon which all other institutions are built and informed. All spheres of society originate from the organizing principle of Ubuntu – these variously include abantu, muntu, ntu and isuntu (people, person, being, things/entities and culture). Ubuntu demands that an accomplished person (measured in deeds) should act humanely and go further to perform this with exceptional care and generosity, always aware that they are interacting with another person who in turn is required to perform this human grace.

Ubuntu in South Africa elicits three general responses, a dismissal of its ideals which are considered a romanticizing of an imagined past, a skeptical curiosity, and aloof neglect. This at a time when the international community is slowly taking interest in an ideal that colored the reconciliatory lexicon of South Africa at the dawn of the new dispensation. Archbishop Desmond Tutu is widely cited as the ambassador of its inscription into the political domain of the nation and its isiZulu adage: "umuntu ngumunthu ngabantu" (a person is a person because of others), which if linguistically traced will lead one to similar axioms across Sub-Saharan Africa. Of course, the philosophy of Ubuntu predates this use in text and more significantly in the oral tradition.

When Archbishop Desmond Tutu established the Truth and Reconciliation Commission under the ethos of Ubuntu it was taking on the form of a tool of healing meant to embody the great task that South Africans had to undertake to move beyond the horrors of their past. Not only was Tutu "introducing a new grammar of framing South Africa's post-apartheid politics and its many possible futures" as James Ogude tells us (Forthcoming 2018, 1), but he was also inserting it into the domain of the post-Apartheid space and reintroducing it as the building block for a new social order. Although Ubuntu had long been part of the lexicon of the nation state it now paradoxically enabled healing and denied people the full expression of that healing. It more dangerously meant that the burden of past injustices fell on Black South African's who had to be actors in reconciling and yet continued to live as largely marginalized bodies while White supremacy ran rampant.

In the 1960's and 70's Black Consciousness was responding to a social crisis that history imposed on Black life. It addresses the greatest challenge to humanity in the 20th century— the systematic destruction of Black life and the expression of humanity itself– Ubuntu. A crisis of this sort laid its claim and legitimacy on existing definitions and narratives of Black people that objectified and dehumanized them. In countering this, Biko redefined Black and repositioned the place of Blackness. He believed that:

> Merely by describing yourself as black you have started on a road towards emancipation, you have committed yourself to fight against all forces that seek to use your blackness as a stamp that marks you as a subservient being (Biko 1978, 52).

Biko was calling upon Black people to see themselves through their own philosophy and not the narrative of erasure. The context under which the concept of Ubuntu flourished may have become unrecognizable after White domination, but the philosophy remained largely intact and could be reignited in even the most daunting of circumstances. Ubuntu was a template which was constantly under threat, but it was the very tool for liberation from a White supremacy that was taking hold of the mind of the oppressed. For Biko then, unless Black people saw the immediate use of Ubuntu embodied in his idea of a Man centered philosophy of being, then the self-creation Black offered would not become manifest.

Modern African Culture

For Black Consciousness, envisioning South Africa or Azania had everything to do with the agency of the Black man and this was to be found in his contribution to modern culture. "Hence in taking a look at African culture" Biko says, "I am going to refer as well to what I have termed the *modern African culture*" (Biko 1978, 45). According to Biko modern African culture acknowledges the contribution Africans have made to the progress of man towards modernity. Modernity therefore, is not exclusive to one race, geography or culture. Biko here makes it a point not to allow the difference and distinction between cultures translate into apartheid. Instead he says: "even in a pluralistic society like ours, there are still some cultural traits that we can boast of which have been able to withstand the process of deliberate bastardisation" (Biko 1978, 50). The resilience of African culture and thought offers us another chance at learning it, Biko says. Perfecting and teaching it to ourselves and the world is a contribution to the breadth of life which Africa is positioned to offer.

To the extent that students today are shifting institutional culture African knowledge is being privileged. Westerners writing on and about Africa and Africans "usually assumed that Africans themselves were not conscious of their own philosophy, and that only western analysts observing them from without could give a systematic account of their wisdom" (Hountodji 1996, 5). Biko tackles the problem of talking about African culture as understood by Africans themselves. This is made all the more necessary since: "Other people have become authorities on all aspects of the African life or to be more accurate on Bantu life" (Biko 1978, 44). Biko makes a pertinent point for African knowledge and culture:

> I am against the belief that African culture is time-bound, the notion that with the conquest of the African all his culture was obliterated. I am also against the belief that when one talks of African culture one is necessarily talking of the pre-Van Riebeeck culture. Obviously the African culture has had to sustain sever blows and may have been battered nearly out of shape by the belligerent cultures it collided with, yet in essence even today one can easily find the fundamental aspects of the pure African culture in the present day African (Biko 1978, 45).

Ubuntu challenges the myth that Africans have no philosophy of their own making. It challenges inheritances from colonialism, slavery and apartheid passed down through missionary education, state structures, church, the law and Christian National Education know as Bantu Education, because it says we had, and still have something that is founded on African knowledge, thought and practice. In fact, this is a philosophy that Western philosophy can learn from.

What Biko says above (if we caution against the idea of a "pure African culture") makes it very difficult to think of Ubuntu as a romanticization of the past since noticeable elements of Ubuntu remain with us. Even if they have been distorted and usurped for other projects as we see in the states use of Ubuntu as well as business enterprise which has been comfortable with appropriating the term but not its principles.

At another level Ubuntu is wrongly considered an academic ideal said to be espoused by African academics who have no real connection to the practice at the level everyday engagement. Van Binsberg who vehemently supports this line of thinking opines that Ubuntu is a relatively recent term with no legitimate foundation beyond this point (Biko 1978, 62). Furthermore, Ubuntu is limited to a concept inspired by the ordinary to serve a global function. This seems to indicate that African scholars have created a concept meant to fall under Anglo-European scholarship thus stripping the knowledge base from African ground and transplanting it into Western centered scholarship which falls short in studying the philosophy. It is not wholly untrue that African scholars have imposed Western readings onto Ubuntu which has distorted a more complex and richer, even clearer study of Ubuntu, and yet crediting contemporary African scholars with creating Ubuntu shows a complete disregard for the origins of the philosophy within the African family and greater community.

The above follows the logic that unless Ubuntu serves the project of civilization and by extension globalization (Zondi 2016, 248), cosmopolitanism (Zondi 2016, 252; Ngcoya 2015) and modernity (Taiwo 2009) then it is pointless to study it. Ubuntu in this regard therefore cannot contribute to modernity because it is not individualistic or premised on individualism. Africans thought and practice that does not subscribe to this model of modernity (individualism) is said to contribute nothing towards modernity. The clearest example of this is in discussions on Ubuntu and Human Rights in Murray's work (Murray 2006). As Sabelo Ndlovu-Gatsheni and Siphamandla Zondi illustrate such thinking is untenable and one might add outdated, as even ideologies such as Marxism are foundational to our thinking on modernity. This is what student movements are in many ways grappling with and in the process, one sees cloaked in the discourse Ubuntu or at least the spirit of Ubuntu.

In reflecting on Black Consciousness and Biko's use of the concept one cannot overlook the gendered reference to a Man-centered philosophy which on face value is almost unnoticeable yet when read alongside critiques by Black Consciousness leader Mamphela Ramphele on the silencing of women like herself who were at the forefront of its thought production and mobilizing it raises the question about what limitations the movement had. The ideology's paralleling with #FeesMustFall and #RhodesMustFall is an opportunity to revisit some of the pertinent issues overlooked not only in the history of women in the liberation but also the silencing of women today. With this firm link established between Black Consciousness and Ubuntu but also the former and current student protest movements we can now delve into the role of women and their leading voices.

The Exclusion of Women Thinkers

The presence of women in the public space is disruptive of androcentric preponderance (Gqola 2001; Boyce 1995; Magaziner 2011; Khan 2017). Whether in private or public spaces women have always been prominent voices, but too often this has been followed by forms of silencing. This is not unique to the current Fallist movement, Black Consciousness leader Mamphela Ramphele notes in her writing how "gender as a political issue was not raised at all," women often had to struggle to be heard and in the process were expected to lose their femininity in exchange for accepted as "one of the boys" (Ramphele 1991, 218). This therefore required of women an assertive and even aggressive demeanor which came with this new-found status. Ramphele recalls how after receiving "honorary male status" she along with her female comrades, deemed "different" were inclined to hold women without this status in contempt (Ramphele 1991, 215; 218). Likewise, she says "I soon learnt to be aggressive towards men who undermined women, both at the social and at the political level" (Ramphele 1991, 218). This highlights the interrelated spaces and levels at which the struggle for voicing by women had to be engaged.

In speaking about the silencing of women's voices and the inability and unwillingness of the oppressor to hear and listen to women who refuse silencing, Boyce draws attention to both public and private domains of address that women are denied voice in. Of the public she says: "Public spaces for speech have been generally identified with paradigms of masculinity, rational discourse, absence or emotion, developed logical arguments, control of representation and so on" (Boyce 1995, 4). As we see with Ramphele women in South Africa's struggle (to say nothing of political parties) have been offered public platform under the mandate of masculine frames and language which have largely been in support of masculine modes of struggle. Reflecting on women movements that have largely defined themselves as militant Wanelisa Xaba cautions against the trend of hyper-masculine resistance which has been adopted by a growing number of Fallist students (Xaba 2017, 6). Xaba argues that part of the challenge when looking at the position of women and their contribution to movements of liberation is that they too have adopted hyper-masculine forms of resistance and negotiation which are closely aligned to neoliberalism, capitalism and nationalism resulting in their solutions in turn perpetuating hyper masculinity and cisgender norms while ignoring an intersectional approaches or negotiations and structures or institutions. While one may be tempted to see this as a red flag, it is more useful to see it as a red herring since these women still operate at the periphery of the Gramscian hegemony.

Indeed, Boyce speaks about a voicelessness that Black women have been subjected to which is linked to how "historically, black women were seen/are seen/have been seen as having nothing important to say" (Boyce 1995, 5). Their contribution is in this manner dismissed. But there exists too and out of this the possibility of moving beyond boundaries which happens when Black women transgress the locations prescribed to by social authorities and norms (Boyce 1995, 8). Under FeesMustFall women carved out a space to deal not only with institutional issues but also concerns that were specific to women and shared by a multiplicity of people with varied identities (cisgender, nonbinary, gender transgressive, queer, differently abled, non-citizen of South Africa) (Khan 2017, 110; Ndelu et al. 2017, 2). As Ndelu et al. poignantly point out, what is distinct from earlier student movements is how womxn have now "brought to the fore a clear and powerful feminist challenge to the cisheteronormative patriarchy in broader society–as well as within the student movements" (Ndelu et al 2017, 3). This is a challenge Darlene Miller laments the previous generation of women activists have struggled to incorporate (Miller 2016, 278).

Developing her thoughts from Boyce, Gqola calls for a collapsing of the binary and boundaries between theory and activism in order that sites that are considered outside of knowledge production are included in a discussion on Blackwomen, feminism and postcoloniality in Africa.[3] No longer concerned with writing back to colonialist or white feminists Blackwomen turn inwards and in so doing appreciate the different locations from which they produce knowledge, write and resist. This presents the possibilities that have been seen in naming oneself (Africa, feminists), situating oneself (as a writer, in postcoloniality) and expressing different ways of designating oneself. The embrace embodied in Gqola's idea is that of contributing to a common cause from multiple entry points.

If we are to understand Black women in Fallism we have to see how they deal with the effects of colonialism and Apartheid and how this shapes their experiences and modes of resistance as well as how these women negotiate differences among each other. Intersectionality is one such method of analysis and

---

3   Gqola defines postcoloniality through the lens of hybridity. It is she says, "a growing body of writing, literary and scholarly, which critiques the implications of the relationship of power between the former colonisers and the colonised" (13).

introspection that has been central to Black women thinkers. Intersectionality can be understood as the interconnectedness of the world, the people who inhabit it and their relations with one another which although different cannot be separated from one another. Informed by Patricia Hill Collins and Sirma Bilge's *Intersectionality* we could say it variously links sophisticated systems and institutions of power to the equally complex lived experiences of people in a study of intersections between gender, race, class, religion, nationality, among others, and offers itself as an analytical tool for discourse on these. [4]

In recent years and with the growing number of multifaceted voices the South African archive of symbols is being repositioned. Black women are not so much destroying the archive of white supremacy as shifting it and resituating themselves as part of a narrative that needs to be heard and paid attention to, if not by institutions of power then by one another. Areas of distinction that must be flagged in women organizations are intersectionality and community and group collectives. In her article on rising women movements and collectives Alude Mahali appropriates Audre Lorde's works to draw parallels between African American radical woman thinkers and the movement #BlackGirlMagic and collectives For Black Girls Only, iQhiya and Feminist Stokvel. These initiatives by women emerge in the last five years operating both in virtual spaces and in general public spaces. #BlackGirlMagic is an online movement that fashions a celebration of achievements that collectively enhance Black women while recognizing that "assimilation to majority or dominant cultural norms is no longer the price of equal respect" (Mahali 2017, 3). iQhiya, For Black Girls Only and Feminist Stokvel are more recent women collectives in South Africa which bring together an array of young Black elite women who

---

4   It is traced to Kimberle Crenshaw who coined it in her renowned article "Mapping the Margins: Intersectionality, Identity Politics, and Violence against Women of Color" (Crenshaw 1991) in which she is concerned with black women in the prison complex and its repressive and social justice elements.

are challenging institutions of art, dominant institutional narratives and anti-Black spaces and institutional barriers of economic access respectively. In large part this has been met with a backlash as was seen in 2016 when alt right white movements threatened to disband the For Black Girls Only event at the historic women's Gaol on Constitution Hill, Johannesburg mostly expressed through social media.

Let us pay attention to one collective iQhiya, isiXhosa for headscarf also called a *doek* in its Afrikaans use. The moniker embodies feminine power, creativity and collective bonds expressed among female artists working together in performance arts, sculpture, video, photography and other mediums. iQhiya Collectives is a network of Black female artist initially comprising of eleven UCT students: Asemahle Ntonti, Bronwyn Katz, Buhlebezwe Siwani, Bonolo Kavula, Charity Kelapile, Lungiswa Gqunta, Matlhogonolo Kelapile, Sethembile Msezane, Sisipho Ngodwana, Thandiwe Msebenzi, and Thuli Gamedze. Like Black Consciousness arts which were "in essence incubators for youth creatives who dabbled in more than one art form" (Peterson 2016, 22) these artists are able to draw from one another's fields to create collaborative pieces while attending too to a political project. They address Black women's marginalization from prominent artistic spaces which are saturated by white male works. In collaboration iQhiya aims to insert themselves and their art into galleries that otherwise rarely if ever represent them. In defining the collective Thuli Gumedze writes:

> iQhiya is attempting to offer an alternative curriculum to Black women artists in South Africa, one that defies the structural injustices (lessons) of *the hidden curriculum* that we all came to uncover in our various experiences of the institution (Gumedze 2017; my emphases).

Through their work they grapple with their various experiences of the institution. iQhiya is thus a direct response to "the hidden curriculum,"—a normalized systemic educational violence which is embedded in "a number of bodies" all of which have "swallowed" the hidden curriculum and proceed to perpetuate it and exist through it (Gumedze 2017). This is the curriculum that runs not only the institution they study through but also informs who will enter the art gallery as creative forces in South Africa and the global arena. To this end the collective has to negotiate the delicate line between being engulfed by the ideologies that support these exclusive sites and breaking the seal to allow more Black art by women. The most challenging of these is the tension between on the one hand, the philosophy and praxis of collective community, collective burden, collective strength which they represent through the support network steeped in Black feminist theory, and on the other the forces of capital enterprise imbued in individualism.

In one of their first collaborations together iQhiya performed *Portraits* (2016) which developed from a photograph of Lungiswa Gqunta's mother and her four sisters in their 20s. The women sit and stand in graceful postures that hide the struggle and pain they were going through in their lives at the time of its taking. It inspires the exhibition by the collective first performed at Greatmore Studios in Cape Town and later at the Athens School of The Arts—Nikos Kessanlis Exhibition Hall both in 2016. The performance was a form of protest against the expectation that women bear their pain in silence. The eleven artists dressed in white and stood on red beer cases containing empty bottles, "this was to inflict pain on the bodies, or feet in this instance, and illustrate the endurance of pain. We were suffering publicly but tried to hide the pain which was later evident", they say in an interview with Layla Leiman (2017). As the performance continues some of the artists climb down from the crates and stuff iQhiya into them leaving a lengthy piece hanging out—a symbol of the petrol bomb—thus drawing a connection between a long history of struggle and weapons of combat. iQhiya is at once an ornament to be wrapped around the head, protective gear when placed on the head to support the weight of a heavy load, an oppressive item required of domestic workers to wear at all times as "uniform" and symbolic of the paraffin-soaked cloth that blows up a parking lot in defiance against Apartheid brutality. Claiming presence and pain is the great task these artists and students have taken up, it is an old struggle in what they have been made to believe is a new dawn and dispensation.

Women still pose a threat to masculine proponents who continue to reproduce untenable conversations. Indeed, voices that early on in the #FeesMustFall and #RhodesMustFall movements at the University of the Witwatersrand and the University of Cape Town respectively, were swiftly silenced. These were the voices of women who called for institutions to address fee increases, curriculum reform, an end to outsourcing university workers, and simultaneously included the contribution of differences in sexuality, nationality, class, race, those differentially-able and marginalized groups. Women collectives that emerge after women are sidelined from these student movements largely retain this inclusive characteristic about them.

In Conclusion

Students in South Africa are going through a phase of self-definition in much the same way Black Consciousness thinkers were. They have identified a crisis, similarly one of education and power brokering. Students have been dismantling power in two forms; what was inherited from the colonial and Apartheid era (Rhodes, colonial education) and that which is imposed by the present government by keeping these colonial ideas and institutions alive and functioning while simultaneously denying access through financial exclusion. Students want to dismantle power by redefining spaces where thought is developed. This is thus also an epistemological struggle. Much of what these students demand is the power to define the terms of engagement with certain knowledges.

As with early Black Consciousness the women of today are seeing that the recovery and re-membering (Ngugi 1986) of cast-off knowledges and practices in the university institution has to take into consideration the world order imposed on the people of the continent and adoptions of certain principles in the struggle in order to be recognized by oppressive regimes and also recognized as possessing independent systems and institutions. The refashioning of Black people is thus multifaceted and involves a multitude of important factors that need to be take into consideration.

Here again Black Consciousness sheds light on the predicament and the struggle waged today echoes. With its philosophical, ideological and political task at hand leaders of Black Consciousness had to deal on the one hand with ensuring the inclusion of Black people into the law and protection of the international Euro-Western bodies of law which South Africa was signatories to, and on the other hand ensuring the recognition of Black people under their own systems which were in turn meant to be adopted in a South Africa inclusive of all who live in it. The emphasis was that whatever the country was to look like, it had to be determined by the majority Black population. White people would be included into this new South Africa, but they would not be its architects since under the Apartheid regime White supremacy had attempted and failed dismally at creating a viable and believable South Africa. Today students have to appeal to institutions that are entangled with capital and the state and simultaneously remain relevant to their everyday struggles and realities.

Students are today asking about those elements of themselves that they cannot recognize in the system and content of education. They are asking about Black pain and why it is not addressed. They are asking about Black bodies and why they still make institutions uncomfortable. They are also deeply invested in destroying the inhumanity that is imposed on them and so they are always engaging with elements of Ubuntu. They are asking to be featured in the knowledge system. Students are questioning where the man or human centered aspect of education is, when it will be taught in the classroom and what kind of a classroom is needed to teach it. Of course, the larger issues of access to education have taken the forefront and met the force of private security hired by universities at the gates of these institutions of learning. What has fallen on the wayside is the deep question of institutional culture. To address this, space must be created for a reflective conversation with the institution. Students are demanding inclusivity in institutions that have thrived on exclusivity. Beyond the thoughts expressed here we must explore what such a world would look like.

Bibliography

Bewaji, John Ayotunde Isola, and M. B. Ramose. 2003. "The Bewaji, van Binsbergen and Ramose debate on ubuntu." *South African Journal of Philosophy* 22: 378-415.

Biko, Steve. 2015 (1978). *I write what I like: Selected writings.* Chicago: University of Chicago Press.

Crenshaw, Kimberle. 1991. "Mapping the margins: Intersectionality, identity politics, and violence against women of color." *Stanford Law Review* 43: 1241-1299.

Gamedze, Thuli. 2017 "iQhiya." Accessed 13 April 2017. http://www.documenta14.de/en/artists/13582/iqhiya

Godsell, Gillian and Chikane, Rekgotsofetse. 2016. "The roots of the revolution." In *Fees Must Fall: Student Revolt, Decolonization and Governance in South Africa,* edited by Susan Booysens, 54-73. Johannesburg: Wits University Press.

Gouws, Amanda. 2010. "Feminism in South Africa today: Have we lost the praxis?" *Agenda* 24: 13-23.

Gqola, Pumla Dineo. "Ufanele Uqavile: Blackwomen, Feminism and Postcoloniality in Africa." *Agenda*, no. 50. 2001, pp. 11-22.

Hill Collins, Patricia and Bilge Sirma. 2016. *Intersectionality.* Hoboken: John Wiley and Sons.

Hountondji, Paulin J. 1996. *African philosophy: Myth and reality.* Bloomington: Indiana University Press.

Khan, Khadija. 2017. "Intersectionality in student movements: Black queer womxn and nonbinary activists in South Africa's 2015-2016 protests." *Agenda* 31: 110-121.

Leiman, Layla. "iQhiya: The black female artist collective taking on the art world." Accessed 13 April 2018. http://10and5.com/2016/03/04/iqhiya-the-black-female-artists-collective-taking-on-the-art-world/

Magaziner, Daniel R. 2011. "Pieces of a (Wo) man: Feminism, Gender and Adulthood in Black Consciousness, 1968–1977." *Journal of Southern African Studies* 37: 45-61.

Mahali, Alude. 2017. "'Without community, there is no liberation': on# BlackGirlMagic and the rise of Black woman-centred collectives in South Africa." *Agenda* 31: 28-41.

Mbembe, Achille. 2002. "The Power of the Archive and its Limits." In *Refiguring the archive*, edited by Carolyn Hamilton, Verne Harris, Michèle Pickover, Graeme Reid, Razia Saleh, Jane Taylor, 19-27. Berlin: Springer Science & Business Media.

Mignolo, Walter. 2011. *Modernity and decoloniality*. Oxford: Oxford University Press.

Murray, Rachel. 2006. "International human rights: neglect of perspectives from African institutions." *International & Comparative Law Quarterly* 55: 193-204.

Murris, Karin. 2016 "# Rhodes Must Fall: A posthumanist orientation to decolonising higher education Institutions." *South African Journal of Higher Education* 30: 274-294.

Mutere, Malaika. 2012. "Towards an Africa-centered and pan-African theory of communication: Ubuntu and the oral-aesthetic perspective." *Communicatio* 38: 147-163.

Naidoo, Leigh-Ann. 2016. Keynote address at The 15th annual Ruth First Memorial Lecture under the theme "Violence and Rage." was held at the University of the Witwatersrand. https://mg.co.za/article/2016-08-17-

leigh-ann-naidoo-delivers-compelling-speech-at-ruth-first-memorial-lecture.

Nabudere, Dani Wadada. 2006. "Towards an Afrokology of knowledge production and African regeneration." *International Journal of African Renaissance Studies* 1: 7-32.

Ndlovu-Gatsheni, Sabelo J., and Siphamandla Zondi, eds. 2016. *Decolonizing the university, knowledge systems and disciplines in Africa.* Durham: Carolina Academic Press.

Ndelu, Sandy, Simamkele Dlakavu, and Barbara Boswell. 2017. "Womxn's and nonbinary activists' contribution to the RhodesMustFall and FeesMustFall student movements: 2015 and 2016." *Angenda*, 31: 1-4.

Ngcoya, Mvuselelo. 2015. "Ubuntu: Toward an Emancipatory Cosmopolitanism?" *International Political Sociology* 9: 248-262.

Ogude, James. 2018. *Ubuntu and the Reconstitution of Community.* Bloomington: Indiana University Press. Forthcoming.

Peterson, Bkekizizwe. "Youth and Student Culture: Riding resistance and imagining the future." In *Students Must Rise: Youth Struggle in South Africa Before and Beyond Soweto '76*, edited by Anne Heffernan and Noor Nieftagodien, 16-23. Johannesburg: Wits University Press.

Pityana, N. Barney, ed. 1991. *Bounds of possibility: the legacy of Steve Biko & Black consciousness.* Cape Town: David Philip Publishers.

Pucherova, Dobrota. 2009. ""Land of my sons": The politics of gender in Black Consciousness poetry." *Journal of Postcolonial Writing* 45: 331-340.

Tutu, Desmond. 2012. *No future without forgiveness.* New York: Random House.

Wa Thiong'o, Ngugi. 1986. *Decolonising the Mind: The Politics of Language in African Literature.* London: James Currey.

Xaba, Wanelisa. 2017. "Challenging Fanon: A Black Radical feminist perspective on violence and the Fees Must Fall movement." *Agenda* 14: 1-9.

Yates, Kimberley, Pumla Gqola, and Mamphela Ramphele. 1998. "This little bit of madness: Mamphela Ramphele on being black and transgressive." *Agenda* 14: 90-95.

NOTES ON CONTRIBUTORS

Aloo Osotsi Mojola is a professor of philosophy and translation studies at the St Paul's University, Limuru, Kenya and an honorary professor as well as research associate, Faculty of Theology, Pretoria University, South Africa. He is the author of *God Speaks in our own Languages*.

Anke Graness is Elise Richter Fellow in the chair of Philosophy in a Global World/Intercultural Philosophy in the Department of Philosophy at the University of Vienna (Austria), and project leader of a FWF-funded research project on the History of Philosophy in Africa at the University of Vienna. She is the author of Das menschliche Minimum. Globale Gerechtigkeit aus afrikanischer Sicht: Henry Odera Oruka (Frankfurt/New York: Campus, 2011). She has also co-edited an anthology on the Kenyan philosopher Henry Odera Oruka, Sagacious Reasoning: H. Odera Oruka in memoriam (Frankfurt/M.: Peter Lang Verlag, 1997; with K. Kresse) and a book on Intercultural Philosophy: Perspektiven interkulturellen Philosophierens. Beiträge zur Geschichte und Methodik von Polylogen (Wien: Facultas/WUV 2012; with F. Gmainer-Pranzl).

Cori Wielenga is a senior lecturer in the Department of Political Sciences at the University of Pretoria and a research associate in the Centre for the Study of Governance Innovation. Her research interest is in the intersection of local, national and international justice and governance systems in Africa. She is currently heading up a comparative research project which has taken her to Rwanda, Burundi, Zimbabwe, Mozambique,

Namibia, Nigeria and South Africa to understand the impact of these intersecting systems of justice and governance on people 'on the ground'. She has held fellowships with the African Peacebuilding Network, the Council for the Development of Social Science Research in Africa and the American Political Science Association.

D. A. Masolo is Professor of Philosophy at the University of Louisville, Louisville, Kentucky, USA. Masolo is the author of *Self and Community in a Changing World*, Bloomington, Indiana University Press, 2010 (Finalist for the Melville Herskovts Award for the Best Scholarly book published on/about Africa in the English language in the year), and *African Philosophy in Search of Identity*, Indiana University Press, Bloomington, and Edinburgh University Press, Edinburgh, 1994. He is editor (with Ivan Karp) of *African Philosophy as Cultural Inquiry*, Indiana University Press in association with the International African Institute, University of London, 2000.

Dominica Dipio is a Professor of literature and film in Makerere University. She obtained a BA with Education and MA in African Literature from Makerere University. She obtained a licentiate in social communications and wrote her PhD on African cinema from the Pontifical Gregorian University in Rome. Professor Dipio has published widely in her crosscutting research interests in literature, film, cultural studies and folklore. Among her most recent publications are: "Art's Subtle, Liberating Ways: Violence, Trauma, and Agency in Fanta Regina Nacro's The Night of Truth"; "Negotiating Transcultural Identities in African Literature: Ngugi wa Thiongo's The River Between and Timothy Wangusa's Upon this Mountain"; "Audience Pleasure and Nollywood Popularity in Uganda: An Assessment"; a monograph, *Gender Terrains in African Cinema*, and four edited books. She has also served as External Examiner and Assessor in universities in eastern, western and southern Africa. Dipio has won several competitive grants and fellowships such as African Humanities Program (AHP), Fulbright and

240

Cambridge Africa Program for Research Excellence (CAPREx). She is a filmmaker with more than ten titles to her credit, most recent of them are: *Word Craft* (2017), *Rainmaking: A Disappearing Practice* (2016), and *Extreme Artists: Ugandan Video Jockeys* (2016). Dipio has also served as a jury member at several international and regional film festivals in Milan, Amiens, Ouagadougou, Zanzibar, as well as in the Uganda Film Festival (UFF) since its inception in 2013.

James Ogude, Professor, is a Senior Research Fellow and the Director at the Centre for the Advancement of Scholarship, University of Pretoria. Until his recent appointment he was a Professor of African Literature and Cultures in the School of Literature, Language and Media Studies at the University of the Witwatersrand, where he worked since 1994, serving as the Head of African Literature and also Assistant Dean—Research, in the Faculty of Humanities. He is the author of *Ngugi's Novels and African History: Narrating the Nation* and he has edited a total of six books and one anthology of African stories, the most recent edited books are: *Chinua Achebe's Legacy: Illuminations from Africa* (2015) and *Ubuntu and Personhood* (2018).

Niels Weidtmann is Director of the interdisciplinary institute Forum Scientiarum at the University of Tübingen. He has studied philosophy and biology at the University of Würzburg and at Duke-University in Durham, N.C., USA, and got his PhD in philosophy from University of Würzburg. His research interests are in intercultural philosophy, phenomenology, hermeneutics, anthropology, and the philosophy of science. He is author of the book *Interkulturelle Philosophie. Aufgaben–Dimensionen–Wege* (Tübingen 2016), editor of several book series and has published a wide range of articles. Weidtmann is a board member of the International Society of Intercultural Philosophy and editor of the online journal *polylog.org*.

Oriare Nyarwath is a Senior Lecturer of Philosophy in the Department of Philosophy and Religious Studies, University of

Nairobi, Kenya. He is the author of *Traditional Logic: An Introduction* (Nairobi: Consolata Institute of Philosophy Press, 2010) and co-author of *Theory and Practice of Governance in Kenya: Towards Civic Engagement* (Nairobi: University of Nairobi Press, 2006).

Unifier Dyer is a PhD student in the Department of African Cultural Studies at the University of Wisconsin-Madison. Before joining the department, Dyer was a Research Associate with the Centre for the Advancement for Scholarship at the University of Pretoria under a project on the moral philosophy of Ubuntu. Dyer has published more recently into the use of indigenous forms of redress for transitional justice in contexts of fragile democracy. Dyer holds a Masters degree from the Department of African Literature at the University of the Witwatersrand, with the thesis title "The Paradoxes of Silenced Trauma in Mongane Wally Serote's *To Every Birth Its Blood*." Teaching and research interests include African storytelling, anti-apartheid literature, indigenous knowledge systems, women institutions, and silence.

INDEX

A

Afrophobia · 16
Apartheid · 140, 153, 218, 223,
    229, 233, 234
Azania · 218, 221, 224

B

Baganda · 20, 147, 158, 161, 163,
    168, 171, 172, 174, 177, 179,
    182, 183, 187, 188, 192, 193
Bantu Education · 219, 225
Basotho · 13
Bio-power · 166
Black Consciousness · 215, 216,
    218, 219, 221, 223, 224, 227,
    231, 233, 234, 236, 237
Burundi · 196, 197, 202, 203, 204,
    205, 239

C

Césaire · 221
Christian National Education · 219,
    225
Communality · 139
Communitarian · 157
Communitarianism · 93
Customary law · 208

D

Dodo · 38

E

European Community · 108
Exclusion · 118, 227

F

Fallism · 216, 229

Fallist · 216, 227, 228

Fanon, Frantz · 28, 62, 115, 131, 218, 221, 237

Friendship · 137

G

Gqunta, Lungiswa · 231, 232

H

Hospitality · 22, 107, 110

Human Development · 119, 132

Humanity · 86, 98, 192, 212

I

Integrity · 86

Interconnectedness · 166

Intersectionality · 229, 230, 235, 236

Intonjana · 8

iQhiya · 216, 230, 231, 232, 235, 236

K

Kaunda, Kenneth · 82, 221, 222

L

Liberalism · 111, 213

Lorde, Audre · 218, 230

M

Ma'di · 157, 158, 159, 161, 163, 167, 168, 169, 170, 171, 172, 175, 176, 177, 179, 180, 181, 183, 185, 186, 187, 190

Mahlangu, Solomon · 218

Migration · 90, 97, 101, 102, 106, 108, 110

modern African culture · 224

Modernity · 86, 191, 224, 236

Mozambique · 197, 199, 202, 203, 205, 212, 239

N

Namibia · 197, 202, 203, 204, 205, 206, 207, 208, 240

Nativism · 222

Nguni proverb · 121, 199

Nyerere, Julius · 78, 82, 87, 129, 132, 143, 221

O

Orality · 148, 149
Owu roka · 177

P

Patriarchy · 171
Personhood · 211, 241
Pretoria · vii, 62, 113, 197, 218, 239, 241, 242

R

Reconstitution · 155, 237
Red women · 9
Religion · 11, 80
Resistance · 5, 22, 127, 163, 193, 219
Responsibility · 111

S

Senegal · 199, 222
Senghor, Léopold Sédar · 40, 41, 63, 143, 222

Social harmony · 68
Solidarity · 68
South Africa · 2, 46, 49, 51, 57, 60, 62, 86, 87, 90, 110, 111, 113, 121, 132, 140, 153, 154, 196, 198, 199, 202, 203, 206, 211, 212, 215, 217, 218, 223, 224, 228, 229, 230, 231, 232, 233, 234, 235, 236, 237, 239, 240
Southern Africa · 14
Ssenga · 20, 164, 165, 167, 172, 173, 177, 187, 190

T

Tanzania · 62, 82, 84, 86, 129, 199, 221
Traditional authorities · 209
Transitional justice · 196, 211, 212
Truth and Reconciliation Commission (TRC) · 20, 139, 196, 223
Tumi · 172, 187
Tutu, Desmond · vii, 19, 20, 23, 66, 67, 68, 69, 70, 74, 87, 121, 122, 132, 166, 171, 193, 199, 223, 237

U

Uganda · 20, 147, 157, 158, 168,
    174, 189, 190, 191, 192, 211,
    240
Ujamaa · 129, 221
universalist · 16
University of Cape Town (UCT) ·
    217, 233
University of the Witwatersrand
    (WITS) · 87, 217, 233, 236, 241,
    242
Utu · 37, 56, 87, 129

W

Wa Thiong'o, Ngugi · 218, 237
Womxn · 237

X

Xenophobia · 98, 110

Z

Zimbabwe · 62, 154, 197, 202, 203,
    205, 211, 239